RENEWALS 458-4574

DATE DUE

GAYLORD   PRINTED IN U.S.A.

The Essential Sales Management Handbook

YOUR
SECRET WEAPON
TO SUCCESS

Gerhard Gschwandtner

Founder and Publisher of *Selling Power*

McGraw·Hill

New York   Chicago   San Francisco   Lisbon   London   Madrid   Mexico City
Milan   New Delhi   San Juan   Seoul   Singapore   Sydney   Toronto

The McGraw·Hill Companies

Copyright © 2007 by Gerhard Gschwandtner. All rights reserved. Printed in the United States of America. Except as permitted under the United States Copyright Act of 1976, no part of this publication may be reproduced or distributed in any form or by any means, or stored in a data base or retrieval system, without the prior written permission of the publisher.

1 2 3 4 5 6 7 8 9 0   DOC/DOC   0 9 8 7 6

ISBN-13: 978-0-07-147602-7
ISBN-10: 0-07-147602-4

McGraw-Hill books are available at special quantity discounts to use as premiums and sales promotions, or for use in corporate training programs. For more information, please write to the Director of Special Sales, Professional Publishing, McGraw-Hill, Two Penn Plaza, New York, NY 10121-2298. Or contact your local bookstore.

Readers should know that all expert-advice interviews in this book present the opinions of the experts. The author and publisher cannot guarantee financial success and therefore disclaim any liability, loss, or risk sustained, either directly or indirectly, as a result of using the information in this book. Readers should know that all contact information in the expert-advice interviews was verified as current at the time of the interviews but may have changed since then due to changes in the experts' businesses.

Contents

Introduction

WHAT MAKES AN IDEAL SALES MANAGER?
How to Identify the Qualities and Skills of Great Leaders

You want to be called leader . . . coach . . . mentor . . . facilitator . . . analyst . . . and the ever-popular VP of something—anything. Anything, that is, but *manager*. The word alone conjures up an image of paper-pushing automatons filling out forms in quadruplicate and making sure all the proper cubbyholes are filled to capacity in an endless sea of cubicles—a Dilbert world where managing means little more than showing up and punching a keyboard.

In such a corporate setting, anyone can be a manager. But what about a *sales* manager? Doesn't that require a bit more on the people skills side? Isn't a sales manager someone who moves the ball forward? A leader, coach, mentor, facilitator, analyst— well, yeah, all those things. And then throw in psychologist, goal setter, motivator, number cruncher, communicator, listener, and a few other functions, and, bingo, you've got yourself a sales manager: an all-around fire starter and putter outer. A sales manager lights the fire under the sales team and puts out the fires that daily life creates.

And what about the bottom line? Yes, the sales manager is a strategist, marketer, and link between the sales team and the executive suite. And, in many cases, one day the sales manager becomes the CEO. So what about it? What does it take?

Be Willing to Wear Many Hats

First of all, sales leadership requires a jack-of-all-trades mentality. The ideal sales manager must be able to juggle the demands of conducting business and directing people.

"Sales managers say their job is really difficult because they have to focus on sales, strategy, and managing their people all at the same time," says Jocelyn Davis, vice president of product development at the Boston-based Forum Corporation, a training and consulting firm. She quotes a comprehensive study the Forum Corporation recently conducted of the best practices of top sales organizations around the world. What else did the study reveal? "All of our respondents were unanimous in saying the most important roles for sales managers today—and also the role they need the most help with—is the coaching and developing of their sales staff."

Typically, sales managers have risen through the ranks, distinguishing themselves as top performers along the way. However, the skills that made them sales stars may not necessarily translate into instant management magic.

"Sales managers often tell us they first got their jobs because they were great salespeople and that their initial tendency is to want to go out and sell," Davis explains. "They know they have to work with their sales teams, but their natural inclination is to want to stay on top of all these different sales situations, stay on top of their salespeople all the time and generally be in the mix, because that's what they love to do. They're used to being self-starters, used to being out with customers, used to the sales role."

Promoting sales reps to sales managers can be a wise choice or a disastrous mistake, depending on the individual manager. On the disaster side, a sales manager who overcontrols can harm more than help. And it can be a typical response when a new sales manager takes over an existing team or, worse, has to hire from scratch. Such a manager may feel the need to help and prod the reps, creating resentment, dependency, or outright hostility. But worst of all, it removes the reps' incentive to produce sales.

Bob Butler, president and CEO of Butler Learning Systems in Dayton, Ohio, says that fear of losing control is understandable but wastes valuable time and energy. "When my wife and I went out to dinner for the first time after our first kid was born, we were petrified," Butler recalls. "We grabbed hold of the sitter and said, 'Make sure you test the milk before you feed him, please be careful not to let him fall, please do this, please do that....' The sales manager has the same fear syndrome. But the sales manager's predominant responsibility is coaching and supporting, not micromanaging."

Amy Gerdnic, an account executive at QRS in New York, agrees. "I feel that every salesperson is like a player on a basketball team, and every team needs a coach," she says. "You need a plan before your game, and your manager will go through all the possible scenarios. The manager will work with you on what obstacles you might come across and what to do about them." Pregame planning, postgame review—all in a day's coaching.

People Matter Most

Second, the ideal sales manager can make the critical shift from managing sales to managing people. Such a manager realizes that positive reinforcement builds a stronger sense of worth.

Like overanxious parents, sales managers who suffocate reps risk stifling the growth of their sales team. Effective managers, on the other hand, spend more energy fostering independence and autonomy in reps. "The managers who are ultimately successful shift their focus from being the top salesperson to realizing, 'Oh, this is about getting stuff done through my people,'" explains Davis. "The key is to make that mental shift from 'I am the lead salesperson' to 'I am the teacher, influencer and coach for my people, and my success consists of their successes.'"

However, sometimes managers let their new positions—and power—go to their heads. "When I first became a sales manager myself it was a badge I felt I had earned," says executive sales coach Marc Corsini, president of Corsini Consulting Group in Birmingham, Alabama. "I would say things that would be distasteful to me today, like 'She works for me, he works for me, they're on my team.' I was puffing myself up by playing them down. I had taken the role. It was my job, by God, to whip them into shape. And you reap what you sow."

Corsini has worked with thousands of salespeople and managers and has seen firsthand the damaging effects of such domination tactics. "I have seen all styles of sales management," he says, "and the kind of old-school techniques of beating your sales force down and trying to modify behavior through intimidation are terrible. It doesn't work long term at all. The companies that I see growing are the ones where the sales managers and upper management have created an environment where people can flourish.

"A good sales manager is not the one who is attracting attention to himself or herself all the time, but is making stars out of his or her salespeople by helping them overachieve," says Corsini. "If you're helping your salespeople overachieve, you will overachieve by default."

Many sales managers are puzzled by what motivates people. "I see it as logic more than anything else," says Chris McDonnell, sales manager for Eureka Broadband in New York. "When I need people to do something, I'm a fan of using the carrot, not the stick. I would use positive reinforcement, praise, and goal setting rather than the hammer-and-nail approach or breaking somebody down. Maybe we'll have to negotiate, and I'll give in a little and they'll give in a little, but I don't like to threaten and take away commissions. I think that demoralizes reps, and it puts managers in a position where their authority and presence are resented."

Be a Part of Your Team

Third, the ideal sales manager works for the good of the sales team, sells to the team, and sells with the team.

Jason Bergman, global account representative with BAX Global in Fort Lee, New Jersey, has worked as a manager and a salesperson and says management is simply a different kind of sale. "The difference between a sales manager and a salesperson is that the salesperson is selling the company's product or service, and the sales manager is selling salespeople on performance," he says. "So one is an internal sale and one is an external sale. Salespeople work for managers, but to a certain extent the best sales managers really work for their sales reps."

As a rule, managers who adopt this kind of mindset also practice highly effective management strategies. Treating salespeople as customers enables managers to capitalize on the skills that made them top performers. The Forum's Davis recalls, "One sales manager in our study told us, 'Whenever I start to panic, I remember that I can still be a salesperson. It is just that now my employees—my sales staff—are my customers. So I try to use the same skills that I would use with customers in influencing them, in listening to them, in trying to uncover their needs, in trying to persuade them through my involvement.'"

In fact, listening and keeping lines of communication open are essential skills for managers and their sales teams. Sales reps commonly give high praise to managers who are readily available to talk and who return phone calls or e-mails promptly. The manager who comes through in the clutch will gain more respect and authority. When a rep wants to talk, the ideal sales manager listens first, diagnoses the issue, and offers solutions—but never imposes them. Often it takes only a little help to solve a problem that may initially seem cataclysmic to a salesperson.

Have an Open-Door Policy

Fourth, the ideal sales manager is a good communicator who is accessible, responsive, and reality based. "I love working with salespeople, but sometimes it's very difficult to keep my door open because I'm so busy," admits Stella Evans, regional director of sales and marketing for Liverton Hotels in Vancouver, Canada. "Yet when I see salespeople coming at me with this look on their faces like 'Somebody has to help me with this' and they have a contract in their hand, I turn away from my computer and say, 'What's up?' That's all it takes. Usually it's something minor, and they just need some encouragement and a pat on the back and they're perfectly OK."

Of course, there's good communication and then there's bad communication. Sometimes managers miscalculate the quality of their interaction with salespeople.

"Everyone agrees that communication is important, and a lot of sales managers will tell us, 'I have an open door policy' or that they communicate with their sales staff constantly," Davis explains. "But for some sales managers that translates to 'communication out'—where they're doing 90 percent of the communicating and the salesperson is doing 10 percent. That means to the salesperson, 'I have an open door policy and you have permission to come into my office whenever you want and have me give you a lecture.' Or, 'I leave voice mails for my people all the time telling them what I think.' Sales managers often overlook the fact that communication needs to be two ways."

Meetings are a perfect illustration of good communication gone bad. Nearly every rep has been to one of those interminable, seemingly pointless meetings, emerging with nothing more than a handful of doodles on a notepad. Sales meetings should be consistent, brief, and focused on reality. Use the time as an opportunity to discuss challenges, motivate the team, and establish or reevaluate goals.

Time Matters

Fifth, the ideal sales manager values the time of everyone on the team. This means not wasting the sales reps' time and not allowing salespeople to waste the manager's time.

"We often schedule time—a half-hour to 45 minutes—anytime during the week that the reps have open," says Eureka Broadband's McDonnell, who manages nine salespeople. "I'm here early and late and always available to sit down and talk. In our meetings, we go through everything from 'How are you today?' to 'Let's talk about what you envision for the month.' Sometimes we can find things that I can help them with, like getting some muscle from management or helping them come up with creative pricing solutions or strategies. But basically I help them get out of ruts. It's sometimes not too hard to get sidetracked, and these are focusing meetings. You discuss a little bit of the personal, a bit of the professional, and balance it out. You can typically develop a relationship and find out what motivates them pretty easily this way. So I make it a priority to sit down with reps one-on-one regularly."

Some circumstances give good managers an opportunity to show how valuable they really can be to their sales teams. Salespeople often need to talk about their lives, whether it's business or at home, and managers must acknowledge that these issues are part of what makes salespeople perform well or not. Consequently, managers must act as counselors when salespeople face challenges they can't work through on their own.

"I need someone to talk to, almost like a therapist," says QRS's Gerdnic. "No one wants to hear you complain, so when I have a problem, I go to my manager and say, 'This is the problem and here are three possible solutions. Do you have any suggestions?'"

What about reps who are struggling to meet goals? This should signal a coaching opportunity for managers. "If you're talking about a salesperson who said he wanted to make $100,000," says Corsini, "then the manager has to come in and say, 'Look, you've only made x number of dollars so far. Based on where you're going, you're probably not going to meet your goal. Do you still want to make $100,000?' 'Well, yeah.' 'OK, so what do you think you need to do to make more money?' 'Well, I need to go out and see more people.' 'That seems logical. OK, let me help you. Who do you want to see in the next 30 days? Let me help you by holding you accountable to doing that, because I want to see you make $100,000, too.' That's a lot more positive than the manager's saying, 'Either get your butt in order or get out.'"

Setting Goals

Sixth, the ideal sales manager helps reps set realistic yet challenging goals. Ideally the goal should strike a balance that revs the team members up and makes them proud when they reach the goal.

Setting goals is one of the critical ways managers influence, motivate, and help keep their sales teams on track. The right approach to helping salespeople set and meet objectives can make the manager's job infinitely easier. Sales reps who feel a sense of ownership over goals will work harder to meet them as a matter of course. "To me, it's important that salespeople set their own goals," says Beverly Knapp, northeast regional manager at Ablest Staffing in Clifton Park, New York. "If I set goals for them, they're my goals that I've given to them, and it's not going to have much meaning."

Mistakes, setbacks, and unexpected changes also present ideal learning and motivational opportunities. "Let's say a sale doesn't go through," says Kim Whitworth, regional sales manager at AT&T in Madison, Alabama. "The reps call; they're upset. Depending on the individuals, we may review past successes or look to the future and opportunities on the horizon, reinforcing their positives and pointing out what they do well."

In times of crisis or disappointment, reps can lose sight of the big picture, so it's up to the manager to make sure they keep the right perspective. "Sales as a way of making a living is full of rejection and ups and downs, so you try to get up, brush yourself off, and move along," says Eureka Broadband's McDonnell. "Every rep out there has had a big loss of something they were really counting on. It's part of the business. The manager is there to help make those losses a learning experience, to evaluate the situation. Typically there are two or three really good reasons for why they lost it, and when that happens, you can help them with what to do next time. You always make it a learning process."

The Bond of Trust

Seventh, the ideal sales manager establishes an atmosphere of trust. Nothing can replace it once it is lost. By going the extra mile to increase their sales team's chances for success, managers create a more level playing field. They exert their authority while eliminating the kinds of micromanaging habits that tend to flourish in a strictly enforced hierarchy. "If you establish things so that you're the boss and the sales reps report to you and that's it, you're not going to get the performance from the salespeople that you need," says BAX Global's Bergman. "Nor are you going to establish a trusting relationship."

Ideal managers also build trust by putting the best interests of their sales reps first. "It's a return on your investment," Bergman says. "When you support a sales rep in that way, you get a level of trust and loyalty from that individual and the event brings down that wall between boss and employee. The sales rep realizes, 'This person really cares about me. This is a good person who is working in my best interest.' Most good salespeople will respond by working harder at their jobs."

Get Them Revved!

Eighth, the ideal sales manager is a master motivator. Because every salesperson is different, it is important to know what motivates each individual. "It is about literally asking, 'What motivates you?' Most sales managers don't do this because they assume they know or because they assume that what motivates them motivates the salesperson," explains The Forum's Davis. "It's true to an extent that everyone is driven by money, for example, but it's also true that each individual is going to be motivated by something different. Sales reps talk a lot about wanting their managers to ask them what they need and what motivates them."

In some ways, successful sales managers see their sales teams as racehorses that need a clear path to reach the finish line. "I don't want them bogged down with things I can handle for them," AT&T's Whitworth says. "If it's paperwork that I can do or phone calls I can return, then let me do it. I want them freed up to be able to be cold calling, prospecting for new business, and working with customers.

"They don't work for me. They work for themselves and they work for the company. My role is to see that they have the resources and the tools they need to be successful and to remove any obstacles in their way."

During unsettling times, managers can do much to reassure their teams. The right attitude can go a long way to softening the blow and help reps find ways to bounce back. "The company I'm with has been sold four times," says Joseph Murtha, a district sales manager in Pittsburgh, Pennsylvania. "When my boss told me not to worry, it made me appreciate him more because there is a certain amount of uncertainty when you're being bought out. Life has no guarantees, but he tries to keep everyone in tune with the changes and help us react to them. When our commission plan changed suddenly—another surprise—I spent three hours talking and he listened to all my complaints and problems. He helped me iron them out and put a different perspective on things because, as salespeople, we're sometimes selfish, spoiled, and maybe have to be hit with a punch of reality sometimes. I look to him for that because he's a leader and I respect him."

When companies must reduce their sales forces to compete during lean economic times, managers have to roll with the punches. No manager likes dealing with the fallout of company layoffs, smaller sales teams, and more competition for fewer customers. It's traumatizing even for the most confident salespeople.

Andy Zoltners, managing director of ZS Associates in Evanston, Illinois, says these challenges are a good opportunity to raise standards. "In a more cautious buying environment, salespeople have to change the way they sell," he says. "The manager has to respond to that as a trainer by listening to the concerns from the field and then figuring out ways to survive in a tougher marketplace."

Above All, Be a Leader

Ninth, the ideal sales manager is a leader. Leadership means keeping your head when the business community, your markets, the economy, the competition, and the customer base seem to be a swirling sea of turmoil. A good leader supplies vision, courage, and discipline.

Above all the other qualities of a leader, nothing is more powerful than leading by example while understanding what it feels like to be in the salesperson's shoes. Liverton Hotels' Evans explains, "I think it's important for managers to walk in the salesperson's shoes in order to understand what they're going through. Empathy for the other person makes it much easier to work together as a team."

Leading at a higher level requires flexibility, diligence, perseverance, and heart. The best managers are constantly trying to improve their performance in order to help their teams excel. "I think you need to make the reps want to do well for you, for the team, and for themselves," says BAX Global's Bergman. "You have to be someone they want to be like and want to succeed for. You do that by treating them well, giving them attention, caring about what they're going through, recognizing their needs, and supporting them. You have to fight their battles for them, especially with upper management, and if you have a good record of doing that, you succeed and the team does well."

You've picked up this book because you want to be the best manager—yes, say that word with pride—that you can be. This book covers all the essential elements that you need to achieve the highest level of personal success and at the same time develop a winning team. Covering all the essential topics—from hiring and training to building teams and understanding sales psychology—this book is your one-stop shop for all your management needs.

Chapter 1

Hiring the Best

THE WHOLE PICTURE

How a Good Job Description Is an Indispensable Asset for Hiring Smarter and Closing More

Ask sales managers and they'll be the first to admit that creating job descriptions is not the most glamorous aspect of their job—and certainly not the easiest. Nevertheless, identifying the tasks that salespeople are responsible for is vital to an organization's sales success.

Where is the best place to start? "The first thing a sales manager should do when creating a job description is determine what the ultimate goal is for that specific job function," says Sharon Collins, sales manager for AutoTrader in Charlotte, North Carolina. "A job description is basically a road map for your sales reps, with starting and stopping points and a clear goal."

Good advice. However, as anyone who uses a map knows, sometimes the most fruitful journeys include a detour now and then.

Specific Yet Flexible

Vague job descriptions are blueprints for disaster, and sales managers should get very specific in terms of spelling out tasks, goals, and objectives, according to Collins. However, just how "buttoned down" is that? "Job descriptions need to be very specific because it's important for sales reps to know exactly what is expected of them from a time-on-task perspective," Collins explains. "They need to know what their boundaries and responsibilities are and what duties they are expected to perform."

However, all salespeople are unique individuals, and they're not all selling the same thing in the same place. Their job descriptions need to take these factors into account. "My Seattle-area sales manager isn't going to be selling to the same kind of customers as the manager in Milwaukee. They're each going to be targeting different markets and may have to do things a little differently," says Jim Surrell, national sales manager for the western division of Fairbanks Scales in Saint Peters, Missouri. "Job descriptions aren't one-size-fits-all, and you have to allow your sales staff some flexibility, while still staying within the parameters of the job description."

David Emmons, sales manager for Electric Melting Services Co. in Anniston, Alabama, also believes that a job description should be specific and closely monitored, yet flexible enough to allow salespeople leeway in performing the specific duties. "In our line of business, we encourage our salespeople to perform all the services they possibly can," he says. "This is especially true when we know we can increase sales with a particular customer by dislodging a competitor's foothold on the account, or we can develop a stronger relationship with a customer we already have.

"A job description should be tightly defined but loosely enforced. This gives salespeople the opportunity to use their imaginations to develop a system that works best for them, but also satisfies all the requirements of the job description.

"Of course, if you allow them this flexibility in interpreting their job description, you need to closely monitor their activities to ensure that they're not wasting time and energy running off in the wrong direction."

To keep everyone on the team on the right track, they need good directions.

A Good Compass

Sales managers should determine exactly what salespeople need to do to achieve their goals, says AutoTrader's Collins. Part of that process includes allotting time for such different tasks as planning, prospecting, actual selling, and developing territories. "Once a job description is broken down into basic tasks with time allotted, a sales manager needs to take it a step further and break it down even finer," she advises. "For example, if you decide that your salespeople have to devote 80 percent of their time to selling, take a look at what you actually mean by 'selling.' It may be that out of the 80 percent, 40 percent is devoted to going after new business and 40 percent is reserved for servicing existing accounts."

Emmons agrees that splitting a salesperson's time between acquiring new business and servicing existing accounts depends a lot upon what type of business you're in. Every company is different. In some cases, continuous service by a sales rep is an integral part of the selling process. In others, service is a different function, handled by different players coming into the loop. Detailed job descriptions, with enumerated time parameters for each task, add to the efficiency of the sales force and the ultimate profitability of the company.

Surrell services a number of different vertical markets and finds that detailed job descriptions are invaluable in maintaining a high-energy, high-producing sales force. "We sell to seven major market segments, and our product line is very deep. That means our salespeople need to be well versed in a lot of different industries," he says. "The first call in the morning may be to a vitamin manufacturer, but one later that afternoon might be to a landfill owner or a slaughterhouse.

"Each of our area sales managers is assigned a territory based primarily on population, and each has a detailed job description with certain criteria. We want 20 face-to-face sales calls a week and seven quotes a week. Those quotes have to fall within a certain dollar level."

To accomplish this, Fairbanks Scales developed an "Expectations and Territory Management" package for their area sales managers that outlines from A to Z what's expected of them and how to do it. The "Compass" details not only the area sales managers' job description, but also covers such subjects as product and application knowledge, preliminary mapping and qualification of territories, actual organization, following up after sales and more. It even breaks down day by day how area sales managers should spend their time. "The 'Compass' helps our area sales managers focus in on what we expect of them and gives them an idea of what they can expect from management," says Surrell.

Even with such an extensive job description and performance handbook, Surrell realizes that, while the core responsibilities of area sales managers are the same across the board, there are going to be deviations in how and when those responsibilities are discharged. "It all goes back to the job description, knowing the markets and industries you're working in, and keeping an eye on what's moving in your territory at what time," he says. "If you're a manager in Kansas City or Omaha, you're not going to talk to grain elevator operators when they're pulling harvest."

Collins also uses detailed job descriptions to keep reps on track with accounts and territories. "We break up all our accounts into larger franchise accounts or mom-and-pop accounts, by geographical area," she says. "That way we don't have to worry about customers getting hit by different reps in the same week. If you're specific in your job description, reps can focus on their accounts, in their territories. They know what their job functions are, and they can do what they've been hired to do.

"Many times, sales reps end up spending more time at what they enjoy and are good at, and that's just human nature. We sell advertising, and our reps are going back to the same businesses week after week. Building and servicing good business relationships are paramount to their success. Consequently, we put a great emphasis on servicing accounts.

"Still, regardless of how well reps service accounts, there's always going to be some fallout, and if they're not out there continuously building new business, the territory is going to end up losing revenue. We have some reps who just love to prospect and love the thrill of cracking new accounts. Sometimes they lose track of what they're supposed to do from a service perspective, and a written, specific job description helps get them back on the right path."

In addition to keeping them on the right path, managers also can help clear away possible obstacles.

No Road Blocks

When it comes to scheduling, Surrell relies on his area sales managers to set their own selling schedules and, aside from the weekly quote requirements, doesn't micromanage. However, he does have stipulations regarding how time is spent and is adamant about making sure that his area sales managers aren't pulled off the primary task of selling.

"As a manager I try to focus people on their job and remove all obstacles and barriers from their way," says Surrell. "I tell them, 'If anyone at this corporation starts throwing things at you that don't belong there, let me know and I'll handle it.' I want 80 percent of my area sales managers' time spent out there selling. It doesn't always work that way, but we try to get them to that level.

"We say that our areas sales managers' office is empty; we want the salespeople in front of customers. The salespeople we have who are really making it happen are working 60 hours a week or better and are in front of customers 40 hours. The other 20 hours is spent doing what needs to be done to make the job function."

In order to squeeze in more face-to-face sales time for his area sales managers, Surrell provides them with sales tools and streamlines the required paperwork. "We give them laptops, contact management software, and a company car and pay for all their expenses, travel, and customer entertainment," he explains. "We require minimal paperwork and have our own e-mail intranet system so they can contact me, my eastern counterpart, or corporate very easily. We try to do and provide everything we can to get them out in the field more.

"We've developed a quote log so I can keep track of what's quoted in all the different market segments. If they sell something, they get a quote number assigned to them. At the end of the month, they have to fill out one page that probably takes about three minutes of work and e-mail the form to us. That's pretty much it."

Approximately 95 percent of Fairbanks' business is new business. Fairbanks has its own service division, which means area sales managers aren't spending precious sales time on service issues. "Basically our guys are selling new equipment and the service behind the sale, which is handled by our service group," Surrell notes. "We teach our area sales managers to introduce the customer to the appropriate person in our service department, explain to the customer what happens next in the process, tell how the process works, and do a professional handoff."

Essential Components

Should you change job descriptions to fit the strengths and weaknesses of individual salespeople? The overwhelming response from the pros is "no." However, savvy sales managers can create a new position that addresses excellence, talent, and ability. "We give people more responsibility based on their performance," explains Collins. "Job descriptions can change, and we can add layers of responsibility. In essence, you're creating a new position with a different job description. For example, you might create a 'manager in training' position where some salespeople not only handle their own business and territory, but also train and mentor new salespeople."

"We recently came up with the title 'senior area sales manager' with its own job description," says Surrell. "It's an earned title and allows us to cross-train managers on different product lines, markets, and better ways to get things done."

Keep a job description in mind right from the beginning when hiring, suggests Electric Melting's Emmons. The benefits will pay off in the long run. "Managers should select salespeople who have the ability to actively reach for and achieve the primary goals and objectives laid out by upper management," he says. "That includes planning, organizing, controlling, and executing a sale at any time, at any level. These criteria should all be spelled out in a job description."

A Good Fit

According to Thomas Fee, president of Performance Management Consultants in Denver, Colorado, job descriptions and hiring go hand in hand. "A job description outlines what is expected of people, not how they should do it," he explains. "Organizations that don't use clear, written job descriptions and good hiring and selection practices are opening the door to incompetence."

Fee recommends the following four considerations when writing job descriptions and using them to hire good salespeople:

1. Determine exactly what your company does and what the target market is. Then you can structure the job description accordingly.
2. Ascertain what space or niche your salespeople fill within your organization. Do they sell only to new accounts? Do they sell and service accounts? Do they sell only to existing accounts? Do they sell to end users? How much responsibility do you expect them to bear in terms of developing new business or taking care of old business?
3. Know what specific tasks salespeople are expected to perform. Can you describe to them what a typical day, week, month, or year with your company is going to be like from a task standpoint?
4. As a manager, what kind of skills are you going to look for in order to find people who are able to perform those tasks? Behind every task outlined in a job description is a set of skills. The job description is a tool for you to use to hire a person who represents a certain skill set or number of skill sets, depending upon your need.

"Sales managers need to determine a job function and description and identify what skills an individual needs to possess in order to perform those tasks," Fee points out. "That's how you make good hires."

SMART HIRING
How to Avoid the Nine Most Common Sales Hiring Errors

To err in hiring is human—and very expensive. Many "standard" hiring procedures are actually common mistakes, so to choose more competent candidates, prepare to revise your hiring methods. Eliminate these nine common errors from your hiring practices to help you choose only the cream of the crop.

1. Relying on Interviews to Evaluate a Candidate

In a University of Michigan study titled "The Validity and Utility of Alternative Predictors of Job Performance," John and Rhonda Hunter analyzed how well job interviews accurately predict success on the job. The surprising finding: The typical interview increases your chances of choosing the best candidate by less than 2 percent. In other words, flipping a coin to choose between two candidates would be only 2 percent less reliable than basing your decision on an interview.

Experts offer three reasons why interviews are such poor predictors of sales success and why they remain the most common selection technique:

1. Most managers don't structure an interview beforehand and determine the ideal answers to questions (develop a scoring weight).
2. Candidates do much more interviewing than most managers and are more skillful at presenting themselves than many managers are at seeing through their "fronts."
3. An interview helps managers evaluate personal chemistry and determine how well candidates might work together with others.

2. Using Successful People as Models

Duplicating success may seem like a good idea, but the reasons people succeed are not clear from just measuring the characteristics of top performers. More important are the differences between top performers and low achievers. For example, a comprehensive study of more than 1,000 sales superstars from 70 companies showed that the top three characteristics shared by high achievers were the belief that salesmanship required strong objection-answering skills, good grooming habits, and conservative dress—especially black shoes.

However, a study of the weakest performers at these companies revealed that the same three characteristics were their most common traits as well. The lesson: You must "validate" critical success skills by comparing large enough samples of top performers and weak performers to find the factors that consistently distinguish the winners from the "also rans." Otherwise, you may select well-spoken, energetic candidates who fail quickly but with style.

3. Too Many Criteria

Only through a method called "validation" can you make more effective hiring decisions. The government originally used validation research to prove that employment selection practices predicted job success and weren't discriminatory. Similar to a process insurance companies use to predict accident risk or the likelihood of health problems, validation can dramatically improve your odds of hiring the right people. Not only does it identify critical job success factors, it weights each factor's importance. Consider these two surprising and important findings from validation research:

1. The most crucial factor for predicting success in any job is usually as important as or more important than all other factors combined.
2. The most accurate prediction of success on the job is based on no more than six to eight factors. Add any more, and you risk diluting your criteria, watering down the prediction of success, and killing selection accuracy.

To hire winners, decide on six to eight factors that separate them from losers. Ignore factors that are not validated, or you may end up hiring nice guys who finish last.

4. Evaluating "Personality" Instead of Job Skills

Certain personality traits—high energy, honesty, a solid work ethic—seem to practically guarantee success, yet they don't. Many consultants and distributors of pre-employment tests maintain that certain personality factors help ensure management or sales success and offer psychological theories to support that belief. However, solid statistical research from many objective sources shows little correlation between any personality factor and any specific job.

Producers of competent and reputable "personality type" tests (like the Myers-Briggs) admit their tests are useful for self-awareness and training but not for hiring. Only tests of job skills or knowledge are proven to predict job success consistently. You might enjoy knowing your sales candidates have self-confidence and energy, but knowing whether they can answer objections and close sales is probably more important.

5. Failure to Use Statistically Validated Testing

In some companies, committees use deductive reasoning or brainstorming to identify criteria for candidate selection. This technique may encourage team building and a spirit of cooperation and participation, and may even focus the organization on the importance of hiring the right people. Unfortunately, two main flaws make it less effective at pinpointing why candidates fail or succeed.

First, the committees tend to focus on theories instead of facts—theories that suggest, for example, that high self-confidence guarantees a better employee. Second, they focus on attitude and experience instead of ability and skills. Skills are a much more significant and consistent indicator of success potential. Incentives can motivate a skilled person, but motivation and good intentions won't improve an unskilled candidate.

To explain why managers often rely on reasoning or common sense to assess candidates' attitude and personality, experts suggest that doing so is easier than measuring their skills. Gauging skill levels often requires carefully developed tests or on-the-job trials many managers are unwilling or unable to conduct.

6. Using Yourself as an Example

Your own sales success might lead you to believe you can spot candidates with potential, but don't count on it. A famous lawyer once said, "The attorney who would represent himself has a fool for a client"—a saying that also applies to managers hiring new salespeople.

Many managers who reached their position by virtue of their sales success believe they can instinctively recognize a good candidate, when they are unconsciously just using themselves as a template. When you use yourself as a model, your ego often gets in the way, and that "bias" can skew your objectivity in judging others—a fatal hiring flaw.

7. Relying on General "Good Guy" Criteria

Everyone may want to hire good people, but being a good person does not ensure success on the job. Sales success skills are now so specialized that you need specialized hiring criteria as well. A coach filling a spot on a baseball team, for example, bases qualifications on the team's skill. At the Little League level, the selection criteria for a player—dexterity, confidence with the ball, desire to play—are broad. As we reach the high school or college level, the criteria are more specialized, focusing on the four general skills required for success: running, hitting, throwing, and fielding. At the professional level, different playing positions require such specialized skills that no pro scout would rely on four general baseball skills to choose a Major League player. In sales, too, reserve broad, "good guy" criteria for entry-level hiring. When you need a more experienced salesperson, use more specialized criteria.

8. Bypassing the Reference Check

Placement agencies report a fairly high percentage of false information presented in résumés and job applications. As many as 15 to 20 percent of job applicants try to hide some dark chapter in their lives. For some positions, one out of three résumés submitted may contain false information. To find out who's pulling the wool over your eyes, make the extra effort to verify the information your applicants provide. An individual who twists the facts to get a job will probably bend the rules on the job. Checking references may seem tedious, but it beats the frustration and cost of hiring someone you need to fire in two weeks.

9. Not Researching Why People Have Failed in a Job

Research consistently shows that people fail in a job due to factors different from the criteria used to select them. Though most managers can list the most common reasons people have failed, they seldom make that information part of the selection criteria for new candidates.

Managers who identify these "failure points" and build them into the selection process can reduce hiring mistakes by as much as 25 percent. In most sales situations, for example, the average prospect buys from a new salesperson only after six contacts. The average unsuccessful salesperson gives up after three contacts. While that salesperson's techniques may be adequate, the tendency to give up after three rejections was never uncovered or evaluated.

৩৩

With the discovery of hiring mistakes comes the opportunity to make positive change. Even if you are content with most of the people you've hired so far, remember that ongoing improvement is the key to success. When you're willing to revamp your standard hiring procedures, you open the door to a stronger sales team that can lead your company in a new and more profitable direction.

EXPERT ADVICE

What Procedure Should Managers Follow to Check References?

A basic good reference-checking process includes three elements. One, find a firm like Equifax and do a credit check, a DMV check, and a criminal county-of-record and federal-level check for felonies or misdemeanors. Two, send candidates a structured sheet asking for names and contact information of the last five people the candidate reported to, plus the nature of the organizational relationship and dates of employment. Don't let candidates choose their references.

Next, send a form asking for contact information and names of subordinates and peers. Now you have 10 or 11 people to call, and when you check references you can observe certain patterns about the candidate. Too often, companies rely on just two or three decent references, but if you speak to 10 or 11 people, a much clearer picture of the individual emerges.

Finally, with the candidate's permission, call trusted friends and customers for more informal references and ask these questions:

- How long have you known the person? What was the nature of your relationship?
- What are this person's strengths? Weaknesses?
- What projects was the person involved in and how did he or she contribute?
- What problems did the person face during the project and how did he or she solve them?
- How would you describe the person's presentation style?
- Have you read the person's written reports and how would you describe them?

—From Michael Zinn, president of Michael D. Zinn & Associates, a retainer-based executive search consulting firm with offices in New York City as well as Princeton, New Jersey. Visit www.zinnassociates.com.

MAKE YOUR NEXT HIRE YOUR BEST HIRE

A sales team gunning for the competition in a fevered marketplace can't afford any duds. But how can you weed out the cold fish candidates to hire only hot shots?

Unfortunately, there is no simple hiring silver bullet, says Bill Enos, a sales manager with Cellular One in Merced, California. But put in a diligent effort, he notes, and you'll improve your odds dramatically.

"A candidate's background is far and away the most important variable," Enos says, "because a person's history is concrete and measurable, particularly earnings in previous positions. We like to say we look for salespeople with the biggest mortgage. It makes them hungrier.

"Then the other part is to get close to some people who have been close to the candidate. Usually I can find an in where I can get enough information on the prospective hires to know what they've done in the past."

Skullduggery and detective work aside, Enos says he still makes effective use of the personal interview. "I look at the interview like it's a sales call," he explains. "Do the candidates demonstrate good listening skills? I like people who walk into the interview with a notepad, like I'm interviewing them and they're interviewing me at the same time. It shows they're interested in what's going on—maybe they take a few notes and use their listening skills to qualify the situation.

"I also like to see that they've done some background homework on our operation before they walk in, because that's an important sales tool that they're going to use with actual customers, so that counts for a lot. I even like to see an attempt to build some trust and rapport with me based on common experiences."

Remember, you're only as good as your last hire. The people you have on your sales team can make or break your company's bottom line and your career. Yet, many managers make up their minds in the first 60 seconds of an interview whether they're going to hire the candidate or not and spend the rest of the interview intellectually justifying the decision.

Here are four rules for hiring:

1. *Identify your market strategy and think about how you sell.* Do you sell mostly by telemarketing, at trade shows and conventions, door to door, or on outbound appointments? Your marketing strategies determine the type of salespeople you need.
2. *Determine the qualities you need in a person to do those tasks.* What type of education, training, and experience does the person need to have?

3. *Determine aptitude.* Decide what combination of personality traits, mental capability, and interests are needed for this person to be a success. How your company markets, to whom, and how the sale is conducted define what the candidate's attributes need to be.

4. *A candidate must be compatible with the values, personality, and culture of your organization.* An individual who has a great aptitude for selling, is highly motivated, and has a lot of education, training, and experience won't be successful if he or she can't get along with the rest of the organization and doesn't have the same values.

EXPERT ADVICE

Tips for Finding and Hiring Top Sales Producers

If searching for salespeople is often frustrating and you find yourself complaining, "I just can't find qualified salespeople!," do not despair. Careful and creative planning can help make the entire process of finding and selecting salespeople more successful. Here are 11 tips to help you find the most desirable candidates.

1. *Look for qualified salespeople before you need them.* When a salesperson leaves, the company is sometimes in a crisis position: you need someone fast to cover the territory. However, moving fast can limit your options rather than yielding the cream of the crop.

2. *Brainstorm the salesperson's duties and responsibilities.* Consider how much expertise is required in territory planning, business management, and servicing current clients. Be sure to include any unique aspects of this sales position.

3. *Establish hiring criteria such as experience and education, then write your job description.* Don't look for a high-powered candidate for a low-powered job. Managers looking for the best credentials for a job with limited potential set themselves up for disappointment.

4. *Look to many sources for your potential salespeople.* Your own company may have someone in the ranks ready to make a career move. Professional recruiters can save you time in locating qualified individuals. Personal contacts at trade shows and conventions can key you in to potential employees.

5. *Once you have those résumés, read between the lines!* Since written presentation skills are important in sales, you should note how each candidate has approached the résumé as a sales tool. If in doubt whether a candidate's résumé belongs in the "to interview" file or the "no" file, proceed to the telephone interview.

6. *Conduct an initial phone interview.* Since salespeople use the telephone to prospect and set appointments, here you have an opportunity to hear them before you are affected by their personal appearance. If you are hiring for a position that is predominantly telephone sales, your telephone interview should be extensive.

7. *Your personal interview style should be thorough and methodical.* Ask open-ended questions and listen carefully to the responses. Explain what your products or services have to offer potential customers. Then present the benefits of working for your company.

8. *Trust your judgment in the personal interview, BUT find out the facts.* Even if the candidate comes highly recommended or your first impressions tell you this is the one, use the interview to probe deeply and back up your intuition with facts.

9. *Treat the sales interview as a sales call—you're the prospect!* The candidate is making a very important call here. You are asking the candidate to do in your sales interview what you want him or her to do as a sales rep—sell!

10. *Conduct role-playing sessions with your top candidates.* These sessions will allow you to see how the salespeople handle clients. If sales reps can perform during a demanding job interview and sell you, there is an excellent chance they can sell your prospects and customers.

(*Continued on next page.*)

(*Continued from previous page.*)

11. *Check references carefully.* Open-ended questions are best to find out the whole story. "How did she perform for the company?" or "Would you hire this person again?" leave room for a wide range of honest answers.
    Based on the pointers above, create a brief sales interview assessment form and then use it in your interviews to help keep track of potential sales superstars.

—From Helen Berman, president of H. Berman & Associates, specializing in sales and marketing and customized sales training, telemarketing, communications, and management development programs. For more information, please write to H. Berman & Associates, 12021 Wilshire Boulevard, Suite 177, Los Angeles, California 90025, or call (213) 820-7312.

ALWAYS ON THE LOOKOUT

How to Cultivate New Recruits to Take the Headache Out of Hiring Salespeople

It's understandable why sales managers with a fully staffed sales team can become complacent about hiring. But then one or two team members quit, another goes back to school, and yet another takes maternity leave—and all of a sudden you're scrambling faster than the egg chef at Denny's in the middle of the Saturday morning rush.

To avoid falling behind on the staffing curve, suggests author Mark David, sales managers should develop an ongoing hiring farm team so that new sales reps can be called up like big league ballplayers whenever the team is in need. The following tips are excerpted from David's book *Coaching Illustrated: A Proven Approach to Real World Management*.

The time to cultivate your farm club of prospective sales hires is while you're fully staffed. By waiting until people leave, you force yourself to depend on newspaper ads and the whims of the job market at that point in time. You will also likely be forced to hurry the decision.

Instead, managers should dedicate four hours each month to developing their farm team. In practice, this means setting a goal for yourself, producing a plan, creating action steps, and then recording it all in your daily planner. Like most goals, if it isn't written down, it likely won't happen.

Try to determine a reasonable hiring goal for your organization. For example, you might decide to find one new player for your team every quarter. How many interviews should you conduct per month to meet that goal? In your daily planner, outline the action steps you'll need to take, like calling prospects and conducting in-person interviews. Do not put this off—hold yourself accountable for confirming and going through with the interviews.

By setting goals for developing your farm team—and following through—you will be in a more advantageous position when, inevitably, some of your best people do leave. Just imagine how much less stress you'll feel the next time someone departs, knowing you already have a number of top-quality candidates waiting to move into the new position.

Chapter 2

Testing Potential Candidates

TESTING THE WATERS

How to Use a Testing Company to Recruit the Very Best Sales Candidates for Your Company

Finding and selecting new salespeople is a critical part of every sales manager's job. Find the right people and, if the incentives are right, revenue will grow. It is not quite that easy, but talented people simply sell better, with much less supervision. And their eagerness to sell can often work around the gaps and glitches that inevitably develop in any sales force.

While most companies have always paid major attention to recruitment, the Internet makes it possible to reach a much wider pool of sales candidates—across the country or even across the world if that is appropriate. And the Internet is doing something else that is transforming salesperson selection: enabling companies to economically screen and test new salespeople much more widely than ever before.

The basics of employee selection, however, still count. Many firms continue to find that the personal touch, in the form of referrals from current employees, is the best source of new reps. As is the case with market leads, referrals are usually the gold of rep prospecting. Still, fast-growing companies need more reps than referrals offer, so they must search more broadly.

Just ask a very busy duck, AFLAC. AFLAC sells accident, dental, disability, long-term care, and other kinds of supplemental insurance to employees of businesses. AFLAC, a Fortune 200 company, now operates across the United States and abroad, including Japan, where AFLAC has a major share of the market. AFLAC goes to market through 55,000 writing agents. It has become nearly as famous as Coca-Cola in its markets—not a bad advantage when seeking new agents.

AFLAC agents may sell other companies' policies, but the AFLAC line has grown sufficiently broad that this division of effort is usually not necessary. AFLAC agents are paid through a commission on new business, stock bonuses, and a percentage of renewal policies.

If success and fame bring larger challenges, John Laughbaum, AFLAC's VP of field force development, has a gigantic challenge. He must oversee the recruitment of roughly 20,000 new agents per year for both replacement and expansion purposes. Laughbaum estimates that AFLAC must start with at least 10 candidates for each person eventually selected. So AFLAC must initially look for upward of 200,000 potential agents each year.

"The number one sources of recruits are referrals, nominees, and personal observation," Laughbaum says. "Our best new hires are people our agents know, friends they meet at church or have seen work." AFLAC also uses a few personnel channels, including career fairs, Internet sites such as Monster.com and CareerBuilder.com, college recruitment, and radio and print advertising.

AFLAC does not try to enforce uniform rules on employee selection, partly because its markets are so diverse. "Our approach is to let local recruiters decide how to recruit and hire," Laughbaum notes.

The most common approach involves two-step interviews. After a person submits a résumé, there is a brief phone conversation. "We try to make sure they have reliable transportation and that they do not have a felony conviction, in compliance with state law," Laughbaum says. Then there is an in-person interview for about half an hour to test true interest in sales.

If that first interview is successful, a second, hour-long session is held that goes into depth on the candidate's goals and AFLAC's training programs. Some local offices combine the two interviews into a group interview with up to five candidates watching an AFLAC video and interacting with recruiters. The aim is always to tailor the approach to local conditions, whether rural or metropolitan. After the second or group interview, a job-offer decision is usually made.

AFLAC thus has a quick, streamlined, and flexible process. Unfortunately, new agents must also meet government licensing requirements. Usually this means studying for an examination and then clearing a background check. The licensing process varies widely among states and is beyond AFLAC's control. "It can take from less than a week to 12 weeks," Laughbaum says.

Some AFLAC recruiters use limited personality testing, but these tests are not a companywide policy. Laughbaum says that drive, rather than education, experience, or credentials, is usually what makes a good AFLAC agent. "Athletic coaches are often very good at sales, and so are firefighters, police officers, teachers, and white-collar workers." Laughbaum worries about any screening step that might prematurely exclude a potentially successful agent.

AFLAC can take chances on new people partly because all its compensation is based on performance. And it can search broadly because training for AFLAC products and techniques is thorough. Laughbaum is confident that AFLAC's training program can fill in experience gaps.

Every new agent first attends a four-day sales school. After that, an online program, AFLAC University, offers more than 100 separate courses. About a fifth of these online courses cover product knowledge. The rest focus intensely on selling, business, and practical skills. This can include anything from how to use an AFLAC laptop to time-management skills or how to think like a CEO. About 500 AFLAC agents use the online university every day. Finally, backing up this Internet-based training are 140 professional trainers, many of them in the field with managers or reps.

Marriott Vacation Club International has a similar recruiting challenge on a smaller scale. But that scale is growing fast.

Marriott now has about 1,000 salespeople, all paid entirely by commission. Marriott needs to add about 600 reps per year, for both growth and replacement. To find the right 600, Marriott will initially seek about 2,500 applications and give 1,500 of these an online test that has been carefully developed to find the best candidates.

Marriott calls its recruiting "talent acquisition," according to Alan Cervasio, VP of global sales strategy and talent relations. "We seek new sales associates through channels and clusters," Cervasio summarizes. These include advertising programs, career nights, college nights, and referrals. "Our best candidates come from asking our successful sales executives to give the recruitment manager a profile of people who would fit within the Marriott culture," Cervasio says. And, as with AFLAC, referrals tend to be one of the most successful sources of top performers.

Another similarity is that Marriott is not looking for experience within its own industry, but for the right type of people from a variety of careers. "We look for talent, not experience," Cervasio emphasizes.

The first step is quantifying the need for new reps and the timing of their recruitment. Marriott tracks its business closely and can predict the volume of sales opportunities well enough to know how many new associates it will need for each upcoming season.

The next selection step is looking over résumés and having short conversations to screen applicants. Then comes the online test.

Working with the Gallup organization for 10 years, Marriott has studied hundreds of its very top performers to develop a Web-based test. The test now has 280 questions and is given to each candidate who passes the initial screen. The latest Gallup test has been given for two years and has proven its worth. Marriott tracks closing percentages, retention rates, and sales volume-per-guest for each salesperson and region. Cervasio reports that the online test has added $275 million in net revenue over two years and has cut sales costs by about 3 percent.

After completing the online test, successful candidates have face-to-face interviews with hiring managers. Some managers do panel interviews with several executives present for each candidate. Only when all managers agree on a candidate does the process move to the next step, offering the candidate a position with Marriott. Cervasio says the entire process, from initial contact through hiring, takes from 30 to 45 days.

Formal tests for sales positions are playing an increasing role in selection. HR Chally has been testing employment candidates, with an emphasis on sales positions, for about 30 years, according to CEO Howard Stevens.

The Chally evaluations focus on predicting job performance, not just on describing the candidates. In sales the aim is to forecast accurately which candidates will perform in the top half of reps. Stevens notes that the predictive power of the Chally test has been confirmed by 300 validation studies from a database covering about 150,000 individuals.

Chally uses one test, involving nearly 900 data elements, for all candidates. The test is given over the Internet and takes about an hour to complete. Although the test is the same, its interpretation differs according to the sales position to be filled. Stevens points out that new-account hunters will need different qualities from farmers of current accounts. Similarly, inside reps sell differently from outside ones, and national account execs or other managers will differ from line sales reps. Chally thus interprets test results differently for each type of assignment.

The Chally test can be taken online because it is not a knowledge test—cheating won't help. And it contains its own validation checks to detect false answers. Most convenient for global organizations, the Chally test is conducted in a variety of languages and has been given in 34 countries.

Stevens says the test can be used at any stage of the selection process. Most clients use the test after reviewing résumés and having a brief telephone conversation with applicants. "They usually require the test before the final interviews of the top three or four candidates," he says.

Chally also uses tests for a major nonrecruiting service, its Organization Development Analysis (ODA). Many ODA clients test all their employees, storing the results in a special database. The ODA may be used in four basic ways. First, it can ensure that the right people are in the best slots for their talents by guiding minor reassignments of duties.

Second, ODA helps select the best people for new job assignments. Third, it can substantially improve career development of employees by assessing their strengths and weaknesses. Fourth and most strategically, the ODA data measures the company's overall employee resources so that top management can plan for long-term growth.

Chally introduced ODA in the middle of 2003. By the end of 2004, the ODA approach had been applied at 90 companies. One major client, auto giant General Motors, credits the Chally program with a significant gain in its market share. As Howard Stevens notes, market-share points for GM add up to some very significant dollars.

The online approach to testing sales candidates has spread about as rapidly as the Internet itself. Most major testing companies now offer online selection tools.

Testing candidates since 1986, SalesTestOnline has focused exclusively on Internet-based testing of sales recruits for the past four years. President David Pearce says the company is distinctive in providing extremely economical online sales tests that are fully customized for each client and position.

"Prior to Internet tests, most companies could afford to test just a short list of applicants, the top three or four people," Pearce notes. "And a lot of Web-based tests are still quite expensive, up to $100 each. With our test, you can test a dozen or more people for every position and speed up the whole process."

Pearce recommends that his clients use his test broadly, to screen all candidates and to focus interviews on only the top candidates. SalesTestOnline starts out at $25 per test but decreases to a few dollars per test when several thousand are tested. An unlimited-use price plan even allows a company to screen every job seeker at no additional cost. Customization for clients is included in per-test fees because Pearce is confident that satisfied clients will renew their licenses.

SalesTestOnline is essentially a personality test. It looks for temperament, motivation, drive, assertiveness, a sense of urgency, and need for supervision. An overall suitability rating is the bottom line.

SalesTestOnline is a minimal obligation for job seekers as well. It takes only 10 minutes, during which candidates respond to two screens of adjectives and instructions. A concise, two-page report of results is immediately e-mailed to hiring managers. Pearce says the test can spot any excessive role-playing by candidates trying to fake favorable impressions.

But Pearce cautions that his online test, like any test, must be used as just one part of a thorough selection process. He reports that clients judge SalesTestOnline to be about 90 percent accurate at its specific goal, describing the personalities of candidates relative to specific sales jobs. About a thousand companies now use SalesTestOnline, including Home Depot and H&R Block, as well as many banks and equipment and telecom firms.

WHICH IS THE BEST TEST FOR YOU?

How to Choose the Best Assessment Test for What You Need in New Hires

Hiring new salespeople can be the most important decision a sales executive makes on a routine basis. Effects of a bad decision can include lost sales, wrecked customer relationships, and the heavy cost of replacing a rep who's below par.

Even average hiring decisions leave money on the table—the money your firm could make by hiring people who have the potential to become top performers.

Expert firms can help you hire better reps by using a variety of tests and assessment methods. The Internet allows more kinds of tests to be given much more economically and earlier in the recruiting process. But the bottom line is, Does the test you're using improve results? The best recruiting experts should be able to demonstrate that their methods work—that they raise the average sales of new hires and reduce the costs of turnover from bad hires.

Shooting for 85 Percent Success

Recruiting assessments conducted by The Gallup Organization focus on five primary areas, according to Benson Smith, global leader for Gallup's Sales Force Effectiveness. The first area is motivation. "The best salespeople are simply more motivated than 9 out of 10 people," Smith emphasizes.

The second area is the candidate's ability and willingness to ask people to do things. Reps must get customers to make commitments.

Relationship skills, which primarily mean gaining trust, are next. Sometimes trust must be gained in a very short time, in other cases it must be maintained over years. Gallup wants to ensure that the potential rep has the skills to fit the market.

Gallup also looks for the ability to organize, plan, and administer. Many people go into sales because they dislike paperwork, Smith says. "Yet in every sales job there is a certain amount of paperwork that has to be done."

Finally, every sales job requires presenting information, listening to customers, and solving problems. Gallup thus wants to know how well recruits take in and process information—that is, how well they think.

Gallup starts by looking for the role-specific behaviors of top performers in each sales force. It then develops questions designed to spot differences and behaviors in either interviews or tests. The results predict the probability that each candidate will match the level of a firm's best salespeople.

Gallup has been studying the relationship between candidates' abilities and the traits of companies' top performers for 40 years. Gallup's senior analysts develop test or interview questions for each client. These veterans have both doctoral-level education and extensive experience in conducting at least 10,000 job interviews. It is cheaper to use generic questions and tests, Smith acknowledges. But accuracy increases dramatically when only the best question for each sales role is used.

Gallup's questions can be asked in a number of ways: in an automated telephone interview for initial screening purposes, through a Web-based test, or during in-depth telephone or face-to-face interviews.

Smith's confidence in Gallup's accuracy is rooted in his experience from using the firm for 20 years in his own career, which included the presidency of a Fortune 500 medical company. He says Gallup's prediction of top-performer potential and actual performance of new hires correlated at about 85 percent. When even the best managers tried to predict success without using Gallup results, they got it wrong about half the time. Good tests and interviews "are simply much more reliable than even the best sales manager's gut instincts."

What is accuracy worth? Smith puts his case simply: "What would your sales results look like if 75 to 85 percent of the people you hire next year perform at the level of your very best producers?"

And assessment can save money in the recruitment process itself. Why waste the valuable time of senior managers on interviewing candidates who do not fit the needs of your sales force?

Recruiting Globally on the Internet

Profiles International offers a psychometric sales profile that also focuses on five key qualities, according to CEO Jim Sirbasku. Profiles looks for competitiveness, persistence, self-reliance, energy, and a combination of these qualities that Sirbasku calls "sales drive." Once profiled, the likely behavior of each candidate in seven critical areas can be predicted.

"For example, we are looking for the way a candidate will prospect," Sirbasku explains. "What kind of closer will they be, how reluctant will they be to make calls, are they self-starting, can they play on a team and build and retain relationships?"

The 75-question profile is given over the Internet and takes 15 to 20 minutes. It is available in 12 languages, and the questions have been customized for local cultures. "If you are hiring a German, you want to use German cultural information." Results are immediately available to U.S. managers in English.

Tests are customized for each client by sales position. "We build a job match pattern for hiring and coaching, validated against the top reps and the lowest producers," Sirbasku says. Attempts to "fool the test" are countered by asking questions with socially desirable answers, calculating a "distortion score," and adjusting results. The profile retails for $50 to $75, with discounts for higher volumes.

With 700 reps selling the profile and Internet testing available 24/7, Sirbasku says, "We are high tech and high touch." Since 1991, he has worked for firms such as Snap-on Tools, Deluxe Checks, and American Income Life. Sirbasku is especially proud of having done validation tests with more than 117,000 applicants and of an 80 percent retention rate by a huge client base.

LOOKING FOR COMMITTED PROFESSIONALS

Objective Management Group has been testing sales candidates as part of its larger services of evaluating and improving sales forces since 1989, according to test developer Dave Kurlan. The result of an Objective Management test is a straightforward recommendation to managers on whether a potential recruit should be hired for a specific sales position.

"We have developed our own criteria of elements that a person must meet to be successful in sales," Kurlan explains. "Then there is a second set of criteria based on what the client tells us is necessary for success in their business."

The test identifies the number of success criteria met and the number failed, which are the candidate's weaknesses. "Depending on the income level of the sales position, we will allow no more than a certain number of weaknesses for a positive recommendation," Kurlan explains.

Successful candidates must have fewer weaknesses as compensation increases. "When the target compensation is a quarter-million dollars a year, they cannot have any weaknesses," Kurlan emphasizes. "But at the entry level, you can have some faults as long as there is a strong desire and commitment to succeed."

Among the most crucial hiring criteria are desire for success, commitment to success, taking responsibility for results, and the candidate's incentive to improve any weak areas.

Kurlan calls this approach an execution test. "The crucial question in selecting a new salesperson is, Will they do what the client needs them to do?" he says. "We look at what the necessary skills are, what can be taught, and whether the person has what it takes to be consistently successful." Sales is a tough environment, so Kurlan is always trying to find out "Will they do it?" rather than "Can they do it?"

The company has invited its clients to have independent firms audit the predictive accuracy of its recommendations. "A year later we ask, 'Is the new person still there, and are they successful in the position?'" Kurlan explains. Measured this way, he says, accuracy is about 95 percent.

The test contains 80 questions and takes half an hour to complete on the Web. Kurlan urges clients to give the test before any interview, to avoid the biases that come from "gut-level opinions" about the candidate. The tool is generally sold through other sales development firms, not directly by Objective itself.

Kurlan offers a free tool that helps managers decide how much a better hiring process can be worth. "We call it a 'ghost worksheet.' You can figure out how much your departed sales ghosts really cost you. Even when they are long gone, those ghosts come back to haunt you. A big hiring mistake can cost six figures."

SIMULATING SALES CHALLENGES

Upward Motion does assessments for recruiting, selecting, and training salespeople, according to the firm's president, Kim Ades. The company has products geared for real estate agents and for business-to-business selling. It is about to introduce an assessment for call center staff.

The real-estate tool, which Upward has offered the longest, has three parts: an intelligence test, a personality test, and a simulation of actual selling situations. The business-to-business assessment also includes a simulation of selling in business markets.

"The highlight is the simulation component," Ades says of the real estate product. "The candidates interact with virtual clients through the whole sales cycle, from building rapport to closing, and we compare them to top performers."

In the simulation of business-to-business selling, candidates deal with typical challenges in this market, including analyzing customer needs, selecting the best course of action, and negotiating prices.

Ades calls it a "competency-based model" of sales ability. "We look for four basic competencies: analyzing customer needs, listening and comprehension skills, ability to manage the sales process, and closing skills," she says. "We believe the best indicator of performance is skills."

Recruits can also use the simulations to decide if they really want to sell. "Companies put a link on their Web site, saying, 'If you are really interested, try our sales simulator,'" Ades explains. "Candidates get an idea of what a sales career is like, get a sense of the highs and lows, and can decide if they are likely to succeed in it." Managers use the results to screen candidates and look for areas to probe in interviews or to address in training.

Sales simulation is done over a high-speed Internet connection, as it includes a video component and takes about 75 minutes. The cost per assessment starts at $300 but goes down to $100 for larger volumes. Or clients can purchase a site license for unlimited use. The eight-year-old Upward Motion has been offering simulations for two years.

Ades is convinced this high-tech, reality-based approach is the wave of the future in assessing recruits. She has signed up Abbott Technologies, an auto-parts company, Ciba Vision, and a Prudential real estate unit. All assessments are validated against actual sales performance before they are offered to clients.

Testing for Improvement

Thoughtful, Inc., offers consulting and software for performance improvement, according to president, Doug Kern. The firm tests the existing staff of a client company, including sales reps, to look for strengths and weaknesses. Sales candidates can be compared to the top performers within each company or to reps in the same industry.

Thoughtful is looking for competencies in specific areas. For example, there is an assessment of persuasion skills that focuses on three competency areas and an assessment of negotiation skills that was developed in collaboration with a lawyer specializing in this field. Another assessment, market intelligence, looks at knowledge of specific markets and industries.

The assessments are given over the Internet and take about 10 minutes each. Salespeople usually take two or three of the assessments, well after the initial screening and interview stages.

Thoughtful's tests are not offered separately, but are part of its overall performance-improvement engagements. The real work is in customizing a broad question list to suit each company, and then making sure the test works and has the managers' confidence. After that, the Thoughtful assessments can be given very economically for as many recruits as necessary.

Kern says the purpose of testing both current and new salespeople is improvement rather than simple selection. "You don't go to a doctor to find out what is wrong with you, but to get cured," he notes. Salespeople often have their own natural style, and all the coaching in the world will not change it. "We try to make improvements where they are weak and to exploit their strengths."

EXPERT ADVICE
Add Winners to Your Sales Team

Hiring new salespeople isn't like making a selection at a vending machine. The choices you make have long-lasting implications. The following tips are for making sure you add winners to your sales team:

- Know what your marketing strategy is and how you sell. Do you sell by phone, by exhibiting at trade shows and conventions, door to door, or mostly by appointment? Your marketing strategies determine the kind of salespeople you need.
- Determine the qualities you need in salespeople to do those tasks. What type of education, training, and experience must they have?
- Determine aptitude. What combination of mental abilities, personality traits, and interests is needed for this candidate to be a success in this position? How you sell defines what the salesperson's attributes need to be.

- Candidates must be compatible with the values, personality, and culture of the organization. Individuals who have a great aptitude for selling; are highly motivated; and have a lot of education, training, and experience still won't be successful if they can't get along with the rest of the organization and don't have the same values.

—From Harris Plotkin, president of the Carlsbad, California-based Plotkin Group, which specializes in hiring, training, team development, and promoting. Visit www.plotkingroup.com.

Chapter 3

Training Essentials

SALES TRAINING 101: HOW SHALL I TRAIN THEE? LET ME COUNT THE WAYS

Done well, sales-skills training can inspire, motivate, and generate genuine behavior change leading to tangible bottom-line sales results. Done poorly, you can wind up spending a small fortune to drag your salespeople out of the field, bore them for a few days with information they either already know or that does not apply to them, and then return them to the trenches more puzzled and alienated than before.

Why Do You Need Training?

So what can you do to ensure that your next sales training venture delivers on its promise? First of all, you may want to check your motivation. According to Gil Cargill, a Los Angeles–based trainer, too many companies look to skills training as a solution to a problem that has nothing to do with salespeople's selling skills.

"You have to figure out what the real problem is," Cargill urges. "When training fails to improve productivity, more often than not the problem has nothing to do with skills. At best, skills training can only improve the skills of the salespeople and managers. It can't do anything, for example, about a compensation program that's out of whack. By the same token, I'm 5 feet 8 inches tall, and no matter how much training I get I'm never going to dunk a basketball in the NBA."

Cargill says that instead of fixating on a single skill or skill set that needs improvement, sales organizations will view training as a panacea to address a host of problems he refers to as the "sales-prevention department."

"The sales-prevention department is a conglomeration of haphazard, inaccurate, sloppy administration, billing, manufacturing, delivery, shipping, and customer support issues," he explains. "So when those functions fail, the customer calls the sales reps, who are then rendered incapable of selling the next deal because they are too busy patching up the last one. The problem is looking to sales training to fix issues that have nothing to do with the salespeople's skills."

Even when a sales organization's problems are skills-based, however, managers may still have difficulty in isolating the point in the sales process where their people are running into stumbling blocks. Linda Richardson, president and CEO of the Philadelphia-based Richardson Company, suggests that companies feeling pain should examine whether their salespeople's skills match up with the strategies they are supposed to be executing.

"Managers will often begin by feeling a deficit," she says. "They know something's not right. Maybe they're not hitting their numbers, people are complaining, or they just want to take their people to the next level. They want to figure out what to do. The best place to start is to look at your sales strategy each year. What are you asking your salespeople to do? And the big question is, Do they have the skills and knowledge to do it?"

As an example, Richardson cites a hypothetical company that has traditionally sold to middle-market customers. However, another company that wants to pursue a more high-end clientele acquires the company. "Selling to small or middle-size companies is a different ballgame than selling to large corporations," she notes. "This is a substantial strategy change. You have to ask yourself, 'Do my people have the skills to successfully implement this strategy?' When you're selling to a smaller company, you can usually get to the senior people—access isn't denied. But with large corporate customers, instead of the CFO you're talking to an assistant treasurer. Is that where you want to be? Probably not. And that's an area where you can provide training that fits the new strategy."

When the challenge is not one of overall strategy, but the breakdown of an individual skill or skill set, Richardson recommends analyzing your sales process to find where your people are most frequently running into a snag. "This option is a little more reactive compared to the proactive approach of analyzing your strategy," she says, "but take a look at your results. Are they not closing enough? Are they not making it to the final presentation? Are they selling at the wrong level? Do they need to cross-sell more? You identify the gap and then figure out what to do."

Cargill believes that sales managers should assess their training needs by administering a skills test to the sales team and then seeing if the results match what is going on in the field. "A skills test can compare your people against unbiased standards," he explains. "There are several good skills tests available on the market. They don't test aptitude, attitude, or behavior. They test your knowledge of selling.

"Let's say the evaluation comes back saying that your salespeople need work on their negotiation skills. If you've been out in the field and watched your people sell, then you've probably seen them flounder through negotiation situations. So you don't go on just your gut feelings or on the test, but now you have corroborating evidence about what needs to be done before you make the decision to bring a sales trainer in."

As both Cargill and Richardson point out, training is most effective when those being trained are excited about improving their skills. Although not the only deciding factor, your salespeople's input should contribute to the decision-making process. Where do they feel the need for improvement? Ask open-ended questions and then follow up—treat your salespeople as though they're customers you're probing for needs. Go beyond the superficial answers to uncover the core issues. A few questions Richardson suggests include "What are the obstacles you come up against most frequently?" "What are the products or services you can sell more readily?" "What are the objections you hear most often? Which are the most difficult to address?" "How long is your sales cycle? Where do you usually get stuck?" and "How many decision makers do you sell to?"

The final step in assessing your training needs is to solicit client feedback. Richardson cautions against sending customers standardized forms because, she explains, salespeople tend to select clients who will only offer positive responses. And clients generally aren't interested in delivering unpleasant news, either. Instead, Richardson suggests running what she calls a "deals won/deals lost" analysis.

"Every time a deal is won or lost, have someone—preferably not the rep involved—call the client and objectively obtain real feedback on why you won or lost that deal," she advises. "Get beyond 'You had a higher price' to explore what really drove the sale. The deals won can help you build a set of best practices that can form the foundation of your skills training, while the deals lost will show you if something's happening in your industry that you hadn't yet identified. Maybe you have a new competitor in the marketplace that's changed competitive pricing. If so, examining your lost deals will expose that fact."

Select the Right Trainer

Figuring out your skills-training needs is just half the battle, however. Next comes the imposing task of whittling down the list of hundreds of training companies to just one—the trainer with the right match for your sales organization. So where should you begin your search?

As president of ETC Connect, an entertainment and architectural lighting manufacturer in Middleton, Wisconsin, Mark Vassallo says he doesn't have to go out of his way to find vendors—the training offers constantly flood into his office for his perusal. "It's difficult to determine. I get inundated with at least five pieces of mail a day from trainers, for seminars, tapes, books, everything," he says. "My people could be going to round-the-clock time management training if I responded to all the come-ons. Their notebooks would be neat but they wouldn't sell anything."

Vassallo says that the company takes care of most training for his salespeople internally, while outside trainers are typically brought in only to work on very specific skills—body language, telephone selling strategies, or trade show selling, for example. "The way we typically choose a program is that we'll either identify a need or a recommendation will come in from another source, or both," Vassallo explains. "But a lot of it is luck. It's not as if your pipes freeze and you need somebody immediately. You just decide you want to do something differently and then you find a vendor. And we've had success with this approach."

For Vassallo, this catch-as-catch-can approach to choosing trainers works because the stakes are relatively low. The company's long-term prospects don't ride on such small, one-time training events. However, for other organizations that are feeling the pinch and need to improve their skills to remain competitive, choosing the right trainer should be done systematically, recommends Cargill. "Once a company settles on the notion of getting sales training, it very often will go for the program that the most powerful manager or clique of managers likes the best, not necessarily the one that best fits the organization's needs," he says. "Or a manager might be new to a company and bring in a trainer he or she had worked with before, without considering whether the trainer provided a good match for the new company's products or culture."

Among the litany of other dubious criteria used to select trainers, Cargill includes meeting someone on a plane and being impressed enough to skip the investigation process, hearing from a third party that someone is "really good," and going with such questionable references as "my brother-in-law knows this guy from his macramé class who was in the Navy with a guy who's supposed to be terrific."

Instead of relying on these notoriously unreliable grapevines, Richardson suggests first letting the Web be your guide: reputable training companies should offer at least basic information on their Web sites about their services. On trainers' Web sites look for strong client lists that indicate a training company's track record.

Nevertheless, when you talk to trainers about their lists, she says, remember that not all clients are created equal. "Anyone can put a name down, regardless of what level of work they did with that client," she says. "Ask them, 'How long did you work with company *x*? How broad was your penetration?' If you're a banking institution, you might be impressed to see that a trainer had worked with Citicorp. But did they just do one day with a small group, or were they responsible for training the entire international division? That makes a big difference."

Admittedly, training your salespeople is a big job, and what would a job search be without references? When you follow up with a trainer's references, make sure to ask not only whether people enjoyed the trainer, but also whether the program generated actual results.

"One of sales trainers' dirty tricks," Cargill says, "is that they know that if the audience enjoys the training experience, it will be valued—not that they got something out of it, not that it changed their behavior, not that it helped them sell more. To avoid this, you need a training plan that says, 'I want to achieve this measurable result. Here's the starting point, here's how I'm going to measure it, and here are the benchmarks I'll look at.' Then when you talk to references, find people who will say that as a result of the training they are selling 5 percent more, 10 percent more, or that their margins have gone up two or three points. You need to find out about tangible, measurable results or it's meaningless."

Narrow your choices to no more than five or six top options, suggest Cargill and Richardson, and then shift the search into high gear. Conduct phone interviews, put out a request for proposals (RFP), and let the trainers begin to sell you on their services. Richardson feels that trainers should be allowed to deliver full-scale sales presentations, while Cargill emphasizes accountability.

"Most sales trainers won't guarantee that their work will produce the measurable result," he says. "They will guarantee that they will show up on time, that your people will have a good time, that they'll cover the curriculum, and that you will be 'satisfied' at the end of the session. But remember, satisfaction without metrics is based on personal appeal."

Whatever criteria you choose to weigh when deciding among candidates, be thorough. As Richardson notes, "This is like sending your children to school. Pay attention to who's training your sales force."

Vassallo agrees. "A training company should really have to sell you on its services," he says. "And for us that's the fun part—watching another salesperson trying to sell you. It's your job to be a tough customer. Go ahead and put them through the wringer."

Select the Right Program

One concern Vassallo voices about allowing outsiders to deliver training is that the trainer may not understand his company's unique culture. "In our corporate culture, we really emphasize taking care of the customer," he says. "The company philosophy is an integral part of the sales training we do internally. We don't go in for the hard sell, and so we don't want our salespeople going outside for training and learning strategies that conflict with that."

As Cargill points out, however, good trainers should be willing to work with you to develop a curriculum that not only matches your needs, but also fits your corporate culture. "If you don't communicate to the trainer what you want, then there's little chance you'll get it," he cautions. "Some may say that because selling is selling, training is training, and it's all equal. That's like saying athletics is athletics, so teaching people to play hockey is the same as teaching them to play tennis. You must teach them differently. Selling to large accounts is different than selling to small accounts. Selling in a relationship mode is different than selling in a solutions mode."

Richardson adds that when it's done well, a customized training program should keep your people in their world, dealing with their products and customers, their challenges and their opportunities, with pointed case studies and role plays that resonate because they come from the salespeople's own experiences. "Everyone says they customize today, but the key is to say, 'Let me see some work you've done,'" Richardson advises. "Is it just the push of a button to change the name on the handouts or does it bring in the company's strategy and the objections their people face? Does it talk about the tough questions the company's salespeople deal with and address how to position answers to those tough questions, as well as the different markets they sell to and the issues within those markets? That's what makes a genuinely customized program."

Depending on the size of your sales organization, before rolling out the sales training to the whole team, you may want to consider a pilot program. If so, Richardson feels that by including your best people you increase your overall chances for success. "You want to populate the pilot with opinion leaders—your luminaries—and then get feedback," she says. "Don't load it with all the cynics in the place. Go with the kind of people you want more of—really positive people. Then debrief, tweak it if necessary, and roll it out with high expectations."

Training Follow-Up

Sending your salespeople through a new sales training program isn't the end of the process, however. It's more like the middle. As any sales manager knows, the number one problem with sales training is not what takes place in the classroom, but what happens after the chalk dust clears and the people get back in the field. The sales trainer you choose should provide a detailed explanation of how the training will be reinforced with effective follow up.

Some programs, like Richardson's, include short Web-based modules addressing each of the topics covered in the training. So, for example, if reps are struggling with effective questioning, they can call up the interactive 15- or 30-minute questioning module that features coaching, a mini-lecture by the trainer, sample role plays, and other performance tools. Cargill suggests that the company's own management team should be responsible for overseeing the reinforcement program with exercises that go on for at least eight weeks—ideally, as long as six months—following the program.

And just as sportscasters talk about the immeasurable factors that contribute to a sports team's success, there are also certain "intangibles" that can make a substantial difference in deciding the success of your sales training effort. What's the number one intangible? Cargill says it's executive participation. "With my best, most on-the-ball customers, the managers are involved in training, development, and coaching," he explains. "Senior management is very involved in what message I deliver and how it's delivered. Another good sign is that management audits the sales reps' course without my inviting them. A less encouraging sign is when I have invited them and they don't show up."

Ultimately, all these components of an effective sales training program boil down to one key factor—a sales organization's commitment to the training process. On one end of the spectrum you find proactive companies that develop long-term strategies and then incorporate an ongoing training program into those strategies. At the other end are reactive companies that discover a problem, whether in the marketplace or internally, and then scramble to find a solution.

"Frankly, most people don't train until it's too late," Cargill says. "They call in a trainer and say, 'We have to make numbers next quarter—what can you do?' By that time the dog's dead; it's lying in the middle of the road, and bugs are crawling out of its nose, and they're saying, 'Make it run.'

"But then there are companies that make a commitment to ongoing training and assess their needs on an ad hoc basis and select trainers accordingly. It's the same philosophy you find in the airlines. Airlines know they have to train every 90 days, and they do so. They do this because it ensures that they have optimally performing pilots. And that's what top-performing sales forces do, too."

GETTING TRAINING RIGHT
How the Right Training at the Right Price Provides the Right Results

Sales training is a lot like learning a second language. Some people know all the vocabulary but not much grammar. Others used to speak with ease but have forgotten lots of phrases. Still others learned just enough to find the bathroom or order coffee, but after that they're lost. All these people need specific teaching at a variety of levels if they are ever to venture into foreign territory and survive. Well, sales training isn't a cookie cutter process either. Some salespeople need a refresher of the basics, others need advanced closing techniques, and still others need specific help with certain types of selling problems. How can you determine what training your salespeople need and what you'll have to spend to give it to them?

There's good news and not-so-good news. The good news is, with so many choices and options available, sales managers can find a solution to almost any of their training needs. On the other hand, they face the constant challenge of applying the proper training at the appropriate price to achieve the necessary improvements.

Needs Analysis

What type of training does your sales force need? Start with what you want to accomplish. "The first thing the sales manager needs to get clear about is desired outcomes," says Gayle Kirkeby, vice president of North American sales for Wilson Learning Corporation in Eden Prairie, Minnesota. "There's a huge difference between thinking about 'What kind of training do I want?' and asking 'What kind of performance do I want to improve?'" Assess the level of performance you are now getting from your people versus the desired performance, Kirkeby recommends. Then target your training to bridge the gap.

To determine the desired performance level you want to achieve, simply use your top performers as models, says Kirkeby. Look at what differentiates the top 10 percent of your sales force from the remaining 90 percent. What do the top producers do that makes them outperform the others?

Jeffrey Alves, sales training manager for tour group operator Collette Travel Services, Inc., in Pawtucket, Rhode Island, takes a different approach. He assesses his training needs on an ongoing basis and focuses on past successes and failures. If Alves sees an aspect of training that works, he continues with it. If it doesn't accomplish what the company hopes for, he changes it.

Sometimes training needs depend on your organization's overall strategy. Bob Brophy, national accounts manager for the Sherwin-Williams Company in Malvern, Pennsylvania, advises sales managers always to incorporate their training plans into the company's business plan for the coming year. For example, if he knows the company is planning a price increase, Brophy will make sure his salespeople get training in negotiation techniques. Why? Because he knows they will need that skill to counter potential customer resistance to rising prices. Or if your company's goal is to increase new accounts, provide your sales force with additional training on prospecting techniques. Training should not occur in a vacuum. Instead, integrate it into an overall company strategy.

Assessment

If you need help assessing the type of training your organization needs, several companies can provide in-depth analyses of your sales process. One such sales training and consulting company, The Woodlands, Texas-based Sales Training International, utilizes a proprietary model involving a sales process with 53 steps organized around 10 phases. "We identify the steps in the client's sales process and then determine whether or not they're doing all the steps," explains Robert DeGroot, president. "Next we determine whether they really need to do all those steps."

In particular, DeGroot points out, training should focus on those areas where customer objections are high.

However, if you want to know firsthand how your salespeople are doing and whether they need training, simply go with them on sales calls. This classic procedure allows sales managers to see where their salespeople are effective and where they need more help. During the first four weeks new hires are on board, Collette Travel's Alves spends four days on the road with them to learn their strengths and weaknesses.

Going on the road also requires another type of training—for sales managers. Sherwin-Williams' Brophy says sales managers must understand their role as observer and coach. Be observant, he recommends, and take notes regularly when on a call. However, don't tell salespeople what they should have done when you get back to the car. Instead, prompt them with questions: "How do you think it went in there? What could you have done differently?"

Conrad Elnes, chairman of the board of the Sales Training Institute (STI) in Kirkland, Washington, says going on joint sales calls with a salesperson is the best way to assess that person's individual training needs. But he is also a big fan of role playing as a means to reveal a person's strengths and weaknesses. Videotaping salespeople in role-playing situations is especially effective, Elnes says, and is a powerful tool for determining training needs.

Sales managers can also look to their salespeople for feedback about training needs. Talk with your sales team—they are an invaluable source of insights and opinions. Elnes urges every sales manager to talk individually with each salesperson, asking, "What skills do you need to accomplish your goals?" or "What skills would you like to see stressed in our training program this year?"

Ibbotson Associates, a Chicago-based consulting company to the financial services industry, surveys its salespeople and regional managers about the kinds of training they think they need, says Mark Kowalczyk, vice president of sales and marketing.

Be prepared for positive and negative feedback, however. Stan Isenhath, director of technical sales and marketing at KM Corporation, a maker of measuring and weighing instruments in Seattle, had STI survey his salespeople. The results surprised him. The sales team admitted they did not feel empowered. "We can train, but if we don't empower it's all for naught," acknowledges Isenhath. "Our reps said we were hard to do business with, and customers said salespeople were not well informed." As a result, the company refocused its training and made organizational changes.

Sherwin-Williams even uses its employees to provide a part of its training. "If you have some people who do something well, ask them to get up in front of their peers to give a presentation on their techniques," recommends Brophy.

The Basics

While there are numerous choices available in training programs, many believe the sessions should include the fundamentals. "Be sure everybody has the basic training and that they all understand the model you are using," comments Elnes.

In addition to helping boost sales, covering the basics also brings consistency to your sales organization, a real management plus. Collette Travel has had a training program for the past two years to help standardize its procedures and simplify managing its sales force. "We have a goal to get all our people reading from the same page," Alves points out. "How to do things, why you should learn these closing techniques, why you need to fill out the forms—everyone has to know these."

Bob Butler, president and CEO of Butler Learning Systems in Dayton, Ohio, points out that such consistency makes an organization more efficient. "When I interview sales reps and ask how they sell, I get as many different answers as there are reps. Sales managers can multiply their efforts by standardizing their sales process."

Training also should not focus on product knowledge alone. John W. Connors, president of the sales consulting firm Connors Partners & Associates in Ballston Lake, New York, says that sales managers often minimize some of the most important training. "Usually, more time is spent on product knowledge rather than skill development," he says. "They should be on a par." Salespeople can be as savvy as possible about the products they sell, but if they really don't know how to sell or are not confident at it, they will not be successful, he explains.

Team Needs

Is it more effective to train your sales force individually or as a group? Ideally, of course, everyone in the sales organization should receive individualized, customized training. Practically and economically, that's often impossible. Jim Matheson, group vice president of Precision Aerospace Corporation in Kirkland, Washington, provides individualized training where there is a strong case for it. Once he had a very effective sales manager who, nonetheless, had a tendency to alienate some of the people he worked with. So Matheson sent him to "charm school" to learn how to get along with people.

Short, modular training is another way to provide customized learning. KnowHow, Inc., in Minneapolis offers a range of courses that run from 60 to 90 minutes each, according to president, Alan Hupp. Sales managers can mix and match different training modules to meet individual needs. The Sales Training Institute also offers short courses, some lasting no more than 45 minutes.

However, for many companies group training is the most efficient and economical. You can capture 80 percent of your sales force's needs in group training, according to Ibbotson's Kowalczyk. Break-out sessions can focus on areas where individuals require improvement, enabling each person to address particular needs while the company contains costs.

If you have a large enough sales organization—one with a minimum of 25 or 30 salespeople—assess individual abilities, and patterns of similar needs will emerge, says

DeGroot. Some of the variables that affect the patterns include geographic location of salespeople, the industries they sell to, and their level of experience. By studying their sales force and discerning these patterns, sales managers can economically target group training to different salespeople who share patterns of similar needs.

Budget Fit

Sales managers must balance economic considerations with training requirements. The first step: Keep your goals in mind. "You have to ask, 'Do I want a one-time training course or do I want to start a performance development initiative?'" says Dan Ellis, vice president of sales at KnowHow. "Training programs per se don't accomplish behavior changes. You need to dig deeper and develop a whole curriculum to meet your goals." In that case, a simple one-time training session is not enough. According to Partners & Associates' Connors, "Behavior changes only with repetition. It does not change overnight. You need to budget for ongoing training."

Ibbotson uses a somewhat flexible approach, setting aside money every year for training, but if sales management identifies a special need during the year, it can usually get the money for additional training. "We have a 'gentleman's agreement.' If we need more money, Ibbotson has been very willing to commit to that," Kowalczyk explains.

On the other hand, Precision Aerospace's Matheson does zero-based budgeting every year. "Say we spent $50,000 last year," he says. "I might keep that in mind, but I build up month-by-month what our expenses will be based on our needs and the benefits we are looking for."

Just like most everything else, training costs can vary widely depending on the length of the course, the topics taught, and other considerations. KnowHow's Ellis says, for a ballpark figure, plan on spending $1,000 to $2,000 per person per training event. DeGroot says most companies budget $250 to $350 per day per person for training, plus the extras—including meals and possibly airfare and hotel accommodations. Elnes says that experienced trainers like himself, who usually accommodate 15 to 20 students at one time, charge $3,000 to $5,000 per day, and usually two days are required.

Of course, there are cheaper ways to go. Elnes also sells prepared courses "in a box" for $595, including a license that accommodates up to 10 students. However, the employer has to provide someone to teach the courses. DeGroot says facilitators who are part of organizations often charge $1,500 to $2,500 per day, while free-lancers will probably charge $250 to $1,200 per day.

To ensure your money is well spent, make certain your training sessions are just that and not some type of "working vacation." DeGroot says the most expensive training he ever saw was a three-day training session where there was little or no training. Most participants partied all the first night and got to class late the next day. The company let everyone hit the links in the afternoon. Students again partied most of the night, arrived late to class the next day, and then left early to go home. "It was a totally mismanaged process," says DeGroot.

Whichever training you choose, Partners & Associates' Connors recommends you do a pre- and post-training assessment. Follow up after the training sessions with a survey asking if the training provided what the employees needed, or if and how it fell short.

For training to be worthwhile, know what you want to accomplish and allocate the needed financial resources to achieve those goals. Planning effective sales training isn't difficult. But it requires time, effort, focus, and money on the part of sales management and the company as a whole. When done well, it can take the company to the next level. When ineffective, it can cost the company money in missed opportunities and lost sales.

EXPERT ADVICE
Dos and Don'ts of Sales Training

Many sales managers say training is important, yet they fail to do much about it. A good training program accomplishes three goals.

First, it teaches the skills necessary for efficient work habits and a high degree of professionalism. Second, it builds a salesperson's knowledge to allow for logical, intelligent action and decision making. Third, it forms attitudes that promote cooperation and coordination with supporting staff and management. The following list of dos and don'ts forms a basis for you to build a better training plan.

DO:

- Let salespeople know you expect them to continue doing things correctly.
- Let them know you are always willing to help them learn.
- Give positive recognition for skills learned.
- Keep them informed, constantly and regularly, on how well they are doing and where they need to improve.
- Ask them, often, what you can do to help them do a better job.

DON'T:

- Assume that all people learn at the same pace. Be patient! You may have to demonstrate a skill several times before it is learned.
- Feel that a task is easy to learn just because you found it easy. We all find certain skills difficult to learn. Be patient with a new salesperson.
- Assume a new person will continue to do something the way you demonstrated it. Skills slip, and you will have to retrain some people.
- Assume the salesperson knows how to do something well just because he or she has prior experience. The incorrect method may have been learned.
- Demand perfection too soon. It takes time for a good habit to develop. Be patient and encouraging.
- Just act interested in your subordinate's learning; be interested. Sales managers can look only as good as the staff makes them look. They are a reflection of the sales manager's competence.
- Ridicule a salesperson for making a mistake. Let the mistakes become learning experiences. You learned from mistakes, too.

—From James F. Evered, CSP (certified sales professional) and author of *Shirt Sleeves Management*.

INVALUABLE TRAINING
Proof That Training Pays!

Need proof that investment in training pays off on the bottom line? According to the American Society for Training & Development (ASTD), investments in workforce training can determine how an organization will fare financially in the future.

The ASTD studied the training practices and results of 575 publicly traded companies based in the United States during the three-year period from 1996 through 1998. Organizations that spent at least $680 more per employee on training than did the study's average company improved their total stockholder return the next year by 6 percentage points—"even after considering other factors," according to ASTD. "It is clear that a firm's commitment to workplace learning is directly linked to its bottom line, and investors, Wall Street, and financial analysts should pay attention," says Mark Van Buren, ASTD's research director.

The study found that organizations that spent more on training reaped other benefits as well. Companies in the top quarter—those investing an average $1,595 per employee in training—saw 218 percent higher income per worker than firms in the bottom quarter. Companies in the lowest quarter invested much less—on average, $128 per employee in training.

Amid the nation's tight labor market, corporate debate has focused on how to keep and attract talent. Training and development constitute a key perk that companies must provide to recruit and retain talented workers, according to another study by ASTD and the Society for Human Resource Management. The research study, called "Recruiting and Retaining Employees: Using Training and Education in the War for Talent," reports that the seven companies demonstrating best practices not only trained greater numbers of employees, but also gave qualified workers more training. At each of the best-practice organizations, turnover was lower and employee satisfaction was higher than at average firms in each leading company's industry. "More companies are discovering that training is critical to their success. For example, at Sears, Roebuck & Co. (an Exemplary Practice Partner company), career advancement and training opportunities for associates consistently rank as key predictors of employee satisfaction," ASTD's Van Buren says.

Need help managing your investment in education and training? Check out ASTD's measurement kit. It's free at www.astd.org/virtual_community/research/. Click on the link to Benchmarking Service. ASTD (www.astd.org) is a leading professional association in workplace learning and performance. ASTD leaders and members work in more than 15,000 multinational corporations and other organizations.

KNOWLEDGE IS POWER: TIPS, TRENDS, DEALS

Your top tier of sales reps has probably received every gift in the book—plaques, money, travel. At your next sales meeting, give them power. "There are different kinds of power; one is knowledge power," says Joan Klubnik, a Klubnik Associates principal and author of *Rewarding and Recognizing Employees: Ideas for Individuals, Teams and Managers*. Give your top producers the chance to share their expertise with their peers, she says, and you'll be giving them power and stature while the rest of the sales force gets to learn from successful role models. It's a win–win situation.

There are a couple of ways you can do this. First, you can ask each of your top reps to give a presentation about an area in which he or she excels and/or what skills have made him or her so successful. If you go this route, says Klubnik, be sure to offer the reps assistance with preparing materials. Another option is to have a panel Q&A where the audience can ask questions of the top performers. In this case, make sure that you have a moderator to guide the discussion and keep things moving. Klubnik also has seen companies successfully use a "carousel" method of sharing knowledge, where each top rep sits at a different round table, and meeting attendees can migrate from table to table. As a preview to any of these events, you can include a short interview with each top rep in the company newsletter to give the rep additional exposure and prepare the rest of the sales team for the upcoming event. It's a low-cost, high-impact way to let your top tier know how much you value them.

Chapter 4

Motivation Strategies
That Work

DON'T HESITATE, MOTIVATE

Ways to Keep Your Sales Team Revved Up and Ready

Although the sports world is full of peak-moment stories, one commonly held theory of unsurpassed performance held fast—until 1954 that is.

The theory went like this: No runner can break the 4-minute mile. All the medical journals said it was "humanly impossible." So there you had it. A barrier beyond which no human being could go. Until May 6, 1954, when Roger Bannister tore through that barrier in 3:59.4 minutes and opened the field for 45 others to go on to break the incontrovertible 4-minute mile.

So how did we go so quickly from believing that a 4-minute mile was "humanly impossible" to saying, "Forty-six people have done it"? Those runners didn't suddenly become that much stronger and faster. Presumably they were already elite athletes who had been training and racing for years. What changed was their belief in what was possible, and that new belief became the *X* factor that pushed them beyond their previous limits. As Jerry Lynch writes in *Running Within: A Guide to Mastering the Body-Mind-Spirit Connection for Ultimate Training and Racing*, with Bannister setting the pace, "the illusion of the impossibility of running under 4 minutes was shattered."

What do running statistics have to do with the science of motivation? Plenty. Motivation was once a matter of "Sell 3,000 widgets before noon and we'll send you to Maui," which worked well enough—as long as you didn't expect to sell any widgets in the afternoon. We now understand that in order to sustain lasting success, salespeople need to feel valued, empowered, and respected. And like those runners trailing Bannister, they need to be in the presence of winners and thus have strong daily reminders of what's possible.

This doesn't mean that the old methods of motivation have gone out the window—hey, everybody still likes Maui—only that these methods need to be reflective of a broader understanding between management and staff.

"Management methods for years were based on the tradition of 'command and control,'" says Alexander Hiam, author of *Making Horses Drink* and *Motivating and Rewarding Employees*. "You'd just tell people what to do, then make sure they did it by creating positive and negative consequences." The negative consequences were usually pretty cut-and-dried: those who didn't meet goals or follow corporate policy were fired.

But most corporate managers preferred the carrot to the stick, and rather than constantly threatening to fire their employees, they instead looked for ways to fire them up with incentives. "The most basic element of motivational psychology is that you reward positive behavior," says Marty Brounstein, principal of the Practical Solutions Group and author of *Coaching and Mentoring for Dummies.*

Brounstein delineates five basic types of rewards:

1. *Incentive programs.* Monetary rewards (or a trip or car) for good performance; employees are working toward a set goal and payout occurs at regular intervals or at the end of a sales contest.
2. *Spot bonus.* A discretionary bonus or gift (such as a gift certificate to a restaurant), which is given on the spot; companies can budget for these small perks, but to the employee it comes as a surprise—an unexpected windfall for doing something well.
3. *Positive feedback.* Praise is a great reward.
4. *Public recognition.* This can include being named "employee of the month," getting a new title, or moving into the corner office.
5. *Private recognition.* An employee is taken to lunch, receives a letter of thanks, or is given unexpected time off.

These types of rewards are what the experts call "external motivators" (i.e., those incentives were initiated and created by the company managers in hopes that they will make their employees more productive). To get the maximum bang for their buck with these methods, managers should make sure these rewards are:

- *Timely.* "The key is to acknowledge the behavior the minute they do it and keep the reward short term," says Brounstein. "The longer a person has to wait for a good performance to be rewarded, the less likely the reward is to have a lasting effect. An end-of-the-year bonus may force employees to wait too long between the effort and the payoff."
- *Specific.* Praise is a key aspect of motivation, but a vague compliment such as "Great job" or "You're doing great" is meaningless. "Don't overdo praise," cautions Dr. Arthur Pell, author of *The Complete Idiot's Guide to Managing People.* "Gushing something like 'What would we do without you?' sounds insincere, so be very specific about what they did correctly. Also, be public in your praise. Some managers praise in private and criticize in public, but you'll have better results if you do the opposite."

- *Well understood by the employees.* "Managers need to clearly define what criteria they're rewarding and how," says Brounstein. "Don't say 'You'll get a bonus if we have a good year' without explaining what constitutes a good year. Employees need to know what percentage of the profits is being paid out, how that number is figured, and when they'll get the check."

- *Tailored to suit individual employee needs.* Cosmetics queen Mary Kay Ash often told the story of how she won a contest in her first sales job only to learn that first prize was a fish light. (As in, "a light you can use to go fishing in the dark.") She was predictably underwhelmed and vowed that when she had her own company she'd create incentives that were valued by women. While your company may not be dishing out roses, jewelry, and pink Cadillacs, it's important to offer incentives that have meaning to the individuals on the sales team. "Not all people are motivated by the same things," says Pell. "You might want to try a cafeteria approach, saying 'We're offering a choice of several rewards—which would you prefer?' That way, individuals choose their own motivator, whether it's money, more time off, or something else."

- *Reflective of the big picture.* Incentives are empty gestures unless they're a reflection of how much management values its employees overall. If a husband ignores his wife 364 days a year but brings roses on Valentine's Day, what's the worth of those flowers? Not much. The wife is likely to see them as an afterthought or even a bribe. Likewise, if a company does not treat its staff fairly throughout the year it's doubtful that a year-end bonus is going to suddenly make everything okay. Rewards should be an outward sign of a good relationship between management and staff— a gesture much like flowers from a loving husband—and not an emotional Band-Aid meant to magically heal all wounds.

The problem with motivating exclusively with goodies is that once the goodies dry up, so does the good behavior. "The downside of external motivation is that when the big sales contest or other challenging assignment ends, the excitement fades," says Pell. "As performance sinks back down to its previous levels, managers constantly have to come up with new ways to reward, and you can't just keep doubling commissions forever. The same incentives eventually get stale. After a while everybody in the company has been "employee of the month" at least once and it doesn't mean anything anymore."

Even worse, managing exclusively through external motivators can create what Alexander Hiam calls *learned helplessness* in the sales staff. "External motivation might work for a while," he says, "but the unintentional side effect of the 'command and control' approach is that employees become dependent upon management to tell them what to do. As the business environment becomes more competitive and challenging, you need people who can think on their feet, take the initiative, and face problems without having to constantly turn to their supervisors for help. We need to reexamine the question of how we motivate."

Money may be a universal incentive to work—after all, you'd be hard pressed to find anyone who wouldn't like a bit more of it—but that doesn't mean it's the only motivator, or even the best one. "People like money and gifts," says Brounstein, "but they also want recognition, challenging work, autonomy, a good company atmosphere, the chance to learn more about their jobs, and opportunities to be creative."

Empowerment is the umbrella term for these qualities, and Hiam defines this as "sharing your power with the people over whom you have power." Empowered employees are involved with planning, provide regular input to their bosses, have the authority to make daily decisions about their jobs, and in some cases have profit sharing or actual ownership in the company.

"Involving people in the business makes them know more, care more, and want to do the right things," says Pell. "The real motivation comes when employees feel they are making a contribution and having an impact. Then motivation moves from being a temporary thing which is inspired by external factors like sales contests to a lasting frame of mind which is inspired by the people themselves."

Turning your sales force into a group of self-motivators is a process that encompasses many elements. The first step is to get to know what makes these people tick.

Talk to Your Staff

"If the old model was 'command and control,' the new model is 'inspire and motivate,'" says Hiam. "In the past, managers didn't care how people were feeling; they only cared about what they were doing. Because we now see the link between how people feel and what they do, it's important that managers ask more probing questions. Not just a casual 'How ya doing?' as you walk past, but sitting down and taking the time for a sincere 'How are you *really* doing?'"

Dr. Paul Pearsall, author of *Toxic Success*, states, "The currency of the new economy is attention, and toxic success is a kind of attention deficit disorder. I suggest that when you get to the office in the morning, the first thing you should do is nothing. Don't check your e-mail or voice mail or go into a meeting. Take one full minute just to sit at your desk and take deep breaths. The second step is to connect with the people you will be working with that day. Not to discuss problems or get the agenda rolling, but just to say good morning and chat a minute before you begin work. Having a manager who pays attention to them initially stuns people. They're so used to the rapid pace of the typical office that they're taken aback. But I promise you that the minute you spend chatting with them will pay big dividends later in the day."

"You can't know your employees as individuals until you're willing to put in the time to talk to them," agrees Pell. "And you have to know them to know what motivates them. Police officers say that criminals have a certain M.O., which means they tend to behave in the same way with each crime. Employees are like that too—they each have their own comfort zone and a tendency to do the same things time and again. Some people like to work in groups; others do their best work alone. Some like direct supervision and constant feedback; others thrive when they're given more freedom. Within reason, managers get the best results when they let people deal in their own M.O."

Tailor the Rewards

"If you start talking with no assumptions, you'll soon find that what inspires Joe doesn't necessarily inspire Melvin," says Dr. Cherie Carter-Scott, author of *If Success Is a Game, Here Are the Rules*. "Connecting with people is a matter of finding out where their sparks lie, what they live for and also what makes them angry, because for most people their passion and their anger are closely related. If you find that someone is upset by violence, pollution, or the breakup in the family unit, that tells you a lot about their value base. Once you know their values, it's easier to create incentives that are appropriate for that person."

Carter-Scott gives the example of an employee who was disturbed by the amount of time she was spending away from her aging mother and two young children. "Just throwing more money at this person won't work," she says. "But if her boss gives her the chance to telecommute two days a week, this woman is going to sing his praises forever. She'll know that she was listened to, and that someone was paying attention about what really mattered in her life."

Help Winners Beget Winners

Remember the Roger Bannister story? It's a safe bet that in the tight-knit community of running, most of the 45 people who subsequently matched his performance had met Roger Bannister before. So they not only saw the allegedly unbreakable 4-minute mile broken, but the person who did it was someone they knew and perhaps had raced against in the past. They may have thought, "Heck, Bannister isn't that much faster than I am. If he can do it, so can I."

In the business world, all those people ahead of you on the track are potential mentors. You can either draw off their experience and energy to bolster your own confidence or, as the manager, pair less-successful employees with their more-successful coworkers. Teaming employees who are at differing places on the food chain can actually inspire both people. The young salespeople have older colleagues to show them the ropes, and the mentors are flattered that you value their judgment and consider them team leaders.

Concentrate on Task Clarity

"The Harvard Business School did a study in the eighties that said that people's understanding how they contribute is more important than salary," says Hiam. "Knowing the connection between what they personally do and the bottom line of the company turns people on."

Task clarity can bring purpose to even the least-glamorous jobs. Pearsall tells the story of meeting a man who literally pumped sewage for a living but who, when asked to define his job, said, "I'm saving the environment." Because he saw the deeper meaning in his work, he was much happier with his job than either of his bosses.

"In order to be self-motivated, people's hearts and minds must be engaged in their work, and they must understand how their task relates to the larger goal," says Hiam. "Without this understanding, any job, no matter how well it pays, is just busywork."

Give Them Choices

Autonomy can work on many levels. "Giving people such simple choices as what order they do things in, the route they drive, or how they decorate their offices can make a difference," says Hiam. "Studies have shown that even something as small as having the ability to change the levels of lighting in their offices helps people stay motivated."

"Managers need to remember that sameness is not the same thing as fairness," Brounstein adds. "The pay structure should be fair and the same for everyone, but beyond that, one of the keys to successful coaching is managing people as individuals. Give them what they want and recognize that in many cases that means letting them choose what they want—both in terms of incentives and having some control over their work environment."

The Walt Disney Company has a policy of allowing theme park employees (who are called, with typical Disney panache, "cast members") the autonomy to fix any problem as it arises. The initial focus of the policy was to please park guests, since the company figured that if the tourists didn't have to wade through three layers of bureaucracy to have a complaint addressed, they could go right back to having fun. But an added bonus was the boost to employee morale. Although many of the cast members were high school and college students, once they were trained and posted in the parks, employees were encouraged to use their own judgment in solving minor issues. Giving employees autonomy is the perfect way to circumvent the "learned helplessness" Hiam warns against. Instead of turning to their supervisors to fix daily snafus, the young Disney workers learned to use their own problem-solving skills. The result was intense loyalty among the cast members, which is reflected in employee retention numbers that are much higher than the industry standard.

Offer Positive Feedback

Some managers operate on a "no news is good news" basis; in other words, if they aren't hearing criticism, they should assume that things are okay. Bad move. "Taking people for granted has never been a great motivator," says Brounstein. "Rather than just praising them, take the time to give very specific positive feedback. Identify the behaviors you want them to repeat and say 'Here's what you did right.' It also helps if you acknowledge, not just closed sales, but also their behavior leading up to the sale. You can give positive feedback on how they're servicing accounts, the amount of prospecting they're doing, or how well they get along with other people in the office."

Hiam adds, "Many managers find it easier to name employees' weaknesses than their strengths, especially if they've come to think of people as a problem. When you turn your thinking from 'George has never been able to do this' to 'George is great in these situations' it becomes easier to give positive feedback."

But what if you have an employee whose performance is skidding so badly that there's really nothing good to say? "Sometimes it's just a matter of building up their confidence," Pell suggests. "Don't throw something tough at them all at once, but rather start them off with small, easy tasks. Let them get a taste of success, and then underline that successful feeling by giving them specific positive feedback about how they handled the task."

Acknowledge Problems

Perhaps you've noticed that the new wave of motivational speakers are not as rah-rah as those in the past, which is a good thing if you're using motivational seminars or speakers to help jump-start long-term changes in your staff. Hypermotivational speeches can bring on a momentary false high that Pearsall calls a "bliss backlash," and he notes that the intense psyching up typical of some motivational seminars is almost always followed by an emotional crash. So the new rule is less cheerleading and a lot more honesty. Many current motivational experts speak from their own experience, including setbacks, and acknowledge that success doesn't automatically happen overnight.

SKILL SET: TIPS FOR RECHARGING THE SALES ENGINE

- Read motivational books; listen to motivational tapes.
- Attend meetings for information, motivation, and networking.
- Talk to other successful salespeople and share leads.
- Keep your body and mind fit through physical exercise and positive time with your family and community.
- Managers need to take time to review slumping team members and suggest changes that will recharge presentations.
- Managers may need to reset goals to include steps that lead to sales.
- Managers should include sales team input in goal setting.

Help Employees Avoid Self-Sabotage

One of the chief characteristics of winners is that they feel entitled to win. But on the flip side, if the people who work for you don't feel that they deserve the best, they'll find a way to make sure they never get it.

"In a way it sounds crazy," says Carter-Scott. "After all, doesn't everybody want to succeed? On the surface we do, but our unconscious minds know that if we succeed we'll have to change, and change can be threatening. Some people fail just so they can stay in their comfort zone. In fact, despite what people say about the competition or their hostile work environments, I'd say self-sabotage is the number-one reason why success becomes derailed."

Success may actually prompt an identity crisis, because few people are willing to look at the question "Who will I be if I succeed at my goals?" Carter-Scott uses the example of her own life to illustrate her point, saying that when her book *If Life Is a Game, Here Are the Rules* first made the bestseller list, strangers suddenly started calling and asking for favors. "There was an onslaught of attention and suddenly everyone, even people who once didn't give me the time of day, wanted a piece of me. I was the same person, but the world saw me differently." Pearsall notes that in his extensive interviews with high-powered sales executives he never met a single one who didn't suffer a bit of what he calls "post-success crash."

People may even subconsciously fear that success will bring out the worst in them. Carter-Scott once had a client whose father had become successful and then abandoned his family for a young mistress. "In his mind," she says, "success made men turn into selfish jerks."

Carter-Scott advises people who suspect they (or people on their staff) have similar unconscious fears to face the issue head on. "Don't brush over your fear of success," she says. "If your beliefs are limiting who you are, you need to talk it out with a trusted friend or therapist. Take the examples of the man who worried that success might tempt him to abandon his family and the woman who believes high-powered women are less attractive to men. These people need to confront the fear and ask themselves if it's realistic. Often, once you vocalize the fear it begins to lose its power over you."

Encourage Persistence

Studies have shown that people who are ultimately successful are those who don't give up. Along the way they may encounter as much failure as their less-successful counterparts, but they keep going.

If salespeople's internal beliefs are that they deserve to succeed, they'll take rejections or losses as temporary setbacks. They're just blips on the radar screen, and they either try again or quickly readjust their strategies. "Ok, so you don't want 100 widgets? How about 50?" And they'll ask the next customer to buy 100, reasoning that they were right to ask for the big sale; it's just that customer number one didn't happen to go for it. In other words, their inner belief in their own worthiness is strong enough that it isn't threatened by a single refusal.

Salespeople who don't believe they deserve success, in contrast, are likely to react far differently to the same scenario. When client number one refuses to buy 100 widgets they take this rejection as an external confirmation of an inner belief. Their self-dialogue runs something like this: "I knew I shouldn't have asked for such a big sale. I looked like an idiot. Next time I'll go in with a smaller number." If you suspect people on your team are self-sabotaging, you'll need to do what Carter-Scott suggests and help them talk it out. Otherwise they will unconsciously continue to prove they are unworthy of success.

Lead Them as a Team

"If people's hearts and minds are not engaged, no external reward will ever be enough," says Pearsall. "If they win a car this year, it has to be a house next year, and this narrow vision of success ultimately drains us. I live in Hawaii and speak at many seminars where the attendees are people who have won sales contests or met extraordinary goals. In other words, they're high achievers or they wouldn't be there in the first place. But I've noticed that you rarely see the same people year after year. The burnout rate is high.

"But there's another kind of success," Pearsall goes on, "that comes when people are motivated by the welfare of more than just themselves. They know that they're contributing to the larger picture, and the whole group is benefiting from their work. To work for the greater good is the greatest joy in the world, and that type of success is sustaining, not draining."

In a way, managers motivate their employees by realizing that it is impossible to motivate them. After all, one person cannot control the thoughts and beliefs of another. But a manager can encourage his or her employees to feel higher levels of connectedness, autonomy, and purpose. As Pell says, "The best motivation is internal motivation, because it doesn't fade with time. Your job as a team leader is to provide a climate in which internal motivation flourishes."

EXPERT ADVICE

Top Performers Motivate Others to Excel

Follow these key tips for using top performers as role models:

- *Proceed with caution.* If you plan to hold up one of your team members as a star performer, make sure that the title is deserved. You might think this person is great, but the sales figures have to back you up. It's easy to think people are great if they remind you of yourself—they think like you, act like you, and sell like you. That's dangerous; it can tilt your judgment about people. If you base superstar status simply upon your own perception, you're heading for trouble, because your other salespeople will know the truth. The superstar—and you—will lose the team's respect.

- *Use a team approach.* Use your top performers' strategies and techniques to help the others in your organization. Star performers become team leaders, sharing their strategies with a few other team leaders. Each team leader trains a group of salespeople in the star performers' methods. Now, instead of just one person "dictating" success methods, you have a number of team leaders. Reps who don't like working with your stars can still benefit from the star performers' strategies. It's simply easier to hear them from someone else.

- *Avoid presenting awards in a way that demoralizes nonwinners.* A popular "motivational" technique in the 1980s suggested that corporations host a dinner meeting where top performers were treated to steak and lobster and expensive champagne. Lesser performers sat at another table and were served beans and franks. The not-so-subtle lesson: If you want to sit with the winners, you've got to be a winner. Otherwise, you are a loser. After a presenter suggested this at a recent meeting, the company's vice president of sales told us that he once worked for a company that held one of these dinners. "The whole thing backfired. Those of us at the 'bean table' were so demoralized I don't think the company ever recovered. I wasn't the top performer that year, but I wasn't a slouch either. I began looking for a new job the very next day. I didn't want to work for a company that treated its people that way."

- *Presenting awards the right way motivates everyone.* To do it right, don't limit recognition to just the superstars. For example, at one awards banquet each winner was called to the stage individually and given an award by the CEO and other company personnel. The first award winner was a woman. When the CEO finished speaking, a video lit up the screen. It was the award winner's husband: "I am so proud of you and what you've accomplished. I don't know how you do it, but you do it all and you do it well . . . ." The video also included clips from her children, her coworkers, and her boss. The same type of presentation honored each of the year's award winners. Afterward, the winners' families joined them on stage. There wasn't a dry eye in the house. One attendee, a nonwinner, said that this ceremony motivated him more than any other he had ever attended, including the times he had won an award: "The company could ask any one of us to do anything after that meeting and we'd do it, because we knew how strongly the company believed in us."

—From Georganne Bender, a professional speaker and trainer, who, with her partner Rich Kizer, specializes in customer retention for all businesses. Visit www.kizerandbender.com.

EVEN TOP DOGS NEED LEADERS
Tips for Motivating Your Best Performers

Having superstars on your sales team can be a mixed blessing. Sure, they throw off revenue like P. T. Barnum at a sucker convention, but handled improperly they also can alienate the rest of your staff, undermine your authority, or defect to the competition. Tim Bucher is a sales manager with Chester Technologies, a computer-based systems provider in Valparaiso, Indiana. The first key to motivating top performers, he says, is to recognize that everyone on a sales team—regardless of performance—deserves individual attention. "You need to treat everyone differently," Bucher explains, "but not in a way that you appear to be giving preferential treatment. 'Different' doesn't necessarily mean 'better.'"

Bucher puts this credo into practice in his compensation plan by giving salespeople options. "I try to offer varying plans that will entice people differently," he says. "I'll let them choose between an aggressive, higher-risk, higher-potential program or a more conservative program with less high-end potential but more up-front guarantees. Top performers are more likely to take the aggressive program, while lower performers will give up some potential earnings for security. But because they choose, no one feels slighted."

Beyond compensation, Bucher suggests that managers can keep superstars happy by feeding their substantial egos. One effective method: added responsibility. "We recently put our top seller on a committee to help us make decisions," Bucher explains. "He seemed to really enjoy that. With top performers the ego says, 'I want to be important; I want to be involved.' When you ask their opinions and get their input you accomplish that goal."

Experience has taught Bucher the importance of keeping top performers happy. In 1997 his two top lieutenants jumped ship to the competition. Though both came back within nine months, the year was still painful. The lesson: make sure your top people recognize the benefits you offer.

EIGHT TIPS FOR SALES MANAGERS TO HELP PROVIDE A MOTIVATION-NURTURING ENVIRONMENT

For salespeople to be productive, they must be motivated to sell. Motivation is a force from within and, although motivation cannot be artificially induced, a positive environment can help to instill motivation in salespeople. Listed below are some tips for managers who want to provide an environment that helps salespeople want to pursue and attain their goals:

1. Get to know each salesperson individually. Understand his or her problems and help with them where you can. Give each salesperson a sense of belonging to a greater cause.
2. Treat each salesperson as an individual and not only as part of a collective sales force. Give individual praise for achievement, no matter how large or small that achievement may seem.

3. Stress the status and trust invested in each one as a sales professional.
4. Introduce your salespeople to important people you know who can make a contribution to enriching their work environment or their sense of accomplishment. This can take the form of secondary introductions like cassette tapes or CDs you find beneficial or books that you might recommend for increasing sales skills.
5. Let salespeople participate in training sessions, sales meetings, and in setting quotas.
6. Read all reports and comment on them individually and promptly.
7. Maintain an open door policy with your salespeople. Be available and open-minded when they wish to contact you.
8. When conducting an evaluation, stress the individual's personal growth and development and encourage it, and comment on his or her percentage of production in the company.

Although it is up to individuals to motivate themselves, as a sales manager you can be an influencing factor by providing a positive environment that encourages motivation and growth.

Chapter 5

Making the Most of Sales Meetings

PROFITABLE MEETINGS

A Five-Step Plan to Get More Than You Bargained for Out of Meetings

When Rochester, New York, eyewear company Bausch & Lomb held its recent national sales meeting, it was looking for more than speeches and a podium full of award winners. In fact, the meeting was designed to produce—believe it or not—a return on investment (ROI).

The five-day meeting followed an ROI process developed by Fusion Productions, based in Webster, New York.

The process enables companies to plan effective meetings and measure their success. Here are the five steps in Fusion's ROI process for meetings:

1. Identify stakeholders.
2. Establish objectives.
3. Develop content based on the objectives.
4. Design ways to measure success.
5. Demonstrate ROI through measurement results.

The lengthy process starts with the meeting planning stage and doesn't end until well after the meeting is over, when Fusion continues to monitor results. The process also involves a wide variety of people, including company executives who are the meeting stakeholders, meeting professionals at Fusion, meeting participants, and, finally, salespeople. They represent the vital link in the measurement chain to determine the meeting's success.

It is essential to identify the stakeholders first because they are the key parties affected by the meeting and will be instrumental in planning and running it. Company presidents, CEOs, sales and marketing managers, and other executives are among the stakeholders. Fusion experts identify such stakeholders at the early stages of a meeting. Leave one of them out and the meeting suffers, according to Hugh Lee, Fusion's president.

Donna Thompson, Fusion CEO, worked closely with Bausch & Lomb and says that determining its stakeholders wasn't easy because there were so many. "There were 15 stakeholders who had a real interest in the outcome," she says. "The two critical ones were the president and vice president of the division, so we met with them first to get the critical aspects. Then the others got involved."

After identifying the stakeholders, the next step in the ROI process is to establish the objectives of the meeting. Thompson says Bausch & Lomb had many objectives to pursue, from training the reps on a new computer system to launching new programs and products to rewards and recognition for the 150-member sales staff. "There were different objectives that all required a different slant but the biggest need was for the vice president to motivate and excite the sales force for new opportunities," Thompson says. "Our goal was to deliver what they needed to win in a motivational, upbeat way."

Fusion accomplished that by bringing all the objectives together with a powerful theme—Journey to Excellence—that was used throughout the meeting.

After determining objectives, the next step in the ROI process is to develop meeting content to meet the objectives. There were two types of content delivered at the Bausch & Lomb meeting, Thompson says: top-line motivation and in-depth training. The motivation was provided by a general session, where company executives discussed the plans for 1998 in an effort to motivate the troops. Then, Jerry Linenger, a U.S. Space Shuttle astronaut who flew aboard the Mir spacecraft with Russian cosmonauts, provided a motivational speech that focused on how problems can be overcome through teamwork and a strong sense of commitment.

"He set the tone," Thompson says. "The reps realized they could pursue the new program and link their personal journey to the journey he was on." When it came time for rewards and recognition, they were linked to the meeting theme, too, by emphasizing that the reps who won the rewards had pursued their own journeys en route to success.

In the training element of the meeting, district managers led 10 small groups though a new program the company launched to position its products. After learning about the program, the reps practiced presenting it to their accounts in the small-group environment.

The last two steps in the ROI process involve measuring the success of a meeting. Traditionally, companies simply analyze the budget in an effort to keep meeting expenses low. But today, companies measure success by determining how much knowledge and motivation attendees take away from the meeting. Such intangibles become apparent when sales numbers start to flow.

Measuring this kind of success is a long-term process that begins before the meeting gets underway and continues after it ends. Fusion designed a series of questionnaires to measure the attitudes of the sales reps both before the meeting took place and after it to determine how the meeting had changed their attitudes. In an effort to measure reps' retention of information, Fusion also conducted interviews with selected reps 3 to 4 weeks after the meeting, Thompson says. Finally, 10 weeks after the meeting, Fusion produced a short video that highlighted the meeting theme. Bausch and Lomb's vice president appeared in the video, reviewing the key elements of the meeting. Another questionnaire accompanied it.

The questionnaires measured changes in attitude and work habits according to the information that was presented at the meeting. For instance, the questionnaire given out three to four weeks after the meeting asked the reps if they could manage their client base better with the new computer system. If enough answered yes, the company knew its meeting was a success and had produced ROI.

Fusion is using the information it gathered during the meeting to plan Bausch & Lomb's next major meeting later in the year. "We're going out to the field to measure how they retained information and look at what they need to do at the next meeting," Thompson says. "Meetings are an ongoing process, not a one-time event."

Fusion's role in the Bausch & Lomb meeting was substantial. More than just being a meeting-planning firm that books hotel rooms and plans meals, it worked with Bausch & Lomb to design the meeting and develop the measurement components. "Meeting professionals should be involved because their role is to be able to capture the message stakeholders design," Fusion president Lee says. "The more we get involved in it, the greater value we add to the organization."

Today, ROI is the hot topic in the meetings industry, and companies are striving to determine how their meetings can produce it. The long-term ROI process demands major input from top executives. But if you follow the process, you may be able to make your meetings more effective—so effective that they will produce a return on the considerable investment all companies make in time and money by holding regular meetings.

TEN RULES FOR SUCCESSFUL MEETINGS
How to Use Meetings to Reach Your Goals

The following are useful tips when conducting a meeting:
1. *Break up your meeting into three parts.* First, recognize efforts and praise performance. Second, show your appreciation and follow with an analysis of

marketing challenges and strategies to successfully handle them. Third, solicit comments and problems in advance of the general meeting, then present solutions at the meeting for everyone's benefit.

2. *Inform and train with news of new products, markets, personnel, sales contests, and campaigns.* Divide and schedule topics into several meeting agendas. In addition to special-focus topics, stress attitude, initiative, diligence, and success at every sales meeting. Maintain attention by role-playing, humor, and participant surveys.

3. *Conduct a motivational presentation and issue a challenge.* Summarize meeting highlights and follow with praise and challenges to new heights of performance. Done effectively, your salespeople will leave energized, optimistic, and ready to sell.

4. *Schedule your meeting appropriately.* Be aware of the body's tendency to look forward to the weekend and to suffer Monday morning blahs. Make fresh coffee (and alternative beverages for non-coffee drinkers) available at the meeting.

5. *Meeting rooms should be air-conditioned and sheltered from outside noise.* Speakers should vary their tone and volume. Avoid droning, monotonous audio materials, as these kill concentration and enthusiasm.

6. *Invite attendees to stretch frequently to prevent stiff joints and sleepiness.* Remember that the best prescription for alertness is an exciting, motivating program, so devote your efforts to this end.

7. *Experiment with different times and places for your sales meetings.* A different setting provides a breath of fresh air.

8. *Add excitement with a sequence of interesting topics, building in pizzazz and challenge.* Start off with an exciting topic to provide you with the momentum to cover some less exciting, but equally necessary, subjects. Always end with the meeting's most important issue.

9. *Conduct your meeting in an upbeat, motivating style.* Appoint someone to record salespeople's questions that need research. Arrive early and dress appropriately. You are the leader. Be gracious in your manners. Whether you like it or not, you are a role model, so act like one.

10. *Make your sales meetings worth the time salespeople take away from selling by investing some time and effort in the entire process.* Your ultimate goal should be to enhance the selling effort through effective meetings that solve problems, bring out hidden issues, and motivate salespeople to go back to the field renewed and refreshed.

MAKE THE MOST OF MEETINGS

Business meetings devour growing amounts of money, time, and energy. But they can produce results, too. Research shows that workers want to create and contribute to agreed-upon goals—and meetings can make that happen, says Marilyn Manning, a trainer and consultant in Mountain View, California.

How do you keep your best performers focused and motivated in a meeting?

- Create events that reflect the needs of the participants.
- Ensure that attendees leave with a sense of exhilaration and a clear plan of action.
- Make the meeting the best use of everyone's time.

From Manning's long checklist of meeting dos and don'ts, here are some highlights for managers striving to put more meaning into their meetings:

- Reschedule if key people cannot attend. In advance, inform all participants of goals, agenda, and results.
- At the meeting's start, agree on ground rules, such as no side conversations and an on-time start and end. Display an agreed-upon agenda and consider assigning time allotments.
- Establish meeting roles. Besides a facilitator and a recorder, identify a timekeeper to keep time and give periodic warnings.
- Resolve conflicts, or risk the consequence—an unproductive meeting.
- At the conclusion, evaluate for a couple of minutes. If you didn't get the desired results, ask why. What worked best and what needs improvement?

A company's talent wants interaction with coworkers they admire. Well-executed meetings are a way to bring an organization's top minds together. Don't just exchange information. Solve problems. Create action plans. Oh, and don't forget: few things motivate better than recognition of employee accomplishments. Seize the opportunity that every meeting offers to acknowledge achievements.

WINNING ALTERNATIVES TO MEETINGS

Do you feel you spend more time coordinating or attending meetings than you do managing salespeople or selling? If so, you're not alone. Meetings are the bane of many companies, not only because they sap time and energy, but also because that time away from selling often equates to major dollar losses. So what can you do about it? Sharon Lippincott, in her book *Meetings: Do's, Don'ts and Donuts*, offers six alternatives to holding meetings:

1. *Phone calls.* Need advice, opinions, or information from just two or three people? Pick up the phone and talk to each of them. You may well get what you need without tying up a larger group whose input is not necessary. When those two or three people are in dispersed locations and talking with them simultaneously is critical, plan a conference call. You won't escape the meeting, but reps at the outstations will avoid some driving time.
2. *Memos or letters.* Sometimes the best way to provide information to people is simply to write it down. For instance, rather than hold a meeting about a new procedure for entering information into your SFA system, put it on paper and distribute it. Not only will reps avoid time in a meeting, they'll have a permanent guide for meeting the new requirements.
3. *Water-cooler conversations.* "Bumping into people in the lunchroom, hallway, or health club can yield a wealth of information that might be difficult to obtain in a meeting," says Lippincott. Why? Most people are more at ease offering ideas in a casual one-on-one environment than in the formal, public atmosphere of a meeting. Additionally, people are inclined to follow the politically correct majority opinion when in a group setting, a tendency that inhibits effective, thoughtful decision making.
4. *Remote-location brainstorming.* When input on ideas is needed from multiple people, try distributing lists of those ideas and asking for written feedback. Reps can work on the task as they have time throughout the day, and you'll wind up with pages full of documented responses.
5. *Delegate.* Do you really need to be the one to handle the issue for which you're thinking about calling a meeting? Or would it be better taken care of by someone else? Where possible, delegate tasks.
6. *Do it yourself.* If it's an issue you can, and possibly should, handle without input, why waste others' time meeting about it? Make a decision and go with it.

EXPERT ADVICE

Meet Up and Heat Up

Do your sales meetings have all the excitement and vitality of a Russian state funeral? Have salespeople been known to fake their own deaths to get out of having to attend? Do some participants fall asleep in the middle of presentations—even the instructors? To bring some vitality back to your moribund sales meetings, consider the following tips:

- *Try half-and-half.* "National sales meetings that go on all day and all night can be a big waste of time because they're tedious and unproductive. Try a half-day of meetings, then let the entire group go off-site for something fun, like golf or a spa. Part of the point is to foster camaraderie and let people blow off steam, and that just doesn't happen as well in a conference room."
- *Open up the floor.* "It's good to have a schedule, but leave some time for sidetracking and questions. And let people know you're eager to take questions. Then get back to your focus and move forward."
- *Do your job.* "As a sales professional, you should be able to give a damned good presentation. Take the skills you use to wow your customers and apply them to your meeting. You should be able to do the same for your salespeople."
- *Keep playing the upbeat.* "There's a fine line between problem solving and a witch trial. Don't let your meeting degenerate into recriminations and accusations about product failures and the like. Keep it instructive but positive. If necessary, take the problem off-line and discuss it privately."
- *Basic training.* "A portion of your meeting should always be dedicated to the basics—the 80–20 rule, the three-call rule, etc. It's like a golf lesson—even the pros need them. You always have to be correcting or you'll switch back into old bad habits. We all need constant reminders."

- *It keeps going and going and going.* "Training shouldn't begin and end at the meeting. If you want your salespeople to think strategically, be proactive and find unique solutions to customer issues. You need to reinforce that. Whenever you call, throughout the year, refer to the training you covered and ask, 'Are you doing this? How can we help you do more?'"

—From Mark Vassallo, president of Electronic Theater Controls–Americas.

Chapter 6

Understanding and Using Awards

CELEBRATE SUCCESS

How to Use Incentives That Motivate

Companies that celebrate successes have more successes to celebrate, claims Mac Anderson, president of Successories, Inc., in Lombard, Illinois, a company that specializes in designing, manufacturing, and selling motivational gifts and awards for businesses. Its roster of clients reads like a Who's Who of Corporate America: McDonald's, Coca-Cola, Anheuser-Busch, Sears, and even the big daddy of Mickey, Pluto, et al., Walt Disney.

People who are good at what they do want to be recognized. They want their families and their peers to know that they are among the best at what they do. When given the right opportunity, they will move mountains to prove just that. That's what a good recognition program is all about, says Anderson, himself a firm believer in positive booster shots.

According to Anderson, a good recognition program follows three basic steps. One, it has to be fairly structured—everyone has to have a chance to win. Two, it has to be presented with a lot of fanfare by a key person in the company, such as the president or sales manager. Three, it should reflect the company's own philosophy of quality and excellence.

The company goal should be to give each recipient an award that he or she will be proud to display to the rest of the world as a reminder of this moment in the sun. "I believe that people remember extraordinary moments, not days, weeks, or months. You want to set the stage for this moment to be special, one that the recipient will remember for the rest of his or her life," says Anderson.

Psychologists have long understood the impact of positive recognition on human behavior. The most important need a person has is human love and acceptance, to know that what he or she is has value to others. The second is to know that what he or she does makes a difference to others.

"When you hear from the athlete who is in the Super Bowl and is trying to win, he doesn't talk about the money he is going to make. He's talking about wearing the [Super Bowl] ring. It's the same for achievers. They have made the money, now they want to be recognized," Anderson explains.

Many companies, unfortunately, fail to tap the full motivational potential of a good recognition program. Anderson speculates that that's because they're afraid to try. A manager may feel uncomfortable about giving someone in a rural area in Idaho an award for making a quota, while someone in a heavily populated section of California may have sold twice as much but didn't make his or her quota.

My answer to that is that the salesperson in Idaho should have a goal, a quota, just like the one in California has. It doesn't make any difference if it is one half as much. The salesperson in Idaho who makes that quota should be recognized. The company should celebrate that success the same way it does the other, asserts Anderson.

According to Anderson, when sales executives aren't recognized, they aren't motivated to their fullest potential. While it's difficult to measure the exact dollar impact a recognition program has, it's a fact that people work harder when they have some goal besides money to work toward.

It's that moment in the sun, Anderson adds, that makes for rich memories and a feeling of real rewards.

"A typical recognition program scenario might be where a sales manager has a force of 100 sales personnel. She sets quotas for them at the beginning of the year. Theoretically, 50 will meet or exceed their goal, 40 will miss, and 10 will quit.

"The 50 people who were recognized go into the next year knowing that they are among the best. They feel great and they aren't going to want to let that fall by the wayside in the coming year. Thus, you've set a psychological stage for them to want to achieve again next year," says Anderson.

Companies that use recognition programs most effectively will give the top 10 sales representatives out of the 50 something special. They may receive more fanfare and their prize may be twice as valuable. And the top salesperson of all will be put on a pedestal and given the very best gift, a great trip perhaps, or a huge bonus.

"The top 10 all want to be that top person, and their goal is to be up there on the stage next year," Anderson says. What happens with the 40 who didn't make it to the very top is that they are now making a personal commitment that it won't happen again next year, and they are going to work harder to make sure it doesn't happen again next year.

In his experience, a company will typically spend $150 to $200 recognizing the top 10 salespeople. The overall best salesperson might receive a $500 piece of etched crystal. The other 40 might get plaques costing $70 to $100.

Professional salespeople know selling too well to think that the profession provides an all-time high. Selling is full of peaks and valleys. When a salesperson is having the lowest day or lowest week and looks up and sees that special thank-you that the company gave him or her last year, all of a sudden he or she remembers that special moment in the sun and how great it felt. The message is: "Get off your rear end and get out there and get to work. It can happen again next year if I make it happen," Anderson claims.

According to Anderson, McDonald's is probably the best example of a company that understands the power of recognition. The multimillion dollar chain recognizes outstanding store managers, assistant managers, and individual employees. It even gives out awards for outstanding landscapes and store interiors.

Recognition shouldn't be reserved solely for employees. Clients appreciate it as well, and thoughtfully chosen gifts can help build good business relationships.

Ideally, what you want to give a customer is something that is going to remind him or her of the person who gave the gift, Anderson recommends.

How does a company go about doing that? Again, Anderson has three suggestions: One is to select a gift that can't be consumed. "Not that people don't appreciate a bottle of liquor or pots of jams and jellies," he says, "it's just that they aren't memorable."

"If you are going to stop and spend the time and the money to say, 'Thank you, we appreciate your business,' you want them to remember it was you who said it. Give them something unique such as a crystal paperweight with a motivational quote etched on it. In addition, if it can be done tastefully, include the company's logo on the gift.

"What makes us unique in the industry is that we include a motivational quote on many of our gifts. Our customers feel that this adds inspirational value to an already beautiful gift," Anderson explains.

Engraving high-quality crystal, metal, and wooden gifts and awards with motivational messages is what sets Graphic Corp., Inc., apart from others in the business-awards incentives field. Sales managers who thumb through the glossy pages of Graphic Corp.'s catalog, "Celebrating Excellence," are apt to buy things like a set of six crystal old-fashioned glasses etched with such sayings as, "In the middle of every difficulty lies opportunity," and "Even if you're on the right track, you'll get run over if you just sit there." The set is called, appropriately enough, "Lift Your Spirits."

"People love quotes . . . because they allow them to focus in on an idea. Like when you have a camera in your hand and you look through it in the beginning, it is kind of gray and hazy, but you twist it a quarter of an inch to the right and click, and it is crystal clear. To me, ideas are the same way. They can be very hazy until we bring them into sharp focus," Anderson the motivator explains.

Among Anderson's favorite quotes is Henry Ford's well-known one about the relationship between success and failure. "Failure," Ford once said, "is the opportunity to begin again more intelligently."

Anderson likes to think that awarding one of his company's products to an outstanding salesperson or client makes for a memorable recognition program—one that keeps producing results long after the lights at the awards ceremony have dimmed. Combined with an appropriate quota system and a presentation ceremony with lots of fanfare, Anderson predicts, you will have a tremendous success on your hands.

KEEP WORKERS HAPPY

With unemployment at historically low levels and employee turnover a thorn in the side of some employers, new research provides simple guidance for businesses anxious to keep workers—and keep them happy.

A survey, sponsored by American Express Incentive Services (AEIS), shows that 18 percent of working and retired Americans polled said they had never received a performance award. "It's unbelievable that nearly one out of five employees has never received a reward," says Darryl A. Hutson, CEO of AEIS in Fenton, Missouri. "If employers are looking for new ways to keep employees happy and on the payroll, it could be as simple as rewarding them for a job well done."

The survey, conducted in June by Wirthlin Worldwide, polled 851 working or retired American adults, all of them members of a randomly selected nationwide sample. Can rewards keep workers in the fold? Maybe. A previous survey sponsored by AEIS found that 63 percent of adult Americans polled said their loyalty to their employers would increase if offered an ongoing incentive program allowing choice of rewards.

Personalized incentives curb turnover most effectively if a company offers rewards over a long term rather than as a one-time pat on the back, says Janelle Brittain, executive director of the Dynamic Performance Institute in Chicago.

But what one person views as a reward may not appeal to another. In the June survey, 1,000 American adults polled differed about what would most motivate them to improve performance if offered a noncash reward worth $1,000. Top motivators included:

A trip to a destination of your choice	40 percent
A shopping spree at stores of your choice	23 percent
Home improvement and beautification	19 percent
Season tickets to a favorite entertainment venue	10 percent
Electronics	4 percent

When asked about their best performance rewards, some gave unexpected responses: a verbal thank you, job satisfaction, career-related training, a letter of commendation, and a good evaluation.

EXPERT ADVICE

Tips to Rev Up Your Selling Engine

Salespeople crave positive reinforcement. That aspect of the sales process is what puts many in the sales profession in the first place! A good sales manager is one who understands that when the engine slows down, positive reinforcement carefully applied is the key to reactivating that selling engine. The focus for that reinforcement often needs to shift from the sale itself to the small accomplishments that build to a sale.

A slump may also indicate that the manager will want to retool the team's skills or attitude. "Skills can atrophy when business comes so easily that the salesperson does not need to really sell." Aubrey Daniels, the author of *Bringing Out the Best in People*, recounts the story of trying to purchase a popular make of car during a time when there were waiting lists for it. "No one approached us. After 30 minutes we left and went to another type of dealership. Someone came out, met with us, explained the car, etc. I bought that car because someone was selling it. They knew how to value customers and present the product. At the other dealership they had forgotten how to sell."

Some aids to renewing basic skills are motivational tapes and meetings, especially meetings with other successful salespeople to trade ideas. Tracking of the small steps to reach a sale will help sales reps reframe mentally so that what was a sign of failure is now a pointer toward success. Daniels notes, "All successful salespeople I have known track their daily ratio of sales to calls in one way or another. They know that if they sell to one out of seven, those six rejections are simply stepping stones to success." In a slump, focus on the calls. Set self-management goals that are reachable. Breaking the ultimate goal—sales—down into a series of steps that are goals—more calls, more presentations—translates into an attitude of success. This is especially true when the marketplace is the cause of the slump. When the market has fewer people buying, good salespeople increase their efforts so that the sales that are made go through *them*! "Long-term goals are not the question here—it's the short term."

The timing of reinforcement is also very important. "Behavior reinforcement from management, and that initiated by the salesperson, must be applied when there are positive results. Don't simply take time off when you are in a slump. That rewards the negative condition. Wait until you have made a sale—then take off some time to recharge, as a celebration of success. Keep such rewards as lunching out, time off, and breaks for when you are doing your best. Keep your nose to the grindstone when things are bad."

When salespeople suffer slumps due to personal depression—things such as the death of a loved one, divorce, reaction to a disaster—or to forces beyond their ability to cope or to the condition of the market, part of the recharge may often involve redirecting their thoughts. "Get them doing something, anything, even outside of sales, that will give them positive reinforcement. One of the best ways is to do good for others. They need to realize that they can remain in charge—if not of their circumstances, at least of their response."

These six tips for crafting effective reward and recognition programs are based on those offered to managers by Daniels:

1. Positive reinforcement has to occur daily.
2. The reward and recognition must be earned. The relationship between performance and reward must be direct.
3. The recognition must have personal value. The dollar value is unimportant as long as it is meaningful to the person.
4. Avoid delay between the valued behavior and the reward or recognition.

(*Continued on next page.*)

(*Continued from previous page.*)

5. Precede the presentation of incentives with some type of celebration, however small.
6. Think beyond money for incentives. Money is soon spent and the memory of it fades.

Management's retooling of goal structures and rewards can be the key to recharging a slumping rep's sales engine.

—From Aubrey Daniels, chairman of Aubrey Daniels International, a performance-management consulting firm based in Atlanta, and the author of several books on management and sales.

Chapter 7

Incentive Plans That Boost Performance

INCENTIVE TO PERFORM

Lift Morale and Boost Sales—Without Depressing the Bottom Line

American companies spend some $27 billion a year on incentives to motivate and reward great performances. In a slow economy, that figure may waffle a bit. Well, maybe more than a bit. Companies look for bargains or often cut back and wait until they really have something to reward. Something tangible that is. Like sales.

But even in tough times, executives in the top spots realize that without incentives salespeople may feel too pooped to pop—especially when markets are drying up faster than a riverbed in Dry Gulch. So as a tough year grinds on, sales managers start looking around for ways to motivate their reps.

Case in point: Spencer Toomey, vice president of special markets for Bulova Corporation in Woodside, New York, says that during his two decades in the incentive field he's never seen incentives benefit from a tough economy—and 2001 was no exception. "It felt like probably the worst year I've gone through," he admits. "The industry came to a screeching halt at the start of the year. But by mid-summer, people began seeking quotes. Companies still take care of their sale forces and still offer incentives, but every single program is reevaluated."

Yes, reevaluate your current programs, but don't throw the baby out with the bath water, advises Karen L. Renk, executive director of the Incentive Marketing Association (IMA) in Naperville, Illinois. "The worst thing companies can do is strip rewards when you need to keep morale high. If there are layoffs, smart companies realize they need to show existing staff that they're secure in their positions and they're appreciated."

So how can companies make sure their salespeople are happy and inspired while keeping a close eye on costs and return on investment? Read on to learn how sales managers, industry experts, and incentive suppliers identify the tried-and-true and ongoing trends in the incentives industry.

Eye on the Bottom Line

When Joan Baranek, sales director at Airgas Safety, a distributor of industrial safety equipment in Bristol, Pennsylvania, talks about the impact of incentives on her company, she can hardly contain her enthusiasm. "It's been incredible," she says. "We've seen the results of what incentives can do for our salespeople. We've learned that if you motivate them, they will sell it."

Airgas Safety, a $250 million division of Airgas, saw its long-time double-digit growth rate begin to slow during the economic slowdown after September 11. With the sales force having to work harder than ever to grow market share, Baranek fine-tuned and beefed up the use of incentives. For example, she increased the value of the American Express Incentive Services (AEIS) cards she used from $50 to $75 in some cases. "Some salespeople work territories hard hit with plant closings. When sales get sluggish, incentives keep people moving in the right direction and keep them focused and stretching," Baranek explains.

While some companies trimmed incentive programs to cope with the tight economy, others tailored high-end rewards, including incentive travel, sometimes shifting funds into more inclusive programs to recognize larger groups of award earners. "Good idea," says Paul Brickman, vice president of marketing and strategic alliances for Heritage Marketing & Incentives (HMI) in Norwood, Massachusetts, who warns managers to resist concentrating rewards only on the company's top 20 percent. "The middle 60 percent has the greatest potential for a performance increase. Without an incentive, the middle 60 percent become more pessimistic. That's probably not prudent for a company trying to protect sales revenues."

During an economic slowdown, it is no surprise that companies want to see the greatest return on their investments. "Budgets are being pared down, and people want to see maximum impact for their dollars," says Bill Termini, national sales manager with Chicago-based Hinda Incentives. Hinda offers one such tool that stretches the reward investment: an e-auction that allows participants to use their points to bid on travel and merchandise awards at bargain prices during nonworking hours. Since Hinda developed the Web-based auction for one company, it has hosted events for other clients. One auction drew 8,000 participants.

Besides maximum impact, incentive managers are also looking for immediate results. That fact helps explain why more companies want short-term sales incentives, says Steve Damerow, president of Incentive Solutions in Atlanta, Georgia. "Everybody wants rewards and results quicker," he says. "The sponsoring company cares about 'What are sales this quarter?' The big thing we keep hearing is, 'We want rewards to provide instant gratification.' If I can reduce the amount of time it takes people to get positive feedback for changing their behavior, the sponsor saves money. That's vital in a soft economy."

And when it comes to almost instantaneous feedback, the Internet is leading the way.

Online Solutions

While the end of dot-com mania fueled caution among some incentive buyers, it hasn't changed the simple fact that the Internet still offers a powerful, exciting technology, according to IMA's Renk. "Furthermore," she says, "the Web is changing how the incentive market works. As more suppliers offer wares and services online to hardworking award earners, chances are better than ever that more recipients will get what they want. And what about overworked, budget-conscious managers? The technology makes the process of rewarding salespeople easier, faster, and cheaper—with better real-time results."

In fact, by providing managers with an easy way to tap into free incentive expertise, assistance, and answers, the Internet is expected to drive increased use of and demand for incentives in a vast, untapped market: organizations with no more than 300 employees. "With the Web there's a huge potential with the midsize and small companies. The Web can provide many incentive services on a scale that will make them more affordable," Renk says.

Hinda Incentives, for example, has developed an online tool specifically for smaller companies. Hinda released the innergE® software program to allow companies with 25 to 250 employees to run employee recognition programs on their own and online. For $2,000 per year and minimal set-up time, Hinda staff help with planning, train an administrator, and provide support via a telephone hotline. "With the advent of the Web, companies with smaller populations can run their own internal recognition programs and not have them cost an arm and a leg to administer," says Termini. "Participants can bank their points. Instead of a pen, maybe they'll get a DVD player. On the Web, administration is cheaper, quicker, and better than on paper. Paper is fraught with error. It's expensive and highly intensive administratively."

Companies are finding more reasons to use online incentive programs. According to HMI, some businesses want Web-based programs that award points to employees for using the Web on the job in order to reinforce a corporate goal of encouraging Internet use in a company's daily operations. Other motives lead companies to online programs. Some of HMI's clients want the immediacy, the flexibility, and the easy setup HMI offers, in addition to the electronic ability to enroll, track, issue status reports, post catalogs, and redeem awards. Last but not least, the Web creates excitement and sustains enthusiasm. Participants receive destination photos, newsletters, program updates, motivational messages, and postcards via e-mail.

To get salespeople firing on all cylinders, AEIS rolled out its Web-based Virtual Rewards earlier this year. The stored-value products—in addition to AEIS's Persona card—are redeemable on the Internet wherever American Express cards are accepted. Paper-free setup is fast, rewards arrive via e-mail, and reward earners can track points at personalized Web sites.

However, HMI's Brickman points out that even with a tech-savvy audience, online communications don't cover all the bases. "Online, it's very easy to delete something and go on with the rest of your day. And if you only use online, you're leaving out reaching the spouse at home," he says.

Online incentives also cannot provide a memorable delivery, and therefore choosing cyber awards does not have the impact of face-to-face presentations. "The presentation gives an award more value," Bulova's Toomey says. "If reward earners just click on a CD player, and no one knows about it, and it just gets delivered to your house, you may as well get money. People like to be rewarded and recognized in front of their family and their colleagues. An e-mail trophy doesn't have same impact."

The best may be combined solutions. "This is the right product for some companies," says Darryl A. Hutson, chief executive officer at AEIS in Fenton, Missouri, of Web-based rewards. "No product is the right one all the time, for everyone. The Web is changing the industry forever, but it will never take over everything. People still like to go out and shop. Giving the award earner the choice of clicks and bricks is very powerful."

Joe Barry, HMI's senior vice president of sales and marketing, agrees. "The Internet is a great vehicle, but it's not all-reaching. It has to be reinforced with paper and mailings. A 3-D teaser gift has greater impact and staying power. You can't beat the visual reminder of a bottle of sand or a pair of sunglasses. The coconut or the bottle of olive oil on the desk, or a poster of a tropical island on their walls, makes them rev up their engines."

TIPS FOR USING GIFT CERTIFICATES AND GIFT CARDS

- *Get a discount.* Of course, you can buy some categories of merchandise at prices far below retail with volume discounts. However, don't forget that many companies offer bulk discounts on gift certificates starting at 5 percent. For instance, Cabela's offers a 5 percent discount for programs ranging from $5,000 to $20,000, 6 percent up to $35,000, and 7 percent for more. At KB Toys, a 10 percent discount applies to any order of $1,000 or more. For Darden Restaurants, discounts range from 5 percent ($500 to $999 per purchase order) to 15 percent ($7,500 or more per order).

- *Put your stamp on it.* Major suppliers of gift certificates or gift cards often provide some customization or personalization. For something as simple as making the certificate out to the individual or for more elaborate services—customized, logoed cards, certificates, or packaging, even customized mailings, for example—just ask. Like other retailers, Best Buy Co., Inc., the nation's largest electronics retailer, will personalize paper gift certificates by including the names of the recipient and corporate sponsor or program plus a greeting and a personalized message of up to 100 characters. While Best Buy offers popular reloadable plastic gift cards as well, the retailer has no plans to eliminate its paper certificate. "There's still a big demand for it. We think it's worthwhile to keep them," says Rich Olson, manager of Best Buy's corporate incentive program. "The personalized certificate reminds salespeople why they won."

- *Never skimp on presentation.* Gift cards and gift certificates are so easy to present, it's easy to overlook the delivery. The paper certificate seems to lend itself to presentation more easily than the plastic gift card. Whether or not you personally present this reward, be sure to take advantage of the supplier's packaging and maximize any personalization. As always, a congratulatory letter from the boss goes a long way to set a certificate or any other nonmonetary award apart from cash.

- *Know when to reload.* To meet budding corporate demand, a growing number of retailers are issuing gift cards that can be reloaded with dollar value. While paper certificates provide a good option for infrequent rewards, reloadable cards can work well when participants receive winnings on a somewhat regular basis, observers say.
- *Click this: redeem gift cards online.* Gift cards seem to be a good fit for retailers with a lot of presence in the brick-and-mortar market. However, some retailers allow redemption of their gift cards in cyberspace. One such national merchant is KB Toys, the United States' largest mall-based specialty toy retailer, with more than 1,300 stores. When KB Toys launched its gift card and stopped issuing paper certificates in October 2000, the retailer provided a currency good both at store locations and on the Web. "The added convenience of being able to use the gift card online has been a huge win," says John P. Reilly, KB Toys manager of sales promotion and public relations. Here's another convenience—if you need to return something bought online, you can take it back to a store location.

Pack Your Bags

When you want your salespeople—and your sales—to skyrocket, there are few substitutes for the positive impact of group travel. In fact, during the soft economy, organizations striving hard to ensure that top performers feel appreciated have helped sustain demand for group travel. "We've seen group travel come back stronger in the past couple of years," HMI's Barry says. "From the company's perspective, it's better for bonding."

At the same time, the increasing numbers of two-career couples have helped fuel demand for shorter, more frequent trips and individual incentive travel. AEIS's Hutson believes that individual travel will climb as much as 20 percent within the next year. And the AEIS line of stored-value products seems well positioned to capitalize on that award trend. AEIS's premium Persona card, for example, is redeemable at leading travel merchants plus well-known retail and entertainment suppliers. Will the individual travel trend continue? "It's hot and promotable," Hutson says. "It makes people excited to work."

Lifestyles and Traditions

Ask industry experts what merchandise awards make people excited about working, and they'll tell you that lifestyle-oriented awards do the job. Electronics still reign supreme as the top merchandise choice. Home improvement items for the kitchen and the home are pleasing crowds, too. "The joke used to be that the incentive industry is the pots-and-pans-and-toaster industry. In many cases we were, because that's what people wanted. But now people are getting high-end pots and pans and high-end toasters," Hinda's Termini says.

Bulova's Toomey agrees that lifestyle rewards are hot. Under the lifestyles heading he includes equipment for exercise, fishing and camping, plus other nontraditional rewards. By contrast, crystal, timepieces, and other traditional awards don't show the strength they had in the past. "We know there's a challenge," Toomey says. "We're an instant society. But a TV isn't passed down like an heirloom clock. A camcorder hardly makes an heirloom. Where are the bragging rights on a nice sweater bought with a gift certificate? Tradition is still going to survive."

Paper, Plastic, and Click

When you want the perfect reward for a short-term incentive program, myriad tools can offer a good fit. However, few enjoy the surging popularity of the easy-to-use and flexible gift certificate. Now available online and in plastic, as well as in traditional paper, certificates can ease the challenges of an overworked manager plus satisfy the recipients' desire for choice.

A survey by the Incentive Gift Certificate Council indicates a big jump in B-to-B sales of certificates. B-to-B sales climbed 22 percent—to $1.5 billion annually—just among the 25 council members responding to the survey. "With the figures representing only a small segment of the entire gift-certificate market, the upside potential is unknown," says Steve Maselko, president of the 60-member certificate council and operations vice president of Marriott Certificates.

For the future, Maselko sees two notable growth fronts. He anticipates an explosion in the use of both online gift certificates and plastic gift cards. Why e-certificates? "Online certificates are easy to manage and present, delivering quick feedback. Plus, communication is simple and the opportunities to personalize are numerous," says Maselko.

Why gift cards? More suppliers are migrating from paper to plastic because the gift card carries greater perceived trophy value and a longer shelf life. "With the new applications, there's more excitement," Maselko points out. "E-certificates and gift cards are about to take off and head straight for sky."

Choices, Choices

Without a doubt, incentives that give recipients more choices are among the rewards that are surviving and thriving. "A sales force doesn't like to be told where and how and when to spend its money. That's why a debit card is so strong," says Damerow. Incentive Solutions created its first debit card eight years ago to satisfy a corporate client that wanted to motivate a large sales force using an alternative to incentive travel and catalog merchandise.

Incentive Solutions now creates debit, or stored-value, cards to fit diverse client needs. For example, cards can be redeemed solely on one cruise line or on the Internet only—or anywhere in the world.

Airgas's Baranek says she has had good results when using various incentive tools—from stored-value cards to Giftscertificates.com's certificates, from TVs and movie tickets to dinners and trips. After four years of incentive success with American Express Incentive Services stored-value products, Baranek especially likes AEIS's Encompass Select card, which is accepted anywhere American Express is welcome. "The salespeople can use it on whatever they want—on vacation, on a large TV, for shopping," she explains. One salesperson bought a home theater system with the Encompass Select card. Another bought plane tickets and lodging for a trip with her husband to the Cayman Islands, and she still had value left over on the card for spending money.

What results have stored-value cards produced on Airgas Safety's bottom line? Baranek offered Encompass Select cards as the reward in a short-term program intended to boost sales of one of Airgas Safety's preferred product lines. The outcome: Sales soared 36 percent in six weeks. "A lot of our growth has come from incentives," Baranek emphasizes. "We firmly believe in incentives."

IGNITE YOUR SALES TEAM—FROM THE BOTTOM PERFORMER TO THE SUPERSTAR

The top 20 percent of your sales force will perform no matter what, or so the common wisdom goes. But what about the other 80 percent? Everyone on the team has to be firing on all cylinders. To rev up steady performers, future stars, and the rest of the team as well, you must provide the rocket fuel that will ignite their boosters.

That may sound like a tall order, but some companies have hit on a mix that has a little something for every salesperson.

Some companies give everyone a chance of winning by offering merchandise, gift certificates, and individual trips—not just the big travel award that spurs the brightest stars to go the extra mile. Other businesses put rewards within the reach of all by allowing salespeople to compete against themselves or by permitting them to earn rewards instantly or over time. By distributing inspiration far and wide, corporations improve their chances of giving the biggest possible lift to the sales force and the bottom line. If you're not convinced, look at how four companies—Allergan Inc., 3Com Corporation, Quill Corporation, and CareerExchange—launched inclusive incentive programs that spurred people at varying performance levels to give their best.

Company: Allergan, Inc.
Incentive Partner: Maritz Performance Improvement Company

Allergan Inc., the health care company, has long awarded high-end group travel to the top sales achievers in its five divisions. In 2000, Allergan's Skin Care Division set out to spread the motivation further—and boost sales of a key product. How? With the help of Maritz Performance Improvement Company, the Skin Care Division launched two short-term performance improvement programs. The goal was simple: to inspire sales reps to reach quarterly product-oriented goals by harnessing the appeal of a wide selection of brand-name merchandise and other individual rewards—while keeping the annual group-travel award in place. Did the "everyone-can-win" approach work?

"Absolutely. We got it right," says Bill Humphries, vice president of sales and marketing for Allergan's Skin Care Division. "The short-term programs are like sprints to add focus and provide immediate gratification for the winners, while the incentive trip is more like a marathon. Our strategy is to use merchandise to add focus and group travel to motivate top performers." Indeed, the results were so strong that the division repeated the two 90-day programs in 2001. "It's been wildly successful. It has benefited the company and the field force," says Humphries.

The short-term programs, called "Just Take It Quick—Tazorac," concentrated on boosting the market share of Allergan's topical gel for psoriasis. As Humphries explains, "It's a focus issue. Our sales force has four different products to sell, and these programs allowed us to provide focus and rewards for driving the strategies we needed to execute with our customers. We were in the process of launching a new indication for our flagship product, Tazorac, and I wanted to put a hot light on that one product to ensure success."

Via weekly voice mail, Humphries updated sales reps on their progress toward the market-share benchmarks, while Maritz handled formal mailings, tracking, fulfillment, and other tasks. The results? Of the 65 sales reps and sales managers eligible to participate, roughly 40 percent met the aggressive goals in each of the two periods. "It's very exciting," Humphries says. "We grew three share points in 40 percent of the field in this very fragmented market."

Upon hitting their benchmarks, sales reps snared points in the Maritz Awards Bank System. By running contests back-to-back, Humphries allowed participants to accumulate enough points in their individual accounts to redeem for big-ticket items. Some reps banked points redeemable for as much as $3,000 in awards. And what do the points buy? Participants can redeem them for merchandise in the *Your Rewards* book, the oversized 375-page Maritz catalog. Its more than 2,000 items carry brand names—and dollar values ranging from $25 to $31,650. Another place to spend points is Maritz's secured Web site (www.awardhq.com) that appeals to Allergan's relatively young sales reps who have the computer savvy to shop and check point balances online.

"Use of the online catalog is easy and it offers discounted specials and seasonal and new items you can't put in a print catalog," says Carol Rogers, a Maritz account manager. "We've found people like the physical hard-copy catalog for browsing; then they order online." Participants also can redeem points by fax, toll-free number, and mail.

However, the award choices don't end there. Participants can redeem for the stored-value Your Choice card, which bears the American Express logo. The card opens the doors to a host of participating retailers, catalogers, theme parks, travel companies, hotels, airlines, and even merchants and restaurants offering gift certificates. Why so many choices? The flexibility ensures satisfaction for a sales force with varied tastes and interests. "It was very diverse," Humphries explains. "You could get a watch, a trip, a washer/dryer, a stereo, a DVD player. Everybody could find something in there that they'd like and would consider a reward for a job well done."

Company: Quill Corporation
Incentive Partner: CultureWorx (Formerly Motivation Online)

In the stressful environment of a call center, employees need positive feedback. While reinforcement can come in various forms, incentives certainly help do the job. Quill Corporation, a B-to-B marketer of office supplies and business products, had been recognizing its top-selling call center reps with catalog-based awards for a couple of years. However, Quill, a wholly-owned subsidiary of Staples, recently launched a new program that distributed reinforcement widely. Using the performance software from CultureWorx, Quill began rewarding every call center associate who showed desired behaviors toward customers—no matter whether an incremental sale resulted or not. And when a rep did make an incremental sale, that too fetched points good for merchandise, travel, and gift certificates. According to Donna Chrobak, CultureWorx director of redemption services, "It's about taking the right steps to get the sale, and if you get the sale there's an extra bonus. What we've found is, if you improve your process the natural result is that you get more sales."

Prior to the CultureWorx program's startup, Quill encouraged incremental sales by rewarding the top 12 performers at each of its three call centers each week. The top 20 achievers for each month and the top 8 for each quarter won awards, too. However, the selection of catalog-based awards grew stale and the program's administration caused hassles. Kim Kelly, Quill marketing and recognition administrator, says, "Quill has gone through a wide assortment of reward options in the last five years—cash, gift certificate, and catalog-based merchandise awards. I was looking for a new and exciting way to motivate our representatives." Luckily, Kelly found what she was looking for in CultureWorx, formerly Motivation Online, and its online performance system featuring Internet-based redemption and more.

The CultureWorx program awards points to associates who offer products to phone customers who otherwise might not take advantage of the specials. Associates also earn points for actual incremental sales. A test program was launched at Quill's Lincolnshire, Illinois-based call center, and was expanded in November to include Quill's two Canadian centers in Nova Scotia and Saskatchewan. In all, about 500 reps were eligible for rewards. For the manager, the online capability simplifies administering a program in multiple locations. In addition, the Web site allows for easy, paper-free communication. The password-protected award site permits associates, whether at work or at home, to track their earned points, see what they can buy, and decide how to spend their points. Employees accumulate points as they work toward bigger awards.

The reps, ranging in age from 18 to 70-plus years, are diverse, yet the award selection satisfies the entire group. Participants shop via direct links to www.ToysRUs.com, www.FansEdge.com, and other sites at the CultureWorx's 30-merchant online mall. Says Chrobak, "We want to provide a broad range, but we want to offer the best."

Quill asked CultureWorx to offer restaurant and merchandise gift certificates in its program. Why? Online shopping requires reps to spend points on shipping and taxes, Kelly explains. "They feel there is a better value if they are able to purchase a gift certificate," she says. "Some are hesitant about online shopping and just prefer to actually go to a store or restaurant." Quill also has used gift certificates in past programs, with a positive response. Kelly gave high marks to CultureWorx's willingness to work hard to satisfy Quill's business needs and startup requirements. "As we have progressed, CultureWorx has gone above and beyond to resolve any issues that have arisen."

Indeed, the program bears the name "Customer Relations Above & Beyond Award Program." The theme: balloons. A helium-filled balloon was attached to the reps' invitations to the kick-off event. The kick-off featured a 26-foot cold-air balloon in the parking lot at the Lincolnshire call center, where the company is headquartered. From a conference room, reps flew two remote-controlled blimps. Has the program given a lift to Quill's sales? "Yes," Kelly says. "More associates are winning awards than ever before, and Quill closed its 2000 fiscal year with a nearly $2.5 million increase in incremental sales. A significant portion of this can be attributed to the CultureWorx program," adds Kelly. "I expect to see even more significant results during the rest of 2001."

When delivering recognition and reinforcement to employees, CultureWorx programs sometimes include incentive rewards, other times not. Nevertheless, the focus is always long-term, sustained improvement, according to Chrobak. "This is about teaching people new behaviors and how to be better employees and better performers," she explains. Other incentive companies help improve performance during the life of the program. We want to help you improve performance permanently."

Company: 3Com Corporation
Incentive Partner: Netcentives, Inc.

3Com Corporation, headquartered in Santa Clara, California, a provider of connectivity products and solutions, wanted to make it easier for its channel partners to do business with 3Com. The solution? In the fall of 2000, 3Com launched the Focus program, which gave United States–based channel partners easy access to online business tools, the latest product information, training, and customized communications. It also provided something more: In recognition of the key role of these VARs (value-added resellers), system integrators, and other partners, the program offered the Focus Rewards program as a sales incentive. Under the points-based reward program, sales reps and other participants earned ClickMiles points for certain accomplishments.

What kinds of achievements drew ClickMiles, a Web-based currency created by Netcentives Inc.? Revenue sales, products sold, events attended, training completed, and participation in a new 3Com certification program. ClickMiles are redeemable for frequent flyer miles, travel, hotel stays, and brand-name merchandise. "The rewards program is not by any stretch of the imagination cheap, but there are strong benefits," says Sylvio Jelovcich, senior director of field and channel marketing for 3Com. "We now have a standardized ongoing process that provides inspiration and motivation. Our goal was to create some real sustaining power. We saw some strong merits in keeping the program long term so people can earn rewards immediately or over time."

The ClickMiles form of motivation certainly got a warm reception from 3Com's target audience. Participants earned more than 20 million ClickMiles and redeemed more than 6 million ClickMiles during roughly the first six months. During the program's first full year, 3Com's Jelovcich expects distribution of ClickMiles worth more than $1 million. Popular redemption prizes include airline tickets, trips, and gift certificates. The online catalog of the San Francisco–based Netcentives offers frequent flier miles on 10 major airlines. ClickMiles are also good for such unusual adventures as white-water rafting trips, African safaris, or cooking classes in Italy. The latest electronics are always hot, especially DVD players. And for the point-holders unable to find exactly what they want, gift certificates can satisfy and simplify delivery of rewards to recipients overseas. "A catalog's wide variety is crucial, because what motivates each individual is different," says Elizabeth Ames, chief marketing officer of Netcentives. "The key is for people to look at a catalog and say, 'I want that.'"

With Netcentives drawing from its ties to airline, hotel, vacation, and retail partners, it can tailor an online catalog to meet the motivational needs of each client. Netcentives also encourages clients to offer things recipients aren't likely to buy—or can't purchase, such as tickets to the company's stadium skybox. "With the Netcentives technology infrastructure," Jelovcich says, "it's been easy to adjust 3Com's program to meet changing needs." For instance, 3Com promoted sales of its Ethernet network interface card by doubling and tripling the number of ClickMiles rewarded for the product's sales. The result? In one month alone, product sales more than doubled.

Before 3Com partnered with Netcentives, 3Com had planned to work with a smaller rewards provider. However, because the scalable Netcentives program could migrate worldwide to accommodate 3Com's global reach, 3Com switched to Netcentives about a month before the program's launch. Plans for a more fully integrated system include automated delivery of real-time feedback and ClickMiles to salespeople for a job well done. "One of the best parts about the Netcentives system design and approach is the online validation and feedback to the actual sales rep," Jelovcich explains. In traditional, paper-based incentive programs, lag times can undercut the effect of reinforcement and rewards. Netcentives, however, says its technology's ability to deliver real-time recognition provides potent motivation. According to Ames, "Having people wait a week or a month leaves them asking, 'Why did I get this reward?' But Netcentives is able in minutes to send, 'Congratulations! You've earned this.' That gives powerful immediacy to a program."

Company: CareerExchange
Incentive Partner: SalesDriver, Inc.

CareerExchange, an Internet career site specializing in high-tech industries, had wanted to keep its five-member sales team better focused on sales goals. At CareerExchange, time-pressed managers have little time to help the salespeople stay on track. However, one of the salespeople heard about SalesDriver's online sales contests. CareerExchange CEO, Jason Moreau, believed SalesDriver's Web-based system would keep the team focused—and provide a welcome tool for communication as well.

"I knew it would get everyone excited," Moreau says. "And SalesDriver would solve the problem of everybody wanting to see what the others were doing." So

Moreau launched CareerExchange's first monthly SalesDriver contest. Did it succeed? Judge for yourself: When the first contest ended, CareerExchange's Moreau launched another monthly program, and ever since, Moreau has continued to renew the monthly contests. Why? "It's been successful for us," he says. "It helps us identify what's doable and what's not. And it's kept people focused. Before, a salesperson would have a good month and possibly fall off track the next month. We're a skeleton shop and we don't have much time to make sure everyone meets quotas. It has probably brought people who were just coasting up to the levels where they should be performing. Bottom line result: the monthly contests have helped the Berkeley, California-based CareerExchange maintain its annual growth rate of roughly 100 percent," Moreau says.

Moreau has customized the SalesDriver contests so that each week $50 in SalesDriver's DriverDollars goes to the account executive who sells the most and meets the weekly sales target. Monthly, another contest spreads out motivation further by awarding $100 DriverDollars to salespeople who meet their monthly quota. Salespeople can earn even more depending on how much more they sell. "You're competing with yourself monthly. Everyone can be rewarded," says Moreau.

One of the most popular SalesDriver features at CareerExchange is the online scoreboard. "It has fostered better communication and fed the sales team's competitive spirit by tracking results and allowing participants to see how they rank," Moreau says. "It's exposed everybody to what each other is doing. Everyone can see you're a top performer or if you're not up to where everybody else is. Salespeople are motivated by dollars and cents, and nobody wants to be at the bottom."

Other handy SalesDriver tools include DriverMail. Via e-mail, it automatically announces the program, then alerts participants to updates and changes. Recently added SalesDriver features include customizable surveys. The polls allow managers to seek feedback on any subject and reward responding participants with DriverDollars.

"Keeping time-short sales directors in mind, SalesDriver designed its system for easy setup and use," says Joel Silver, vice president of marketing at Maynard, Massachusetts-based SalesDriver. What's more, the basic setup and operation of a program costs nothing—a benefit that Silver says can save 20 percent or more on the cost of a traditional paper-based program. One of the biggest challenges for a manager trying to design an inclusive incentive program is how to distribute inspiration to everyone, not just the top 20 percent. SalesDriver offers a couple of solutions in the form of customizable contest templates that give all participants the chance to earn rewards. For example, the Activity-Based contest structure rewards salespeople each time they finish an assigned task. The Hit-the-Target contest template allows everyone to aim for the same target—or it can feature individualized targets that take into account each individual's history and client base.

"In the old world, usually just the top people got the trip, or managers got buried dealing with 200 salespeople getting awards. The power of an online program is that it's easy to give anybody the chance to win."

And what can they win? DriverDollars are redeemable at SalesDriver's 1,500-award online catalog of merchandise and trips. Besides such crowd-pleasing categories as electronics, toys, and housewares, SalesDriver offers some unusual rewards. Who hasn't coveted a Porsche or Harley Davidson? Here's your chance to see the Daytona 500 or the NFL Super Bowl. Ever wanted to take an Amazon River adventure or a Thailand odyssey? How about experiencing zero gravity in the Russian IL-76 MDK or traveling to the edge of space in the legendary MiG-25 Foxbat? Drawing from partnerships with various reward fulfillment partners, SalesDriver updates its online catalog monthly to keep it fresh. "A sales audience is demanding. Selection, brand names, and quality are important," explains Silver.

At a program's end, managers pay only for the DriverDollars their sales teams have earned. SalesDriver makes its money on the rewards, which SalesDriver buys in volume. At CareerExchange, SalesDriver's currency is so popular that the company gave out bonuses for the holidays in the form of DriverDollars. Moreau says participants have redeemed the currency for name-brand items from the electronics, sports, luxury, and housewares categories. With back-to-back programs, they try to save up points to shop for $400 and $500 items. "They love the rewards," says Moreau. "They may be small when you compare them to their commission checks, but it's instant gratification."

AN ADDED INCENTIVE

Put the Motivating Power of Incentives to Work for Your Team

Even if your team members have the knowledge and selling skills to take them to the top, whether or not they fulfill their potential may depend on their level of motivation. Managers may think that a simple thank-you note or a few words of recognition are no big deal, but they mean a lot to salespeople in the trenches.

Implement an effective incentive program to reward your salespeople's efforts and ignite their desire to achieve like never before.

- *Link incentives to performance.* An effective incentive is more than just a handout distributed to every member of the sales force. Rewards should be reserved for above-average performance. Let your salespeople know that the greater their performance, the greater the reward. Design your incentive program so that the value of the rewards and the degree of recognition match the level of the recipients' achievements.

- *Add variety—be creative.* A variety of rewards helps maintain your salespeople's interest in earning them. If you offer the same award for a particular achievement time after time, your salespeople may come to expect it as an ongoing benefit. For example, instead of always rewarding your salespeople with half a day off when they meet their quarterly quota, try rewarding them with the half day the first quarter, offer no reward for the second quarter, then have an ice cream party when they meet the quota the third time. Variety keeps a motivating incentive from becoming a predictable expectation.

- *Emphasize nonmonetary incentives.* Studies show that the greatest increases in productivity come not from cash alone, but from such nonmonetary recognition items as merchandise, plaques, and lifestyle items. Believe it or not, many employees rank their manager's personal thanks at the top of their list of motivating rewards. Don't be stingy with praise. Realize how much your salespeople need to hear from you that they're doing a good job. Be specific when you offer praise—tell your salespeople exactly why you're recognizing them and single out those who earn your praise.

- *Match the incentive to the salesperson.* When your salesperson can see that a reward was thoughtfully chosen specifically for him or her, it takes on greater meaning. If you know the award recipient is a football enthusiast, let the award (season passes to a local team's games, a unique piece of football memorabilia, or tickets to the Super Bowl) reflect that knowledge. Incentives don't need to be expensive, but they should show that care and consideration of the recipient went into their selection.

- *Be generous with praise.* Don't save your praise for a performance review. It takes very little effort for managers to compliment salespeople on a job well done, but the praise means a lot to the person receiving it. To make sure your people hear praise from you more often, try thinking of your salespeople as things to do. List the names of all your salespeople on your weekly to-do list and cross off each name only after you've offered that person a compliment on some aspect of his or her performance.

You don't have to reward your salespeople with all-expenses-paid vacations to Hawaii to keep them motivated. An incentive program's value is measured by how it makes your salespeople feel and perform—not by the monetary value of the awards. As long as your salespeople know their achievements and efforts won't go unnoticed, they're likely to keep up the good work.

EXPERT ADVICE

Rewarding Tips

Do you throw rewards at only your sales stars? How big should rewards be? Should everything be handled in cyberspace? Here are some incentive tips:

- *Target the right people.* You've heard the 80/20 rule, no doubt. That rule says that 80 percent of your business comes from 20 percent of your sales force. However, Dittman says, "If you start throwing stuff at the top 20 percent, you're throwing motivation at self-motivated people. You should aim at the 60 percent in the middle, especially the top half of the middle 60. They are the people who need an extra reason to do what they should do—to make a last client call at 4 p.m. on Friday or sit down Sunday to prepare for the workweek. A merchandise program allows these people to reap rewards."
- *Give value.* The booming economy has fueled high employee turnover. Here's another implication for merchandise awards: You need to increase award values. What's Dittman's rule of thumb? He advises

(*Continued on next page.*)

(*Continued from previous page.*)

clients to select products equal to 5 to 10 percent of a sales rep's pay during the contest period. For example, a salesperson who earns $15,000 during the course of a three-month incentive program would find motivation in products perceived to carry a value of at least $750 to $1,500.

- *Paper, please.* An incentive program's online capabilities certainly speed up promotion, communication, feedback, and other activities. Web-based catalogs, redemption, and fulfillment offer ease, convenience, and more. Nevertheless, Dittman's agency has discovered one advantage in paper: performance statements and status reports delivered via e-mail consistently have less impact than feedback on paper. "There's something about physically getting a piece of paper in the mail. We see the activity and what happens after a paper statement goes out. There are more redemptions, people ask questions, it gets attention, and it's not mixed into the other 50 e-mails that came on a given day. Most people we're targeting turn on their computer in the morning and they have 40, 50, or 60 e-mails."

—From James B. Dittman,
president of Dittman Incentive
Marketing in Edison, New Jersey.

Chapter 8

Managing a Variety of Personalities

HOW TO MANAGE THE SEVEN MOST DIFFICULT (BUT PROMISING) SALES PERSONALITIES

When you can identify the strengths and weaknesses of each member of your sales team—and you know how to enhance the strengths and diminish the weaknesses—you'll be well on your way to a record sales year. This chapter provides a hands-on how-to manual for molding the minds and behavior of your most difficult salespeople.

The characteristics of the salespeople are those of real salespeople. It is likely that people on your team possess similar characteristics; however, no one individual will have all the characteristics of any one personality type. By increasing your understanding of the psychological forces at work, you will find it easier to create a winning team, stimulate individual growth, and help your company reach higher levels of sales success.

1. Grandstand George

Positively sales superstar material, people like Grandstand George (or Georgette) want to run the show, but don't want to take the responsibility of being the sales manager. They are backseat drivers. Their favorite statement is, "You need me more than I need you!"

- *Behavioral giveaways.* Grandstand Georges are assertive to the point of being aggressive, self-assured, arrogant, action-driven, forceful, and expressive. They have the tendency to be disrespectful of authority figures and often challenge your authority as a manager. Yet they have the amazing ability to be highly diplomatic. Grandstand Georges are masters at building trust and rapport with customers.
- *Nonverbal signals.* Grandstand Georges love to display visible signs of success. Their gestures are expressive and signal power. Watch for nonverbal clues: pointing into your face, invading your personal space, bonecrushing handshakes (men), tendency to lean toward you, direct and unwavering eye contact, very engaging smiles, dressed for success, expensive accessories, monogrammed shirts, personalized license plates, high-status cars.
- *What motivates Grandstand Georges.* They want to make the biggest sale, to win the biggest award, to achieve the highest sales volume, to become a member of the President's Club, to buy a faster car, to get the best car telephone, and to acquire anything else that can satisfy their appetite for grandiosity.
- *Greatest strengths.* Grandstand Georges are not afraid of cold calling, are great closers, and do whatever it takes to make the extra sale that will push you over the

top. They don't need your input, and you don't have to help them sell. They can do it all themselves.

- *Greatest source of problems.* When people like George become dissatisfied, you—the manager—will be blamed. They can hold you hostage and may threaten to take other salespeople along with them when they leave or join your competition. Grandstand Georges may demand extra compensation, first-class air travel, or almost unlimited expense accounts.
- *How to manage Grandstand Georges.* Grandstand Georges respect power and strength. To maintain your authority, your assertiveness needs to match or exceed theirs. If you feel threatened by this type of salesperson, don't hesitate to call in expert help—lawyer, accountant, personnel manager, or industrial psychologist. Georges respect people who call their bluff. They expect you to set fair limits and enforce those limits. They responds well to managers who don't overreact to power games.

2. Fearful Fred

Fearful Freds (or Francines) have not yet grown into the professional salesperson role. They show cold-call reluctance, are weak in handling objections, and are afraid to close the sale. Fearful Freds think they need to give extra discounts or special concessions to get the sale. Their favorite phrase is, "I've got a lousy territory!"

- *Behavioral giveaways.* Fearful Freds have difficulty with displaying enthusiasm. Their low assertiveness makes them retreat very quickly from any serious challenge. They avoid asking tough business questions because they are afraid of not having the right answers. In sales meetings, Fearful Freds are quiet and passive.
- *Nonverbal signals.* Their speaking style is characterized by a soft tone of voice. They wear clothes that don't attract attention, often appear ill at ease with the world, and hate it when people make comments about their appearance. Fearful Freds appear meek with slumped shoulders, weak handshakes, and averted eyes.
- *What motivates Fearful Freds.* Salespeople like Fearful Fred respond well to things that make their jobs easier. They love sales support programs and sales assistance, like telemarketers who schedule appointments for them. They love writing long proposals and sales letters. Their tendency to procrastinate often causes them to lose sales.

- *Greatest strengths.* Fearful Freds are eager to complete their paperwork and are steady workers. They never offend a customer. When they do make a sale, their customers tend to be loyal.
- *Greatest source of problems.* Fearful Freds can easily lose half of their sales opportunities to more assertive competitors. Their lack of enthusiasm can often be de-motivating to other salespeople in your company.
- *How to manage Fearful Freds.* Provide Fearful Freds with a series of small success experiences. Fearful Freds need a safety net. They need to learn how to crawl before they can begin to walk. Sales managers begin with teaching Fearful Freds how to master the basics. Begin by setting and rewarding activity goals (like completing 20 cold calls per week). With the help of structured activity goals, Fearful Freds can learn each step of the sale with a larger sense of security and greater feeling of competence. It is important to teach Fearful Freds the techniques of self-assertiveness.

3. Slumped Sally

Salespeople like Slumped Sally (or Sam) have lost their former glory. They may be going through a period of extreme stress. Your job is to determine if this is a temporary or permanent condition and decide if it is worth your efforts to help them recapture their greatness.

- *Behavioral giveaways.* They show up late and leave early, won't complete paperwork, and take long lunch breaks. They have low energy levels. In sales meetings they look as if they stayed up too late the previous night. They often talk about the good old days. With their customers they tend to skip steps. Rather than calling customers, they want the customers to call them. You will have customer complaints about Slumped Sallys.
- *Nonverbal signals.* They sigh a lot, slump, look depressed, and their shoulders hang down. They have a sloppy appearance, their suits need to be pressed, and their shoes need polishing. They have shallow breathing and flat emotions.
- *What motivates Slumped Sallys.* They are motivated to seek and rediscover old glory. They want to look good to their old friends and talk about the good old days. Slumped Sallys want to avoid fights and disagreements. They want you to be a strong leader with meaningful answers and insights. Slumped Sallys will respond well to coaching.
- *Greatest strengths.* Their experience and insight can become valuable assets to the company. If you can help Slumped Sallys recapture their former glory, you will have

great sales producers on your hands. Slumped Sallys often make good sales trainers because of their many successful selling experiences.

- *Greatest source of problems.* Slumped Sallys can easily infect others with their pessimistic attitudes. Other people may follow the example of Slumped Sallys and become sloppy with paperwork. Productivity may be threatened. Since Slumped Sallys were once top performers, their words have some credibility and, therefore, their criticisms can be very unsettling.

- *How to manage Slumped Sallys.* Discuss goals and plans. If Slumped Sallys do not care about themselves, get them to improve for the sake of their families. Reward them with vacations, even if they are only three-day weekends. Take unnecessary assignments away. Reprioritize and teach Slumped Sallys time and territory management. Some Slumped Sallys have no idea of how much time they waste on nonproductive jobs. They sometimes work long hours but get very little accomplished. Don't leave Slumped Sallys alone. They need to be involved in new, but limited, challenges. Don't overburden Slumped Sallys with high expectations.

4. Excited Eddie

Excited Eddies (or Ednas) enjoy chasing nearly every new idea, dream, or opportunity. They will start many projects but fail to complete most of them. They have a tendency to flatter people and will glowingly praise your work as the sales manager.

- *Behavioral giveaways.* Excited Eddies are highly enthusiastic, outgoing, and expressive. They are the first ones to sell a newly introduced product or service. They are unafraid to talk to any prospect, no matter what the rank, status, or geographic location. In their pursuit of exciting new opportunities, they may cross into another salesperson's territory. They are undeterred by reality and naive about how much effort is necessary to reach consistent levels of success. Excited Eddies are capable of reaching temporary peaks that often fizzle quickly. Opportunity addiction blurs their focus and dilutes their strengths.

- *Nonverbal signals.* Excited Eddies are fast talkers who tend to lose their breath when speaking. Unable to slow down, they get excited to the point of speaking almost incoherently. When you don't pay attention, they quickly raise their voices or wave their arms. Their gestures are unrestrained, wide open, and expressive. Their eyes are wide open, they flash big smiles, and they'll shake your hand for a long time as they talk to you. Excited Eddies slap you on the back.

- *What motivates Excited Eddies.* Excited Eddies are motivated to be the first to sell a new product or service. They love to be pioneers and are hungry for new experiences. They love sales incentives and short-term sales contests. They love constant change, variety, and new challenges.
- *Greatest strengths.* Excited Eddies are your best people for introducing a new product. They are great at penetrating a new market and developing new leads at trade shows. They never procrastinate, and often work overtime or on weekends. They will call anyone on the phone to arrange a meeting where they can share their excitement.
- *Greatest source of problems.* Salespeople like Excited Eddie are poor with follow-up tasks. They hate paperwork. They overpromise and are poor listeners. Because they see themselves as progressive individuals, they change jobs more often than other salespeople. Yet Excited Eddies often go nowhere fast. They may alienate prospects because they do not understand why other people are reluctant to change. They often overstate the capabilities of the product and tend to overpromise and underdeliver.
- *How to manage Excited Eddies.* The best way to keep Excited Eddies producing is to give them a healthy dose of new challenges. Be careful not to overload their capabilities and avoid letting them go in too many directions at once. Ensure that Excited Eddies do not overstate the performance standards of your products (or services). Beware of their inflated sales forecasts. They tend to neglect details and hate paperwork. Try to be patient with their frequent requests for the latest high-tech equipment and offer these tools as incentives for above-quota sales performance.

EXPERT ADVICE

Simple Steps to Management Success

To motivate your team to get out of the excuse mode and into the selling mode, follow these three key steps:

1. Announce a full-disclosure communications policy—how you'll communicate. Lay out visions and expectations. Talk about performance

evaluations and providing feedback. Introduce yourself and forge a bond.

2. Make things happen right away by eliminating barriers. Ask yourself if there is anything you can do today to remove two or three barriers. This will help you gain trust.

3. Establish consequences for those who continue to make excuses. Reward and acknowledge those who do the job well. Know who your top performers are and ask for extra effort.

—From Frank Pacetta, speaker, trainer, and author of *Don't Fire Them, Fire Them Up: Motivate Yourself and Your Team.*

5. Disorganized Debbie

It is easy to identify salespeople like Disorganized Debbie (or Doug). They are unclear about who they are and where they are going. As a result, they are confused about their true values. Disorganized Debbies are floating through life. They often appear to be working like rocking horses, always in motion, but never advancing. When presented with too many choices Disorganized Debbies easily get confused. They often end up in sales because of their friendly and endearing natures and because they can't clearly imagine that they could master the challenges involved in other careers.

- *Behavioral giveaways.* Disorganized Debbies are scattered, their desks are disorganized, and their reports are always late and frequently incomplete. They often lose things, forget follow-up calls, or let their cars run out of gas. During sales calls it is not uncommon for them to match the wrong benefit to a given sales feature. They seem incapable of setting goals and try in vain to develop consistent working methods. They are easily influenced, and their attention spans are short. They are loyal, however, and given proper coaching and training, they have the potential to do well.

- *Nonverbal signals.* Often you'll see Disorganized Debbies walking briskly in one direction, then stop, shake their heads, mutter something unintelligible, and walk back slowly to where they came from. They often show signs of frustration with themselves. They apologize for their shortcomings in an endearing way. Their speech patterns are characterized by rambling sentences. They habitually dilute the essence of their ideas and look troubled when they can't make their points clear to you.

- *What motivates Disorganized Debbies.* Disorganized Debbies respond well to people who are disciplined and focused. They love to work for managers who issue clear directives and help set goals. You should divide their work into small, comprehensive steps and provide them with a series of structured success experiences. Disorganized Debbies are not motivated by money, but by meaning. They are most successful in companies that offer a strong training program and provide a step-by-step selling process. It is important to realize that they need to rely on work systems that limit choices, reduce confusion, and prioritize tasks.

- *Greatest strengths.* Salespeople like Disorganized Debbie tend to be very likable, down-to-earth, and agreeable. They are unselfish employees, make friends easily, and never push customers too hard. They are good team players and very loyal to the company. Even if business is slow, they won't complain and will cheerfully do their jobs. They have a high capacity to be enthusiastic. A congenial nature makes Disorganized Debbies nonthreatening and easy to work with.

- *Greatest source of problems.* Disorganized Debbies can create more unfinished business in one hour than another member of your staff could create in a day. Because they are unfocused and easily distracted, they tend to be weak in closing the sale. They are weak with follow-up work and may lose some leads that they have been given. Their poor sense of priorities can turn customers off. Too many loose ends in their lives tend to reduce their work efficiency.

- *How to manage Disorganized Debbies.* Disorganized Debbies need your personal attention. Begin by teaching them step-by-step how to prioritize their work and manage their time. Invest in a time management system and make sure they clearly understand how it works. Next, ask them each day to turn in a photocopy of their daily activity schedule and monitor their progress. If their time management system is incomplete, meet with them and have them complete the job. For a period of four weeks, set clear activity goals for each week (such as the number of leads to qualify, the number of prospects to call, and the number of sales to close). Never say "Do the best you can do." The more room you leave for uncertainty, the more confused they'll get. Be very specific and continually help them focus on the most important and most urgent tasks every single day. Reward them for reaching their goals and for increased personal efficiency.

6. Perfectionist Pete

Salespeople like Perfectionist Pete (or Paula) have unrealistically high standards that lead them to procrastinate on almost every project. When faced with uncertainty, they get anxious or panic. Perfectionists are always afraid of making mistakes and get easily angered when their work is criticized.

- *Behavioral giveaways.* Perfectionists appear hesitant, deliberate, and overcontrolled. They take little risk and double-check everything. Their capacity to express emotions is underdeveloped. They are afraid of change, critical of new ideas, and lack flexibility. They love to sell your tried and proven product line but resist selling new or untested products. Perfectionist Petes keep close track of their time and always show up early for appointments. Perfectionists are too hard on themselves and others. Since they tend to measure and weigh the statements of others carefully, they usually exceed other salespeople in the area of needs analysis. They are good long-term planners.
- *Nonverbal signals.* Perfectionist Petes are neat dressers, every hair in place, shoes spit-polished. Their files are neatly organized and stacked, and each file has a typed label. Their speech patterns are very precise, and they often correct your grammar. They show little emotion in their speech. Perfectionist Petes tend to use words like *should* and *ought* as in "You should have been more careful," or "You ought to check their credit."
- *What motivates Perfectionist Petes.* Perfectionist Petes are motivated to control themselves, their territories, and their customers. They love computer software and any tool that increases control and certainty. Perfectionist Petes enjoy planning. They complete all their assignments on time and write detailed reports. They love awards, plaques, and certificates. They like to participate in highly structured meetings with typed agendas. After completing a course, Perfectionist Petes will be the first ones to ask for a certificate of completion.
- *Greatest strengths.* Salespeople like Perfectionist Pete tend to be very knowledgeable about their products and services. Their presentations are complete, but often too detailed. Their proposals are sometimes too elaborate; they tend to produce fewer proposals than other salespeople; and they will take much more time to develop them. Perfectionist Petes, however, will never overpromise or lie to a customer. They tend to plan their activities meticulously. Given the right kind of training, they can be very loyal and profitable salespeople.

- *Greatest source of problems.* Failure is seen as a big blow to their personal identity. They often engage in fatalistic thinking, When they make a mistake, they "awfulize," whine, or see it as a catastrophe. They often suffer bouts of depression because nothing meets their standards. Since they become overly concerned with details, they are slow in completing proposals and often procrastinate. Their lack of enthusiasm and somber moods can make customers feel uncomfortable.
- *How to manage Perfectionist Petes.* Perfectionist Petes respond well to a confident and reassuring manager. They need to know that the world will not come to an end if they make a small mistake. Encourage them to be more tolerant and more accepting of themselves and others. Teach them to see the bigger picture and encourage them to take more risks. Reward Perfectionist Petes for getting things done on time, even if they are not perfect. Salespeople like Pete need to know that you are not as critical of them as they are of themselves.

7. Worried Walter

Salespeople like Worried Walter (or Wanda) worry about anything in their environment. They often see themselves as inadequate or incapable of handling everyday challenges. As a result, they have a tendency to pull back from life to protect themselves. They loathe taking risks and rarely buy stocks or speculative investments. Worried Walters lack the ability to think positively about turning even minor problems into opportunities. Their favorite phrase is, "What if something goes wrong?"

- *Behavioral giveaways.* Worried Walters do not want to reject any bad idea outright, nor do they have the courage to fully endorse a good idea. They can find something wrong with any project, any customer, or any product. Their worries warp their perception of reality. They have difficulty in making a commitment to your company, your sales team, and you as the sales manager. They sometimes worry how long you are going to last. They worry about their own bodies and tend to be hypochondriacs.
- *Nonverbal signals.* The speech patterns of Worried Walters are hesitant. They often clear their throats before speaking. They pause frequently and use a lot of "qualifying" words before making a point. They use words like "I am just guessing," "I am not sure," "But," "You may think differently," and "I can't blame you." Worried Walters walk gingerly in small, hesitant steps. They move cautiously and hold their arms rigidly to their sides. Their handshakes are limp and often sweaty.

- *What motivates Worried Walters.* Provide them with a safe, controlled, and predictable environment. They are comfortable selling the tested and proven bread-and-butter product line. They are motivated by a good health plan, annual physical examinations, a life insurance policy, and retirement benefits. Since they are motivated by certainty, they love effective sales training tools such as scripts, closing manuals, and powerful customer testimonials.

- *Greatest strengths.* Worried Walters can be steady producers. They will often rehearse and practice a presentation until late at night. They always show up early for appointments. Walters are good sources of information on how to improve your product or how to improve customer service. They are tuned in to every minute customer complaint and are familiar with the weaknesses of your competition. They know well what can go wrong with their design and service. Worried Walters tend to be good listeners and can be very understanding of people who are experiencing difficulties.

- *Greatest source of problems.* Worried Walters often tend to start rumors. Unable to sort out the issues, they may procrastinate and delay taking action until the sales opportunity has been seized by the competition. Worried Walters also tend to infect other people with their worries. They are often jealous of other people's success and sometimes even give negative advice on purpose to sabotage other people's chances for success. Worried Walters often fail to take action because they worry too much about being rejected or turned down.

- *How to manage Worried Walters.* Worried Walters respond well to careful and patient coaching. Managing them requires a two-step approach: First, build awareness; second, build self-confidence. To build awareness, have them write down their worries. Ask them to rank the worries in the order of their importance. Let them focus on the most important worry for a day. To build self-confidence, have them write down their success experiences. Ask them to write down their personal strengths next to each success experience. Then have them write their personal strengths on a 3 × 5 card, which they can carry in their wallets or cars, or keep in their top desk drawers. Next, provide Worried Walters with safe success experiences, like calling on prequalified prospects. Ask them to predict the degree of difficulty with each customer on a scale from 1 to 10. (Ten is the greatest difficulty.) Then ask them to complete each of these calls. After each call ask them to rate the actual difficulty of the call from 1 to 10. This exercise will help Worried Walters realize that their abilities in predicting future events need fine-tuning. They'll learn to anticipate the future with less pessimism and with a greater sense of reality.

OH, GROW UP!

How to Manage the Babies and Whiners on Your Sales Team

It doesn't matter what company or industry, management structure or compensation plan, economic conditions or territory plan, some salespeople will always whine about something—or everything. These are the team's sales babies, the reps who never want to take responsibility, who always want preferential treatment for the problems that only they have to face. When a problem arises, where do they turn?

To their sales manager, where else?

"Why can't they think for themselves?" asks one national sales manager. "They're smart enough to do the work. That's why I hired them. But whenever there are any complications, they come running to me. Do I look like their mother?"

Sound familiar? Do you find that you're spending more time dealing with tantrums and excuses than serving customer needs? According to many experts, managers are partly to blame. Behind almost every workplace "baby" is a manager who accepts the behavior.

"People become babies because we let them. They'll kick up a fuss, so we'll do whatever they want," says San Jose-based Hank Trisler, a consultant who has written about "no bull" selling techniques in two books, *No Bull Selling* and *No Bull Sales Management*.

So, maybe it's time to put a stop to the Romper Room antics. To start helping their sales teams motivate themselves and get out of the excuses phase and into the selling phase, managers must lead the way. Larry Schulz, a Huntington Beach, California, marketer and author of *Selling When You Hate to Sell: A Guide to Getting in Gear When You Fear Sales* compares the relations of managers and sales babies to those of parents and children. "A child is quick to blame someone else," he explains. "It's up to the manager to point the employee in the right direction."

Excuses, Excuses

Eileen Brownell, president of Training Solutions in Chico, California, says, "People will come up with umpteen excuses for not getting the work done."

Mitch Paluso, a vice president of sales for Echopass Corporation, a Salt Lake City–based application service provider of contact center solutions, has heard all the excuses: "This doesn't fit with this market." "I don't have good accounts." "Everything has already been sold to this customer." And that's just the beginning.

"These are common excuses, but if you're a good sales manager you'll find out what's beneath the excuses," says Paluso. "These excuses can usually be tied to one of two things: First, they may not understand what the customer is trying to accomplish or the customer's driving mechanism. Second, they may not really understand the product."

So how do you find out what lies beneath the excuses? Paluso has monthly meetings with each member of his team. He guides the reps as they learn more about their customers, so it becomes easier to call on them. Paluso also makes sure the sales team really understands its product, so all team members become experts and have a comfort level with what the product can do for their customers.

The Fear Factor

"I can't because I'm afraid." Nothing stops a sale faster than fear.

"We didn't tell ourselves that lie when we were kids," says Steve Chandler, motivational speaker in Gilbert, Arizona, and author of *17 Lies That Are Holding You Back and the Truth That Will Set You Free*. "For example, when we were kids, we were afraid to ride a bike, but we did it anyway. We just said, 'This is something I really want to do, and I'm afraid.' Then we did it.

"Lies are very convenient because they keep us out of action. But a good sales manager can point out these falsehoods and allow someone's self-esteem to keep climbing. You can tell someone on your team, 'Being afraid to cold call or close a big deal doesn't have to prevent you from doing it. Every time you do it you'll be less afraid. But avoiding what you're afraid to do will drive you deeper and deeper into a self-concept of cowardliness and laziness.'"

Many times, Chandler points out, salespeople will try to sell the sales manager a picture of themselves as victims by making excuses: "My territory doesn't contain any good business," for instance. If sales managers are action oriented instead of excuse oriented, they will know that this excuse is a fear of action, and they need to encourage action by taking away excuses. Says Chandler, "When people are getting things done it's exciting, and they will want to do more. Give them access to their own desire."

How does a sales manager give access to desires? Frank Pacetta, vice president of sales and marketing for SinglesourceIT, a B-to-B e-commerce company in Columbus,

Ohio, and author of *Stop Whining and Start Winning: Recharging People, Reigniting Passion and Goosing Profits*, says, "The way to motivate is, first, to show your energy and your desire to succeed and, second, to get inside each person's head. Don't use a cookie-cutter approach. Ask each person what he or she wants. Build a relationship with this person."

Chandler adds, "Ask the salesperson, 'Why are you selling? Why are you here?' If you can get to the basic desire, you can get the person to get out and sell. But if you get lost in all the fears and company politics, then you're lost as a sales manager."

Nip It in the Bud

Bob Davies, a Lake Forest, California, consultant who, among other techniques, uses skydiving to teach performance enhancement and overcoming fear, believes that back-sliding behavior is a matter of internal conditioning. According to his bell curve theory, 2 percent are top performers, 70 percent are average, and 2 percent are very poor. The rest fall between the extremes and the middle. "Most of us are driven to avoid pain and seek comfort, which is why salespeople complain, shuffle papers, or do other busy work instead of making calls," he explains. "They're afraid of rejection."

However, elite performers "recognize that sales is a numbers game and welcome the challenge of making and even beating the odds." Davies compares their attitudes to flying a plane that, due to the physics of aeronautics, naturally drifts to the left. "I must compensate by pressing down the right rudder pedal to keep it straight. It's the same with people. They need to modify their perceptions to counteract their built-in limitations."

Lead by Example

What about sales managers? Do they set an example by making excuses themselves? How much do they want to see their sales teams succeed? Or are they just trying to get through the day by resembling sales managers—doing what their superiors think they should be doing?

According to Barbara Pachter, a consultant and author of *The Power of Positive Confrontation: The Skills You Need to Know to Handle Conflicts at Work, at Home and in Life*, "Managers need to look at themselves. Are they confrontational or bullying? Do they tend to avoid problems? Neither approach produces good results, so it's important to be honest with yourself."

"A common sales manager excuse is, 'I inherited these people,'" Pacetta points out. "My answer to that is to get performance evaluations in place and start each salesperson working toward goals. Decide who you think can make it and who can't, and show me the documentation behind it. What is your corrective action to make them better?"

Another excuse Pacetta hears from sales managers is, "I don't get the support I need from headquarters." He explains, "If this is your excuse, what are the three most important things keeping you and your team from doing business? What are the barriers? Of those three, is there anything in your location that you can control? On the other things, whom have you sat down with to explain the problem? Have you given a solution, a proposal by saying, 'Here is how I think we should go forward?'"

Chandler adds, "Realize that you are totally responsible for the performance of your team. If you try to make yourself a victim of how your team is performing, or of your resources, then you're lying to yourself about why things are going wrong. If the team is not selling, the sales manager is the problem—either by not getting to the truth or by having made a bad hiring decision. The good thing is, if you're the problem, you're the solution."

WAC'Em Upside the Head

Pachter has developed a formula for dealing with contrary team members. Basically, the WAC approach involves finding out:

(W)hat's really bothering you, the manager;
(A)sking the other person to do or change something and defining what would solve the problem; and
(C)hecking to see how the individual feels about the proposed solution.

To prevent dependency, managers must be specific, she advises. Rather than reprimanding workers like a stern parent, gently point out their problem areas. "Are they not calling on enough people? Not closing? Speaking too softly or quickly?"

Other issues might include failing to provide enough or giving too much information, not following through or being overly aggressive, or poor utilization of body language. An example of the latter includes a man whose customers complained that he had a harsh and off-putting appearance. "Once he softened his facial expression and started blinking, he was able to establish rapport."

Match the solution with the problem. If time management is an issue, for example, have the salespeople get electronic notebooks or personal organizers and help them prioritize.

Managers also must deal with salespeople according to their individual frames of reference. "Some like the direct approach. You simply sit down and explain what can and cannot be done," Brownell explains. "Others need more coaching. You work with them closely, in increments, and monitor their progress."

Independence Day

Most salespeople are capable of resolving their own difficulties, but the rub is to teach them how to think on their own two feet. Trisler spends at least 20 minutes a month with each worker. "I give them my total concentration. I want to know what's going on in their world."

Before they come to him with a situation, however, he tells them to ask themselves four questions: "First, what's the problem? They need to be able to understand it enough to write it on the back of a business card. Second, what caused the problem? This allows reps to sit back and reflect upon the roots of their plight. Third, what are the possible solutions? Here they need to brainstorm about what they can do to get out from under it. Fourth, what is the best solution? By the time they've answered these, they no longer need my advice," he says. "Instead, they will have come up with a recommendation, and I usually say, 'Go do it.'"

Jay Conner, CEO of Morehead City, North Carolina–based Leader Homes, has an open-door policy even though he supervises about 175 salespeople. "If they're whining, it may be because they require some attention," he observes. "When people have problems, they're not necessarily looking for you to solve them. Sometimes they want a sounding board and need to know someone cares."

"What they're griping about may not be the real issue," adds Schulz. "Managers need to do some deep listening and help people look within to find out the true cause of the unhappiness. When they regard their work as a job, they run into trouble. Sales is all about internal motivation and meeting goals," he says, rather than just putting in the hours and passively waiting for results.

Also, address problems quickly but thoughtfully. Conner says he tries to be slow to speak: "Even if I immediately know the solution, I think about it some more and get back with the person within 24 hours."

Hire Right

Suppose you're being brutally honest, you set a good example, and you still can't get certain salespeople to sell. What do you do now? Chandler says it's just as important to take a look at your hiring process as it is your managing process.

"When sales managers work with people day and night and see no improvement, what they really have on their hands is a hiring mistake," he explains. "They didn't take the time up front to get the right people. Maybe those people don't really want to sell, but are in sales anyway. And maybe you were in too much of a hurry to hire to even notice."

Pacetta suggests that you check references, look at track records, and get a group of people to interview the person. Go through a detailed process before you hire him or her.

Motivating Moments

Sales managers can provide the tools to push performance higher. "The great leader makes the great performer even better," notes Pacetta. "A really good manager will lay down the guidelines without being intimidating. The great leader sets the stage, makes a statement, and then follows up. Find a way to make them feel like you're with them. Communicate with them every week to see how things are going."

Says Chandler: "Keep strengthening a picture of them that is very positive and powerful so their self-esteem goes up. Paint this picture of them and base it on the good things they've done at the company. Tell them about your fears and how you struggled. Don't intimidate them. People have to feel that you do understand what they are going through."

Motivation comes in many forms, but removing any excuses comes first. Get beyond the lies, and the truth is that your team will soar.

EXPERT ADVICE

The Marine Corps Way to Manage

Before shipping employees off to boot camp—or giving them the boot—consider how the Marine Corps handles its raw recruits. Both former Marines themselves, Dan Carrison and Rod Walsh of Semper Fi Consulting in Sherman Oaks, California, have built a management philosophy based on that particularly macho brand of the military. And it's surprisingly gentle.

Insists Carrison, "You get nowhere by intimidation. And who in their right mind would go an extra mile for a tyrant?" Instead, "Marines are inspired to act courageously because they want to excel. They work together, and their leaders cultivate each individual's resourcefulness and talents."

"Officers encourage solution-seeking," Walsh points out. "They take them out of 'babyhood' and teach them how to handle difficult situations," mostly by having them assume personal responsibility for each task and utilizing inner strengths.

"Rather than immediately rappelling down a 30-foot wall, recruits start with a small section," explains Carrison. "That way, they build confidence by mastery of each step." Everything is done as a group, "so there's no chance of backing out." The instructor goes first, providing leadership by example.

The generals eat last, with the lower ranks being served initially, according to consultant Brent Filson of Williamston, Massachusetts, another former Marine. Higher-ups are also the first to rise and the last to go to sleep. "The Marines recognize the importance of small-unit esprit de corps and how it can strengthen an organization from the bottom up."

"Rather than focusing on the individual, managers might do well to emphasize team players," Walsh suggests. "That way, everyone is given credit and is provided a sense of unity."

"They need to be there during the bad times, too," adds Carrison. "Too often, failure is interpreted as 'the other guy's problem.'"

In the Marines, "Officers do whatever they can for the team's completion of the mission," Carrison says. "There are no secrets. It really is a brotherhood."

—From Dan Carrison and Rod Walsh of Semper Fi Consulting. They are also the authors of *Semper Fi: Business Leadership the Marine Corps Way.* For more information visit www.semperficonsulting.com.

Chapter 9

Coaching Your Staff

DEFINING YOUR ROLE AS A COACH

The sales manager should build sales … right? Wrong. The sales manager first, last, and always should concentrate on building a productive sales force. That's job number one no matter how large the company or the sales force.

Specifically, this means developing and leading a team equipped with outstanding selling skills and market knowledge— plus strong motivation to achieve and grow, fine-tuned sensitivity to prospects as human beings, flexibility, creativity, self-confidence, and self-discipline. Sales managers who live by this book and work at improving their ability to practice it chapter and verse will see their sales records soar.

Yet many sales managers, under the pressure of generating volume quickly, get bogged down in a day-to-day struggle to rack up the numbers. This leads them to focus on short-term business development to the exclusion of long-term people development.

Many sales managers are unable to kick the hands-on habits they acquired coming up through the ranks. They sit in a manager's chair, but they go on thinking like sales-people. Remember, selling by remote control is a very challenging process. It requires the talents not only of a professional football coach, but also of a green-thumb gardener and a symphony orchestra conductor.

The Lombardi Touch

Perhaps the most important reason Vince Lombardi deserves his fame as a master of masters is the fact that the Green Bay team he built into a legend was essentially made up of the identical player material he found when he arrived.

Sales managers face the same situation. They must work with what they've got. This means they must ask not what their people can do for them, but what they can do for their people. Basically the answer boils down to coaching.

Every sales manager will have his or her own definition of coaching. To me, coaching is not a compartmentalized process that takes place in curbside conferences after sales calls. It is any and every interaction between sales manager and salesperson who have professional growth and improved job performance as goals.

Coaching can be a discussion of objectives, a review of prospect selection and account management strategies, an examination of techniques at each step in the sales contact from qualifying to close. It can even include lending a sympathetic ear to personal problems that are having an impact on the job.

Whatever the context, the most important element in coaching is definition. Salespeople must be presented with concrete and objective standards to compare their performance against, measurable goals to aim at, and specific ways of elevating all their essential job skills.

Unfortunately, too many sales managers spend too much time telling their salespeople things they already know, such as where they are month-to-date, quarter-to-date, or year-to-date. They limit their communication to reviewing the numbers. That's not coaching. If you were a football coach and all you did was read your team the scores, you wouldn't like the scores you'd wind up reading.

Let's examine this in a little detail. Two stock-in-trade questions sales managers ask are: "How did it go?" and "Will we get the business?" First of all, this indicates that the manager is interested in business development, not people development. Beyond that, such vague questions can only get vague answers that serve neither the manager nor the salesperson.

In comparison, look at what can be accomplished by questions that recreate specific elements of the sale: "How did you open?" "What did he say?" "How did you interpret that?" "What was your response?" "Did you feel she was showing resistance or indifference?" "What would you do the next time something like this comes up?" When you inspect in depth the way your salespeople apply their skills and expect them to continually strive for improvement, you are placing their work on a professional level.

Does Your Garden Grow?

Coaching also has to be forward looking. It's not enough simply to work with salespeople on correcting deficiencies; from a development standpoint, that's basically running hard to stand still. Just avoiding mistakes is to operate at perhaps 50 percent of full potential and to waste the other 50 percent—a loss that your salespeople, your company, and you as a sales manager cannot afford.

The good news is that there's no level of performance that can't be reinforced for the better. And here is where the job of the sales manager resembles that of the gardener. Every day there are weeds to be dug out. But, even more important, there are seeds to be planted, fruits to be harvested, new ground to be broken.

Here are two useful techniques for translating this metaphor into on-the-job practice. I call the first *asymptotic limit*—building a series of progressive steps that lead in the direction of the desired performance goal. On the well-proved principle of learning to walk before you can run, we prescribe a series of gradually lengthening small steps instead of instant giant strides. Let the salesperson build self-confidence through scoring a series of small victories. At the same time, we stress aiming at perfection even while knowing it's unreachable. The saying that seems to apply here is: "Only when we choose perfection will we be able to capture excellence."

I call the second approach *ongoing positive feedback*. Salespeople are entitled to be told, on a regular basis, how well they are performing. It is the sales manager's responsibility to say: Here is how you are doing today. Here is what I expect you to do differently tomorrow. Here is what you can do to come closer to achieving your goals. In essence, the manager is paving the road for the salesperson's future. If there is no feedback, and if there are holes in salespeople's education, both they and their sales manager are going to fall into them.

The Leader of the Band

Finally, you can look at the sales manager as a maestro on the podium. Even though a symphony conductor doesn't play an instrument, he or she is responsible for the quality of the music through helping each individual reach the highest possible artistic level and fusing all the players into a totally coordinated team. In real-life selling situations, the manager similarly establishes the tone, the pace, and the style of the sales staff.

In a five-year study of the factors that can improve sales performance through coaching-based management, I found four imperatives:

1. The creation of an individualized professional development plan for every salesperson on the team
2. Frequent open and honest communication between manager and salesperson
3. High-quality, specifics-oriented feedback coming from solutions
4. Reinforcement of the value and importance of the work, and understanding support for the people doing it

Admittedly, coaching in the terms defined here is no easy job. But it is indispensable. Salespeople are on the inside looking out; from their position they cannot have a fully objective, correctly focused perspective on their own performance. It is up to the sales manager to provide them with this vision.

What are the results the sales manager can expect from selling by remote control through people development? A sales force with higher numbers and better earnings. A sales force with increased motivation and stronger commitment. A sales force that works smarter as well as harder. A sales force on the way to reaching management caliber.

FOR SUCCESS IN COACHING, KNOW WHEN TO HOLD BACK

Everything was going smoothly as his sales manager, Mike Smith, observed John Ward, salesman for ABC Equipment Company, on a call to a prospect. Smith was impressed with Ward's style. He had already established a strong rapport and trust with the prospect. It even turned out they shared an interest—sailing. Ward skillfully led the conversation from general matters to the client's needs.

He asked good fact-finding questions, and through more questions determined that the man he was meeting with was in a decision-making position.

Ward was discussing the benefits of using ABC's computers when the prospect interrupted with a question: Would ABC be able to service its equipment in his branch office 200 miles away? Ward hesitated a moment, and his manager jumped in with information on the company's remote service policy. After a few more minutes of discussion, the prospect said he'd need some time to think it all over. Ward said fine, and told him he'd telephone him in a week or so to follow up.

Smith just about held in his anger until he and Ward were out of the prospect's building. Then he burst out with criticism: "How could you let the sale go? Why didn't you ask to give him a demonstration? By the time you get back to him next week, the competition's going to have him. And why didn't you know about our servicing policy for remote locations? I covered that over and over in our training classes!"

Is this salesman going to look forward to his next joint call with his manager? Will the manager's criticism and advice help the salesman to overcome the weak points in his presentation style?

The answer to both questions is a resounding "No."

This example shows sales managers just how counterproductive the wrong kind of joint sales call can be. This sales manager may have good intentions—he may want to evaluate his salesperson's performance and offer advice from his many years of experience.

But his critical approach defeats those objectives. The most likely results: the salesman's self-confidence will be wounded, and he will resent and reject his manager's advice.

The key to successful joint-call coaching is to get salespeople to see themselves not as they are, but as they can be.

Through coaching, a sales manager can:

- Strengthen the salesperson's selling skills
- Build up the salesperson's self-image or self-concept
- Demonstrate his or her interest and concern for the salesperson
- Get the salesperson involved in and committed to the improvement process
- Help the salesperson solve problems and set goals

The steps in the coaching process are the following.

Preparation

Review all significant aspects of the salesperson's past and current performance, including prior call reports, prospective sales reports, and the notes on your last coaching session.

Determine your coaching objective—which skills you feel need special attention.

Notify the salesperson that you will be going on calls with him or her—and explain what kinds of calls you want to observe. This is important so the salesperson doesn't just set up a comfortable call with an old satisfied customer. Tell the salesperson you want to go on a "cold" call, or to a prospect he or she has been working on for several months.

Note: When you notify the salesperson that you will be joining him or her on these calls, focus on your purpose of helping, rather than the aspect of critique.

Pre-Call Planning

This step takes place in the field with the salesperson. Go over his or her records with the salesperson to see how well prepared he or she is for the call. Are you calling on the decision maker? Does the salesperson have a specific objective? How organized is he or she?

Remember, your presence may make the salesperson nervous. It is up to you to set a comfortable and supportive mood in order to help build enthusiasm for the call. Help your salesperson relax by offering positive reinforcement about his or her strong points.

There should be no surprises during the sales call. An essential part of the pre-call planning is telling the salesperson what your role will be during the call—whether you plan to participate or just observe.

The Joint Call

Observe the salesperson's behavior, attitude, and style. Use a standard form to make notes about performance in the field. How does the salesperson get past the receptionist to the purchaser? How does he or she get to see the decision maker? What does he or she do while waiting for the client in the reception area? What is the salesperson's conduct with the client?

The most important, and the hardest, job of the sales manager is simply to observe rather than participate. It's difficult for sales managers to keep quiet on a joint call. They always feel the sale is being lost and want to interject and save it.

But when a manager takes over, he or she defeats the purpose of the coaching session. If the salesperson loses the sale, he or she will think, ironically, "I already know how to lose sales. I could have done that myself." If the manager takes over and closes the sale, the salesperson may say later, "I was going to say that, but you interrupted me."

My advice to managers: Resist the temptation to interrupt. If you feel you must say something, be sure to return the conversation gracefully to your salesperson. And if the client turns to you for an answer because you are the manager, say something like, "Well, Jane is quite experienced in handling these matters," and turn the question back to your salesperson.

The "Street-Side" Conference

This takes place immediately after the joint call. It's not necessary after every call, however. Sometimes a simple, "Good work," or "Good sale" will be enough.

Be sensitive to your salesperson's feelings. Don't launch into a recitation of everything that's wrong with him or her. Mention a few key points—positive as well as negative.

Remember: Your goal is not just to point out areas needing improvement. It is just as important to reinforce good behavior and techniques. Start with praise; then mention one or two points of criticism in a positive, helpful manner. End on a note of encouragement.

Rather than telling your salesperson what went wrong, the ideal way to help your salesperson improve is to lead or allow him or her to be the one to discover the mistakes.

Many times the salesperson already knows what went wrong. Wherever possible, make him or her comfortable enough to figure it out independently. Ask questions: "How did you feel about the call?" "How do you feel about the way it ended?" "What do you think the customer wanted or expected you to do next?"

Keep asking questions until the salesperson sees for himself or herself what went wrong in the presentation. Then it's the salesperson's own idea—and he or she feels good about realizing what happened and becomes motivated to handle the situation better the next time.

Summary and Critique

Meet in your office, or any quiet place, to review the session. Reserve a block of time so you can discuss everything in an unhurried manner.

Don't expect the salesperson to agree with your conclusions and don't use your managerial power to force agreement. Discuss each point. Listen to what he or she has to say and come to some points of mutual understanding. Your prescription for improvement will not work if the salesperson does not accept or comprehend your evaluation.

Together define problem areas and steps for improvement. Work out a schedule for corrective action. Finish up by telling the salesperson your expectations and reviewing the purpose of the coaching session.

Follow-Up

This step is as important as all the others. Salespeople respect what you expect and inspect.

File away your field reports on your joint calls. Mark the agreed-upon dates for action by your salesperson on your own calendar. Write a memo to the salesperson summarizing the steps you have both agreed upon. Then be sure to meet with him or her again at a later date to review and assess development.

EXPERT ADVICE

Six Tips to Turn Your Amateur Sales Athletes into All-Star Performers

At 5 feet, 8 inches tall, sales trainer Gil Cargill can't dunk a basketball. No amount of prodding, begging, screaming, training, or inspiration is going to help him dunk. Yet it is this type of thinking, he says, that leads sales managers to try to train, cajole, and berate poorly performing salespeople who lack the raw materials needed to become selling superstars.

A good sales manager should know whether a bottom-tier performer genuinely has the potential to make the grade. For sales managers looking for methods to help those reps live up to potential, Cargill offers the following six suggestions:

1. *Work on the worst.* "It's always more fun to go out on calls with top-tier performers," Cargill says. "Those are the fun calls. But at the end of the day you'll get a better return on investment working with that poor performer. Practice, repetition, and coaching are the keys. Always work on the worst first and get them to be better. If they can't get better, help them to go work for someone else."
2. *Match the buying style to the selling style.* "Research has shown that you need a completely different type of person to sell in a demand-fulfillment environment as opposed to a demand-creation environment. An apt analogy would be to say that we need a basketball player for one type of sale and a football player for the other. Both are athletes, and both can be stars in their respective games."

(Continued on next page.)

(*Continued from previous page.*)

3. *Segregate your sales force.* "In some sales situations a three-tiered sales force works best. Former top performers who find themselves having to sell differently often have trouble. Many times they're doing poorly because they just can't get into an account. That's why I divide the sale into finding the opportunity, closing the opportunity, and keeping the accounts. I call the three distinct types of people who can handle these three segments 'scouts,' 'hunters,' and 'chefs.' Scouts are immune to rejection and don't mind prospecting. The hunters have the thrill of the kill, the close, but they won't cook. The demand-fulfillment person is a great chef—good at dotting i's, crossing t's. The problem most companies have is they ask one person to do all three, and it's like playing quarterback, lineman, and receiver all on the same play."

4. *Let them fail—almost.* "A good sales manager is like a parent helping a child learn to ride a bike. You have to let your lower performers wobble but not fall. A manager should spend an entire day going on calls with the rep. After each call you should debrief. But the hardest—and maybe most important—part is to shut up during the sales calls. The real art of managing is letting the sales rep almost fail, but not quite. Let the rep feel that discomfort, that sense of 'I'm losing control of this sales interview' before you step in. That's when you're coaching at the peak of effectiveness."

5. *Think globally, motivate individually.* "You can't motivate a sales force; you can only motivate each individual. For example, it is impossible to make a salesperson want to earn more money than he or she wants to earn. All the bonuses, spifs, brouhaha, and ballyhoo won't cause any behavioral change. You have to motivate by understanding, by coaching, by communicating, and by discovering what will turn that employee on. That's motivating individually."

6. *Tie increased expectations to activities.* "You have to help reps understand the correlation between their activities and the results their activities produce. Far too often managers say, 'You've got to sell $100,000 more a month.' But what we should be saying is, 'In order to sell $100,000

more a month you have to make two more sales calls a day, publish five more proposals a week, and give six more demonstrations a month.' It's a smart manager who will do it this way because then you're assigning activities that are understandable, digestible, and manageable for the salesperson, as opposed to the traditional approach, which is 'Go get'em, Bubba!'"

—From Gil Cargill, president of Cargill Consulting Group of Culver City, California, a sales effectiveness consulting organization specializing in business-to-business sales, sales management, competition, marketing, and sales process engineering.

DOUBLE THE BENEFITS

One of the best ways to coach your sales team is to accompany them on a sales call. "If I'm modeling on a call, then I will run the show and the reps will observe me so they can learn," explains Bev Knapp, northeast regional manager for Ablest Staffing in Clifton Park, New York. "If I'm coaching, I let them take the reins and I watch to see what I can do to help their performance."

The preparation beforehand also provides effective training. "Before any call, we spend a lot of time doing research on the company," Knapp says. "We'll formulate a full call plan and strategize about openings. Then we'll role-play—I will be the salesperson and the rep will act as the customer. You have your game plan so that when all of a sudden you're expecting to do one-on-one defense and someone goes into a zone defense, you're able to adapt. You can't call a time-out to regroup on a sales call. To me, the most important part before going into a call is planning, because very few calls will go exactly how you expect them to."

Often managers gain an added level of trust in salespeople's abilities after seeing them in action. "A lot of the trust I have in salespeople I gained while training them," says Knapp. "I try not to make it as if I am coming in and looking over their shoulders to make sure they're doing things properly. We both look at it like we're selling as a team."

Joint sales calls are an ideal way for managers to flex their coaching muscles. Chris McDonnell, sales manager for Eureka Broadband in New York, tries to keep the focus on the sales reps' performance. "If they're really struggling, I'll ask if I could come along and see if I can help them close an account," he says. "But in general I say, 'Hey, I'd love to join you on a call,' or I let them come to me and ask for help. I think it puts them on the defensive if you're going with them to their customer, with whom they've initiated a relationship, and you take the lead. I would say on a call I try to make it a 70/30 split, where I try to be secondary and chime in just to direct the conversation."

MANAGEMENT TIPS FOR HANDLING SLUMPING SALESPEOPLE

"The skills that help salespeople probe customers for needs and buying signals can prove equally effective when a manager needs to find out what's troubling a slumped sales rep," says Lavin Associates president, Hank Lavin, a consultant who works with independent sales associates.

"When you talk to that slumped rep you should act like a salesperson talking to a customer," he says. "Ask probing, open-ended questions. Look for underlying issues. Listen for the pain or where the struggle is. That can help point you to what may be causing the problem."

Helping solve a salesperson's troubles, Lavin emphasizes, requires personal involvement by the manager and avoiding confrontational tactics that rarely work.

"Blasting a sales rep doesn't work," he says. "Nor does comparing the salesperson to others on the team. You also shouldn't give warnings or ultimatums. The salesperson wants to get back on track—it's your job to help make that happen, and combative tactics won't get you there."

Instead Lavin suggests going on sales calls with the slumping rep and looking for answers there.

"The manager should be going on sales calls with the sales staff anyway," he points out.

"When you both call on the customer, the sales rep has to do all the selling. Even if they do a rotten job, you hold your tongue until afterward. Then you can offer constructive criticism to direct what the salesperson may be missing or doing poorly.

"The other possibility is role playing. In your sales meetings have your people talk about what problems they're having, and then have them act them out. The manager should just observe. Next, let the reps talk it over among themselves and see if they can pinpoint the problem."

EXPERT ADVICE

Quick Tips to Become a More Effective Sales Coach

The basic premises of coaching always hold true. So use the following six tips to become a more effective sales coach:

1. *Set goals.* Establish observable, time-specific, and measurable goals for each salesperson. Once you set the goals, speak often with the salespeople about their progress.
2. *Teach the skills.* People do not know how to do these things intuitively. It's your job to give them the tools they need to be successful.
3. *Build relationships.* This is a matter of "trust or bust." Trust takes years to build but only seconds to destroy. It's not about being friendly, but about being honest and fair with all your people in an effort to earn and keep their trust.
4. *Motivate your players.* Catch your salespeople doing something positive and reinforce them immediately. The quicker the reinforcement follows the behavior, the more powerful it will be.
5. *Monitor performance.* There isn't much point in going through the first four steps if they don't result in better performance. Use your eyes and ears and look at actual performance constantly.
6. *Provide guidance and additional training.* Catch people doing something right, provide comments in a positive way, and direct behavior in the direction you want it to go. Use one-on-one or more formal training to reach your objectives.

Any coach will say you'll need to work hard if you want to win. That means having an incredibly motivated team that constantly delivers results in the form of sales.

—From Jim Dion, president of J.C. Williams Group Ltd. in Toronto, Canada.

TEN COACHING TIPS

1. Coach all your people all the time—top performers, those in the middle, and those at the bottom.
2. Coach each person at least once a month.
3. Coach at the peaks, the valleys, and in the middle.
4. Don't wait until sales are down—your people may resist.
5. Avoid jumping in at the first sign of trouble on a sales call. Don't let the reps drown either.
6. Find something positive in every sales call you make with your people.
7. Have your reps analyze their sales calls first—what they liked best and least.
8. Ask your people what would have made a particular sales call more productive.
9. Recommend and model a preferred sales method.
10. Continue coaching—practice, practice, practice. Role-play different situations one-on-one and in group settings.

Chapter 10

The Essentials of Team Building

TEN TIPS FOR LEADING YOUR TEAM

"Beyond tools and techniques, the most important team-selling challenges are still 'people' challenges," says Lee Shelton, a highly respected sales seminar leader, consultant, and president of Lee Shelton Associates. Shelton learned that rule in a varied sales career, which included heading up marketing for Coors Brewery and American Hospital Supply.

The most common mistake in team management, Shelton says, is "hiring the wrong people for the team and then sticking with them. Usually, you know they're wrong and they know they're wrong for the team in the first day."

But managing a team correctly by "listening to people and praising them when they deserve it," Shelton says, can bring large rewards. Shelton finds that few people will leave a team they like for less than a 30 percent pay hike—and most would want much more than that to leave a happy team. How do you build that kind of team? Here are Shelton's top 10 rules:

1. *Feel good about yourself first.* Check out your own assets, including creativity, commitment, a comfortable manner, and communication skills. Then, get ready to lead others.
2. *Hire right to give the team a chance.* Look for honesty, reliability, and enthusiasm. Ask yourself, "Who would I feel comfortable inviting home to dinner?" You will spend more waking time with your team than with your family.
3. *Train, train, train.* Show team members how to do their jobs; do the jobs with them; then let them do the jobs. Make sure you include sales support staff in the training as well.
4. *Set goals.* Do the goal setting together, rather than handing out goals. Make the goals challenging and specific. Report regularly on how they are being met.
5. *Give team members lots of rope.* Let them make mistakes, learn from them, and grow. Keep the rope just short enough to avoid big trouble.
6. *Expect the best.* Good teams want to be held to high standards. Set your sights high and let your people know if they are falling short.
7. *Appraise, appraise, appraise.* Shelton suggests a weekly chat and pat on the back. Team members will want to know how they are doing. In addition, "free those who do not fit into the success of your team."
8. *Create a climate.* Have fun and let team members know it's okay to have fun. Reward and celebrate every milestone and achievement.

9. *Brainstorm.* Let discussion, without rules or boundaries, pursue solutions to the team's challenges.
10. *Make customers part of your team.* You should strive for a selling team that is so upbeat and contagious that your customers will want to be connected with winners!

PEAKS, NOT PLATEAUS
Tips to Keep Your Sales Team Moving Onward and Upward

When the people on your team with unlimited potential hit a wall and sales level off, that's when effective sales managers earn their pay. According to John James, a sales manager with Thulman Eastern, the nation's largest fireplace distributor, the first step to solving the plateau problem lies in figuring out exactly who has plateaued.

"It usually shows up in the numbers," he says. "Our company is incredible with reports. I know what they're quoting, what their closing ratio is, their sales numbers, gross profit dollar numbers, UDAs, market penetrations. Also, I look at the individuals themselves. Do they lack motivation, enthusiasm, and focus? Some people develop bad habits—a negative attitude—and little things set them off. They're not following up on certain issues with their customers. These are all clues I look for."

The problem identified, James next suggests sitting down with the rep to figure out why the stumbling block has cropped up.

"You have to recognize what the situation is with each individual salesperson," he explains. "One reason is that they get caught up in the same old routine. Salespeople are notorious for needing new challenges to feel successful. Another stumbling block is a lack of objectives. We used to set an annual excellence goal in the beginning of the year, but then we wouldn't mention it again until the year ended. Now we put that goal in front of people on a monthly basis, to let them know where they stand at all times.

"Then you've also got the salespeople who are spread too thin. In our company, at about the $2 million mark our people tend to plateau because they have too many customers to handle. They spend all their time servicing existing accounts and stop chasing after new business. For them we've developed a whole new compensation package that rewards them for old business, but keeps them in the hunt for new accounts, too."

Though solutions to the plateau problem vary according to the root causes, James says that the best tactic is to avoid the problem altogether. "Ideally you'll recognize the problem before it really crops up," he says. "To do that we've developed a sales council with six of the top salespeople in the company. We discuss this and many other issues and then develop programs to address these situations so that salespeople never even get to that point."

EXPERT ADVICE

Ten Tips for Effective Team Leadership

1. Being in charge is not a popularity contest. Make your decisions without any concern for whether people like you or agree with you.
2. When making changes to the status quo, explain your reasons and emphasize that the results will prove beneficial for the organization. The people who want to achieve the same goals will get on board.
3. Building a successful organization requires two things from you: a clear plan for the future and the courage to stick with that plan.
4. The most important building block of team success is attitude. If your organization has an attitude problem, address that situation first.
5. Team unity should exist both on the field and off. Create avenues for your people to gel outside of strictly business environments.
6. It may be impossible to treat everyone the same way, but it is possible to treat everyone fairly. Make fairness your ambition.
7. Superstars should not receive special treatment. This is a sure ingredient for a breakdown in team cohesion. When you talk about paying the price for success, that means everyone.
8. Follow your instincts. There is no textbook for leadership success. Sometimes you will find unorthodox methods that work for you. If it works, keep it up.
9. When things do go wrong, recognize that small, incremental changes may be all that is needed to right the ship.

10. As the leader, you set the tone. You have to want to win more than anyone else in the organization. Set that winning tone and it will penetrate everyone on the team.

> —From Dennis "Denny" Green, the current head coach of the Arizona Cardinals. He was previously the fifth head coach of the Minnesota Vikings from 1992 through 2001. Green is also one of seven current African-American head coaches in the NFL.

SIX TIPS FOR EFFECTIVE EMPLOYEE RELATIONS

What makes a great manager? Besides being able to communicate well and offer mentoring, it's often someone who's able to make a great working environment for his or her employees. The authors of *On the Ball*, David Carter and Darren Rovell, offer tips about what it takes to be effective at employee relations.

1. "Recognize the professional and personal value in quality, long-term relationships," say the authors. "What is in the best interests of a business in the long run must not be in conflict with what is required to succeed in the short run."
2. Maintain employee happiness. "Even in tough economic times, when your employees are less likely to jump ship, employee happiness is still linked to increased productivity," say Carter and Rovell.
3. Remember that it is cheaper and less time-consuming to keep an existing employee than it is to hire and train a new sales representative.
4. Communicate and involve your sales staff. "Take a page from the NFL's playbook when dealing with change," say the authors. "Incorporating vested parties in the process, whether formally or merely by providing a heads-up, can help changes be received more formally."
5. "Surround yourself with people you trust, and if they are new to a company, make sure you've done your homework," say Carter and Rovell. "Companies should

strive to be pragmatic instead of symbolic when agreeing to long-term contracts with top executives. Hire the right person for the right reasons rather than extending or entering into an awkward relationship."

6. Finally, say the authors, always be proactive when it comes to employee relations. It will spare you the time and resources associated with hiring and then having to replace the wrong person.

Chapter 11

Implementing an Effective Sales Process

PERFECT THE PROCESS OF SELLING

How to Apply Engineering Principles to Sales, Marketing, and Customer Service

Salespeople pride themselves on being intuitive. Sales management is no exception.

However, according to Paul Selden, author of *Sales Process Engineering*, management often rushes to automate the sales process for the sake of "improving" it, without taking the time to examine the process itself, expose its underlying flaws, and set measurable goals for improvement.

Selden proposes that the principles of engineering can and should be applied to sales; that sales is a process that can be controlled; and that systematic inquiry into the sales process—raising questions and solving problems step by step—is necessary in order to effect meaningful change.

THE NEED TO MEASURE INTANGIBLES

In order to improve the process, says Selden, all the variables in the process must be measured, even such intangibles as customer relationships. Managers can measure these by operationalizing them, or defining observable behaviors. In customer relationships, for example, a company can measure customer satisfaction by determining its customer retention rate—what percentage of customers are continuing to buy from it versus purchasing from the competition?

Once these variables are operationalized, management can then assign them a cost. Only by measuring the costs can management objectively prioritize which portion of the process to improve. When the costs have been evaluated, the decision of which part of the process to change is based on such factors as how much it will impact the customer, how important it is to the business, or even how easy it is to change.

APPLYING QUALITY CONTROLS TO THE SALES PROCESS

Selden maintains that quality theories that apply to the manufacturing process apply just as well to the sales process. He cites as an example the work of Shigeo Shingo, author of *Zero Quality Control*.

Shingo's solution for reducing costly errors in the manufacturing process was to automatically inspect 100 percent of the parts under construction at the source of their initial construction or assembly and to automatically prevent the defect from occurring. In the sales process, a company could achieve this "zero defect" solution by implementing an electronic configuration system.

Just-in-time methodology—delivering exactly what is needed in the right quantity and the right quality, just in time for when it is needed—also applies to the sales process, claims Selden.

For example, companies have eliminated the need for office space for their salespeople by equipping them with mobile computing tools that allow them to get the information they need while on the road. Telemarketing firms have adopted call center technology that allows them to triple the number of contacts per day per telemarketer from 25 to 30 to 75 to 90. Eliminating all forms of waste in the process means that only the truly useful work remains.

IMPLEMENTATION OF EFFECTIVE CHANGE

Once a company has selected a solution, management must implement solid techniques for it to be successful. Selden gives an example: "A well-known electronics manufacturer once rolled out a sales automation system. Its analysis of the initial problem was sound. Its implementation, however, was terrible. The system was released to meet a target date before testing was complete. In effect, the entire sales force was used as guinea pigs. We don't have time to do it right the first time, but we always seem to have time to fix it later."

The solution, says Selden, is to test any new approach in a controlled setting. Pilot a new system with a small group. Modify the system until all the specifications are met. Roll it out one group at a time, fine-tuning the system as needed. Hold it up if the specifications are not met. "Throughout, if your original specification called for a business result, don't accept mechanical achievement as a substitute. Mechanical achievements take the form of hooking up computers or testing software until it is bug-free. Being bug-free is not the same as accomplishing a business goal."

PROCESS IS A SNAP

Four Ways to Rethink the Sales Process for a Better Return on Your Sales Effort

"Customers are becoming more demanding," says Dr. Michael Hammer, president of Hammer and Company, Cambridge, Massachusetts. "More products are becoming like commodities. If you want to distinguish your company from competitors, you need to differentiate through your sales process."

"Technology also has a lot to do with change, if it is used right," Hammer adds.

"The old rule, 'automating a mess gives you a mess,' still applies. Throwing technology at something doesn't help. Just putting up a Web site doesn't change much. But there is a potential to do things really differently if you go through a fundamental rethink."

Old, familiar problems are growing less tolerable in fast-shifting markets. "There is the lack of an efficient integration of the parts," Hammer notes. "In some companies, to put together a quote, you must have a million cooks—the reps, the finance department, someone from engineering to configure it and from logistics to deliver it."

The pure number of kitchen helpers can lead to miscommunication, misunderstanding, and inconsistencies. So, "You have to integrate the process better," Hammer states. "That means fewer people doing it or at least doing it more consistently. Very frequently, you just need fewer people. If you use technology right, you can integrate a lot of backroom work into the rep's laptop."

Delay is the big cost of overgrown sales bureaucracies. "By integrating the process, you can shorten the sales cycle enormously," Hammer urges. "That's critical because we now have shorter product life cycles. Some products live for only a few months. Getting from the first sign of customer interest to closing the sale always speeds up cash flow. In many cases, it may significantly extend the product's life on the market."

Where do you start fixing all this? Below, several top consultants and sales execs provide different angles from which to approach—or think about—improving the sales process.

RETHINKING THE SALES PROCESS

1. Create a vision of what the new process should be.
2. Communicate it to your people.
3. Make people understand it is necessary and inevitable.
4. Incent them to do it.

Think About Time

"People ought to be thinking first of what can they do to create more selling time," emphasizes Gil Cargill, president of Cargill Consulting Group Inc. of Culver City,

California. "A lot of salespeople confuse what you do on a sales call with the sales process. The process is also what you do before and after the call."

Cargill estimates that the average salesperson spends only 20–29 percent of the day pursuing revenue from prospects or customers. The biggest nonsales element, consuming 34 percent of sales force time, is administration. And what really annoys Cargill is that "60 percent of this time is spent on correcting someone else's mistakes. So you spend two hours a day correcting errors."

Reducing administrative burdens or simply eliminating mistakes could lead to a significant increase in selling time and revenue.

What leads to unnecessary administrative burdens? Cargill lists several causes:

- *Inadequate automation or automation training.* Bad systems suck up sales time. Badly understood systems drive frustrated salespeople to keep double records, one on the system for management, another on old-fashioned paper, for their own use.
- *Inadequate support.* Cargill recalls his early days working at a nationally known company, when there was one experienced sales secretary for every four or five reps. Modern word processors reduce the burden of doing letters, reports, proposals, and quotes. But you cannot automate away these jobs completely. Some companies have thrown the whole administrative burden on their reps and the reps' laptops. As a result, says Cargill, "The administrative work doesn't get done, or done well, and the salesperson wastes selling time."
- *Transportation.* Simply getting there can be a frustrating time vacuum, and not just for long trips. One of Cargill's clients had high-performing reps who were spending three hours a day in traffic searching for parking when they visited their Washington, D.C., customers from their office across the Potomac. Cargill reckoned the lost selling time might have made it cost-effective to have the reps chauffeured to their calls.

Confusion about technology also blocks improvements. "In the first 10 years of sales automation, there were a lot of computer glitches," Cargill says. "So they now define a successful system as all the laptops glowing when we push the buttons. But they should be asking, 'Are we selling more?'"

The Internet created a revolution in sales. However, Cargill points out, "Sometimes the Internet dilutes the issue. You can't tell whether your salespeople are selling more, or if it is coming from the Internet."

That sort of confusion is what really bothers sales productivity experts like Cargill. To improve any process, you first need to define it, then measure it and control it, he urges. "If you can define and control the sales process, you can control results."

"Every other business function has a set of documented processes that, when followed, produce predicted results," Cargill emphasizes. "Sales usually does not. There is nothing written down."

The solution is definition of responsibilities. "You have got to say who does each job, how it is to be done, and how it will be measured. You have got to put all this down on paper first and then ask, 'Do these jobs work together?'" A very good question, as Delta Air Lines discovered.

Think About the People Who Have to Make It Work

In some businesses, process changes must work through skilled support staff who simply cannot be replaced. The trick here is to educate, persuade, and motivate. Often, the best incentive is not money, but just understanding these supporting players' jobs. Delta Air Lines faced this challenge as it prepared to provide much more personalized service for the 9 percent of its customers that account for about a third of the airline's revenue.

Delta recently installed an expensive new computer system that flags these "top-flyers" as they hit airport ticket counters and check-in gates. "The ticket agent will hit a couple of keys, and up pops a profile of the passenger, what he or she likes to eat or drink and where they like to sit," explains Vince Caminiti, Delta's senior vice president of sales and distribution. "It will even show if we have ever lost their luggage."

The new tool is potentially quite useful in letting special travelers know they are appreciated and thus keeping their business. Delta is making a major commitment, $300 million in new hardware costs alone. But some very time-pressured employees, the agents who get late-arriving passengers on board fast, must use the tool.

Caminiti knows he can't just dump a new PC screen on a pressured employee. "We have to get the message out that the new system will also help them do their current jobs better," he says. "It will help our agents expedite things, avoid assigning duplicate seats, know where the connecting passengers are, and so forth. It will help them better balance the decision on when to close the door. If I can show them it will do all that, they will see the system as a positive support, not as an intrusion. That is the key to making it work."

Think Like a Start-Up

Sometimes, a sales process is so inefficient that inspecting it for little time wasters or motivational challenges is no solution. In Mike Hammer's view, "Often, things are so messed up that just tinkering around the margins won't work. You must break all the rules and think creatively. You need to start with a clean sheet and ask, 'How should it be done?'"

That is one reason, Hammer notes, for why it can be easier for a start-up company to get the process right than for an established firm to reform successfully. "Start-ups do not have as much to unlearn. In process reform, everybody has to change, people need to work with shared accountability and interactions. Salespeople need to work with backroom people. There is the messiness of emotions. Frequently, you must dump managers who don't get it. Sometimes, you must dump whole departments."

Hammer has heard two reactions again and again from the "victims" of process overhaul: "They all say that the transition to the new process was the worst experience of their lives. And then they say, 'Now, I would never consider going back to the old way.'" He draws a simple lesson. To minimize the misery, "don't drag it out. It is a very bad idea to make it gradual. It will be more painful if you slow it down."

Hammer knows top salespeople have special qualities that must be preserved throughout change. "You don't want to break their spirits. We are not talking about creating automatons. Salespeople must retain their independence and creativity, but they must learn how to work in the context of a team."

Making sure it is truly a team is the toughest part. One key to making it real is what Hammer calls *process ownership*. "One person must be accountable for the whole process from beginning to end, not just sales but the support work as well," he argues. "We are not talking about an individual sale or account, but for the whole activity of sales, crossing the boundaries of business units or divisions."

The process owner must usually be a senior executive, the CEO, a very senior sales executive, or someone else responsible for sales, marketing, and distribution.

Think About Your Customers' Customers

Some process changes are driven by new market opportunities, new technologies, or both. Selling is going to change—there is no choice about that—but the company does choose how fast, how completely, and how well it will adapt its selling methods. The boom in Internet sales has brought an accompanying boom in the express cargo business. United Parcel Service (UPS) ships about 55 percent of Internet-ordered packages, a nice position to be in. The veteran shipper also leads the business-to-business shipping market, helping Internet selling companies keep their shelves full of components and inventories for fast order fulfillment.

But the package business is fiercely competitive, and there are new, hungry rivals for UPS's dominant position. How does UPS distinguish itself from the new entrants? UPS had long known that "information moves with every single package, and the information is just as valuable as the package," explains Jordan Colletta, vice president of electronic commerce sales. A business customer of UPS wants reliable delivery, of course. But the customer also wants to know where packages are and when they will get to their destinations so that it can run its own operations efficiently.

UPS developed a suite of powerful computer tools for managing its business. Why not let customers use them to track this vital part of their own businesses? The new rule is, if you want to sell to a customer, think of the customer's customer. It applies with special force to business-to-business shipping.

Access to UPS's own tracking tools helps business shippers in several important ways, Colletta argues. "First, think of their customer service departments. Think how powerful it is, when they are taking orders, if they have all the current information on their inventory shipments."

Second, UPS's major customers have their own Web sites that their customers can visit. UPS can arrange a link from those Web sites to its own shipping tracking site, allowing the "customer's customer" to view the shipping status as well. "This adds tremendous value to the customer's Web site," Colletta notes. The UPS tools also improve management of the customer's account receivables and return operations. "It puts information about shipments at the customer's fingertips," Colletta summarizes. "It saves money, improves image, and improves service."

All this is easy enough to see in principle. Making it work in practice required major efforts. UPS now invests about $1 billion each year on technology, far more than it spends on trucks. More than 15,000 customers have downloaded at least some UPS Internet tools from the company's Web site. But were they getting the full value of all the tools? And what about the rest of the 1.6 million UPS customers that receive daily pickup service?

For both the customers and UPS to get the full value out of the e-commerce tools, these tools had to be explained and "sold" to each business shipper. UPS realized that its 2,500 regular reps and 200+ national account managers could not do that alone. It decided to create a special unit, an electronic commerce salesforce of 40 reps, to do this job better.

The E-C reps were chosen from UPS managers based on education, prior training, and proven ability to do consultative selling. Selection and e-commerce training took about four months.

Every E-C rep was trained in the value of all the online tools UPS had developed. "We wanted to make sure the entire solution set was available to every customer," Colletta says. "In this New World of information, you need to understand the whole picture. You cannot do it piecemeal."

The reps trained interactively with all the E-C tools. They used them every day during training in a simulated sales contact with a business customer. Colletta explains: "The team sat down afterward and asked, 'What did we learn about the customer? What do they need? What's the solution set? What is the best fit?'"

Training finished up with a final sales call and recommendation to the customer. The E-C teams competed for making the best recommendation to each of their simulated customers.

Soon, UPS was ready to roll with both its tools and its reps. Technology had changed what the shipping business could be. That business first became selling information, then selling use and control over the information to improve each customer's own business.

In short, better technology demands different and better selling. In Jordan Colletta's business, "at some point, it become the price of admission."

EXPERT ADVICE

Reps Should Be Asking Different Questions

Reps, as well as managers and consultants, must think outside the box to restructure sales processes. One way to get out of the box is simply to ask

(Continued on next page.)

(Continued from previous page.)

different questions, says Paul Selden of Performance Management.

- *Money.* Instead of "How much money can I make off this deal?" ask, "What is the lifetime value of this customer?"
- *Time.* Instead of "How can I close quickly?" ask, "How can I satisfy my customer to assure we get that lifetime value?"
- *Selling technique.* Instead of "How do my company's top-revenue reps sell?" ask, "How can I use technology and imagination to sell better than any other reps now sell?"
- *Contact.* Instead of "How can I increase 'face-time' with my customers?" ask, "How can I blend all my communication tools together to satisfy my customers most economically?"
- *Team.* Instead of "Who signs my checks?" ask, "Whom do I need to work with in my company to sell better?"

—From Paul Selden, the chairman of the international training and consulting firm, Performance Management, Inc., a four-time recipient of Ford Motor Company's Marketing Excellence award for professional services. He is also president of The Paul Selden Companies, a firm specializing in sales process analysis, improvement, and training.

Chapter 12

Choosing and Implementing Effective CRM Technology

ENTHUSIASTIC ACCEPTANCE

Five Keys to Implementing a CRM Solution
That Reps Embrace with Love and Loyalty

If salespeople have to be forced to use a computer system, there's something wrong with the system. Many early CRM implementations were awkward and complicated and served the needs of sales management more than the needs of the sales force. No wonder sales reps were unenthusiastic! Today's CRM systems are much more focused on the needs of sales reps, so today the big question isn't how to force people to use CRM but rather how to create the kind of enthusiasm that will make the CRM project a big success. Here are five keys to ensure that your CRM implementation will delight and amaze your sales team.

Key 1: Simplify, Simplify, Simplify

Early CRM implementations were characterized by a wealth of features and functions, all laid out on dozens of complicated screens. Sales reps, however, don't care about bells and whistles. What they want is a system that's streamlined and gets the job done. "All too often the CRM vendors have gotten involved in feature wars with one another, while the end-user community really only wants something they can use quickly and easily," observes Larry Caretsky, CEO of Commence Corporation, a CRM vendor headquartered in Oakhurst, New Jersey. He also notes that "an overly complex system can actually impede sales and ultimately result in failure of a CRM project."

To create enthusiasm among your team, you need a system that's easy to use. Insist that your CRM vendor provide you with a customized system that presents only the features and functions that are absolutely necessary to your sales process. No matter how neat a feature seems, it doesn't belong on the screen if it doesn't drive more sales or save a significant amount of money. Once you've got a system stripped down to the essentials, provide top-quality training to your sales team so they will really understand how to use that system effectively. Ideally, you should provide CRM training through a variety of methodologies, including classroom and online instruction. "Several large high-tech sales forces are using sales simulation to train their sales force and then identify specific skills they need to develop," observes Erin Kinikin, vice president of CRM at Forrester Research, a technology-research company headquartered in Cambridge, Massachusetts.

Enthusiasm is a natural by-product of CRM systems that combine simple design with easily understood training programs—especially if both the CRM design and CRM training reflect and reinforce your organization's sales methodology and processes, according to Caretsky. "For the past few years, I have recommended to dozens of customers that they implement CRM in conjunction with sales training, particularly in the areas of prospecting and pipeline management," he explains.

Key 2: Introduce the System in Stages

Once a company's executives decide to go forward with CRM, they understandably want to get things rolling as quickly as possible. The most common way of speeding up a CRM implementation is to give the sales force access to a generic, out-of-the-box version of the CRM software while simultaneously working on the customizations. This is a bad idea.

Cutting corners during the rollout alienates the sales reps, according to Dave Golan, vice president of Sales at Salesnet, a CRM vendor headquartered in Boston, Massachusetts. "It's like going to a dealership to test-drive a sports car, only to find out that all they've got for you to try out is an SUV," says Golan. "You simply aren't going to be happy with the experience, and you certainly aren't going to be ready to buy."

Successful CRM implementations—the ones that generate enthusiasm among the salesforce—always begin with the customization process, followed by a pilot program with a small sales team, and finally a gradual rollout. The pilot program is the key element of the process, because the sales reps that participate in the pilot will spread the word about whether the CRM system will be useful or not. The pilot program also offers the opportunity to get invaluable input from sales reps about problems with the system that need to be fixed before it's rolled out to the larger sales force.

A successful CRM implementation doesn't stop with the rollout, though. A CRM system is never done. Instead, CRM must evolve and change as your sales processes evolve and change. "Sales methodologies and motivational programs tend to change frequently, and sales implementations need to be flexible enough to reflect new constructs without requiring reimplementation," says Robb Eklund, vice president of CRM Product Marketing at Oracle Corporation.

If this sounds like a lot of work, don't worry. Today's CRM systems are far more flexible and customizable, according to Joe Galvin, vice president of CRM at Gartner, a market-research firm headquartered in Stamford, Connecticut. "CRM used to be a rigid application that attempted to enforce a theoretically best sales methodology, regardless of the skills and experience of the actual sales team," he explains. "Today's systems allow sales teams to reconfigure the application to match an evolving sales process, without costly programming."

Key 3: Offer More Carrots Than Sticks

If you want your sales reps to be enthusiastic about CRM, you should never, never, never punish reps who have trouble using the system, for whatever reason. Instead, do the opposite. Give early adopters and enthusiastic users additional perks and bonuses. Establish a special prize for the sales rep who uses the CRM system most effectively. Publicly praise sales reps who embrace CRM. Make sure enthusiastic CRM users are given extra credit in their employee reviews. "Make CRM processes and behaviors part of the sales reps' bonus and annual evaluation processes," says Dale Hagemeyer, research director for CRM at Gartner. "If CRM is in their objectives and part of their bonus, they will do it."

Compensation and recognition aren't the only carrots you can offer. Ideally, the CRM system will have features that create enthusiasm among the reps. For example, many companies manage their forecasts by compiling data from various spreadsheets—a process that's frustrating, time-consuming, and extremely prone to error. Today's CRM systems can collect forecasting data automatically, eliminating many hours of busywork. Similarly, at some companies the paper mechanics of moving a sale from opportunity to product shipment is so burdensome that sales reps can only handle a limited number of deals in the pipeline. "CRM allowed our firm to increase its pipeline tenfold, which means more sales for everybody," says Paul Lavallee, executive vice president of worldwide sales and marketing at MARC Global, a software vendor that uses Salesnet to manage the sales of its warehouse-management and supply-chain products.

The fact that today's CRM systems are much easier to use than earlier CRM implementations can also be a carrot of sorts. For example, most of today's CRM implementations minimize data entry, drawing instead upon the wealth of corporate data that's already stored in your company's computer systems. "The best examples of successful CRM implementations incorporate the software as an enabler of existing processes—so the software is seen as an aid rather than an inhibitor," says Jon Van Duyne, senior vice president and general manager of Mid-market CRM at Best Software, a software vendor headquartered in Scottsdale, Arizona. "CRM should truly reflect how people want to work, and those most serious about implementing CRM need to know this and the degree of detail they desire."

Key 4: Emphasize How CRM Increases Sales

This sounds obvious, but you'd be surprised how many sales managers don't do this. While most CRM systems save money and boost sales, sales reps really don't care all that much about cost savings. They're only likely to get enthusiastic about a CRM system that truly helps them sell. This means that whenever you talk about the CRM system to your sales reps, don't spend much time on cost savings. Instead, emphasize how much easier it will be to sell using CRM than without it.

For example, if the CRM system has group calendaring, show how it will now be easier to schedule the resources required to close a sale. Similarly, if the CRM system has a library of downloadable sales tools, show how easy it will now be to get sales materials into the hands of prospects. "If you've thought the implementation through, there will be multiple ways for you to show off how the system increases sales," says Golan.

It shouldn't be too hard to make a compelling case. According to independent research, implementing a CRM system can result in around a 20 percent boost in sales. One of the best ways to show how CRM increases sales is to apply the system directly to the challenges faced by each individual sales rep, according to Jeff Summers, general manager of sales products for Siebel Systems. "Siebel provides an excellent platform for tracking skills development across the sales organization. Individual skill plans can be defined, executed, and tracked," he explains. "The centralized skills database is then available to accelerate resource identification for critical sales opportunities, and in this way, the right people are aligned with the right opportunities at the right time."

Key 5: Cultivate CRM Champions

Finally, it's important to remember that word of mouth is your greatest ally. Sales reps are by nature gregarious communicators, so any scuttlebutt about the CRM system is going to spread quickly. To make certain the rumors and opinions are positive, actively cultivate one or more champions among the sales teams who will tout CRM around the watercooler.

The best candidates to play this role aren't the young, gung-ho technology types, though. The people you want to cultivate as champions are the successful sales reps. "Ideally you want somebody who is a little resistant to technology," says Lavallee. "That way it will be all the more dramatic when they embrace CRM." One caveat is necessary, though: you want someone who is only somewhat resistant to technology. Don't make the mistake of trying to cultivate an employee who is actively "technology-phobic." "Your cause won't be helped if you put a curmudgeon in the position to gum up the works," Lavallee warns.

In short, building enthusiasm among the sales reps means selling the CRM system to the sales team. Rather than thinking of yourself as a manager, twisting your employees' arms, treat the sales reps as customers who need to be convinced that your product will help them become more productive. That shouldn't be too hard. After all, the reason you became a sales manager in the first place was because you know how to sell.

ROUNDTABLE OF TOP CRM INDUSTRY LEADERS

Selling Power recently chaired a spirited roundtable panel discussion at the DCI Conference in Chicago. During that session, I asked top executives from 18 leading CRM vendors to share their wisdom and perspectives on a wide range of CRM issues, including implementation strategy, business process reengineering, the role of management, and return on investment (ROI).

Here are the most insightful highlights from that discussion.

How to Get the Most Out of CRM

Question: There's no question that CRM is a powerful technology that can change the way salespeople do business. That being said, it's not always clear how sales managers should proceed in order to ensure that their CRM implementations are successful. What's the best way to make sure that sales groups get the most out of CRM?

- **William Green (Pivotal):** Companies shouldn't assume that CRM is the answer. They should first find out what the problem is, or what the opportunity is, and then figure out whether they actually need CRM. After that, it's important to build a cross-functional team that can evaluate the different vendors. The thought process should be "think big, but act small," with the ultimate goal that every time customers contact your organization, they have a positive experience and feel that they are being well served.
- **Ellen Olson (E.piphany):** I agree. Sales groups must have a vision of what they want to accomplish from a business perspective. But then they should start slow and look for areas where they can get a quick ROI. Ideally, the cost savings or revenue improvements should be impressive enough to provide justification and funding for continued improvements of the CRM system. It's also important to set expectations appropriately. It's better for everyone involved to undersell what the system will do so that the installation not only meets but exceeds expectations.
- **Tim Vertz (Oncontact):** Quick wins are definitely what it's all about. If a CRM vendor can install a system and do a few customizations in a few key areas, and then let the management and other departments see the positive results, the overall CRM system is far more likely to be effective.
- **Peter Dios (Optima):** You have to be careful with the customization, though. Initial projects are more successful when they don't require major alterations. When we're in the early stages of a CRM implementation, we tend to use a standard set of custom add-ons, so that we don't have to invent anything new. Complicated customizations add unnecessary risk to the equation.
- **Joshua Lackovic (Clear Technologies Inc.):** It's all about focusing on the "sweet spot," the area where the vendor is certain they can add value and where they've been successful in the past. For example, our implementation teams, our specialists, our consultants are most knowledgeable in working with manufacturing/distribution companies with approximately $100 million in yearly revenues. That's where we fit in the best, and we try to stay within those parameters.

EXPERT ADVICE

The Panelists

The panelists for this roundtable were selected based upon ISM Inc.'s annual ranking of top CRM solutions. They are, in alphabetical order:

Finn Backer, CEO, Software Innovation Inc., Toronto, Ontario, Canada

Michael Belongie, Senior Vice President of Sales and Marketing, Axonom Inc., Minneapolis, Minnesota

Rebecca Czupryna, Senior Business Consultant, Saratoga Systems, Campbell, California

Jeremy de Silva, Director of Sales, StayinFront Inc., Fairfield, New Jersey

Peter Dios, CEO, Optima Technology, Irvine, California

John Durst, Vice President of Sales and Marketing, Interchange Solutions, Toronto, Ontario, Canada

Jon Van Duyne, Senior VP and GM for CRM, Best Software, Scottsdale, Arizona

David Golan, Vice President of Sales and Marketing, iET Solutions, Framingham, Massachusetts

William Green, District Sales Manager, Pivotal Corporation, Vancouver, British Columbia, Canada

Steven Hamden, Sales Manager, Ardexus Inc., Mississauga, Ontario, Canada

Joshua Lackovic, Vice President of Sales, Clear Technologies Inc., Dallas, Texas

Tony Martinez, Director of Business Development, SAP AG, Walldorf, Germany

Zach Nelson, President and CEO, Netsuite, San Mateo, California

Ellen Olson, Senior Vice President of Worldwide Marketing, E.piphany, San Mateo, California

Michael Pessetti, Vice President, SalesPage Technologies Inc., Kalamazoo, Michigan

Bob Tyler, Vice President of CRM Solutions, S1, Atlanta, Georgia

Tim Vertz, Business Development Manager, Oncontact Software Corporation, Cedarburg, Wisconsin
Everton Wallace, Staffware, Maidenhead, Berkshire, United Kingdom

Changing the Business Processes

Question: It strikes me that long-range planning is just as important as short-term wins. One of the strengths of CRM is that it can help sales managers think through their sales processes and make sure that they make sense. That's going to involve a deep discovery process, to understand how things work today, how they should be working, and how a CRM system can help get the sales organization from A to B. Isn't there a danger that the focus on short-term results might give short shrift to the larger issues of improving the overall sales process?

- **Rebecca Czupryna (Saratoga Systems):** It's all about prioritization. You need to start with the biggest problems, implement the system in manageable chunks, and get more sophisticated as time goes on. And, yes, measurement is extremely important. A large percentage of failed CRM projects are the result of failure to set clear and attainable goals. They are without a way to quantify whether the project was successful.

- **Michael Pessetti (SalesPage):** A company has to have a clear, if not complete, vision of what it ultimately wants to accomplish. That may mean simply understanding the problems that need to be fixed, but it can also be a deep understanding of all of the different systems that they will eventually need to integrate. Frankly, unless they do this kind of homework prior to talking to us vendors, CRM customers are likely to run into trouble. Because when a company's vision for its CRM implementation shifts and changes, there is no clear target, and the project is likely to get lost in the mist.

- **Jon Van Duyne (Best Software):** It's my experience that the risk of CRM failure is directly correlated with the complexity of the system. The minute you start adding a lot of features and functions, the job becomes much more difficult. The size of the organization is also a factor. When you're dealing with a smaller organization, you're typically working with a smaller implementation. What's more, there's always the chance that your sponsor will also be the decision maker, which makes it much easier to get things done.

- **Steven Hamden (Ardexus):** Companies need to understand the big picture, but also simultaneously break the implementation into manageable chunks. It's also absolutely essential to have measurable goals at each stage of the implementation. For example, you might set a criterion that a project is successful if it achieves 100 percent adoption among the sales staff.

- **Jeremy de Silva (StayinFront):** The way I like to think of it is that you put the short-term initial wins into the context of a "blue sky" definition of how you'd like things to be in an ideal world. That being said, it's important that the CRM team doesn't overpromise and thereby set expectations too high. You have to whittle down the "blue sky" definition of what's possible to what is actually achievable at this point in time, with the available funds.

- **Tony Martinez (SAP):** All this talk about short-term wins can get companies into trouble if they're not careful. I prefer to think of a customer as a complete entity—not just sales and marketing, but an entire, complex operation that runs all the way through the taking of the order to the final delivery of the product or service. You have to think about the overall business processes and then decide how to build out the implementation.

Setting Appropriate Goals

Question: So the key is to implement something that works in the short term but still have your eyes on the long-term goal.

- **Zach Nelson (NetSuite):** That's exactly right. There's an old saying in business: "Don't pave the cow path." The phrase comes from Boston, where they poured concrete into the cow paths when they built up the city. Now it's costing them $10 billion to try to figure out how to move traffic through Boston. The lesson here is that, if you aren't willing to make some changes in a company's business processes in order to make them more efficient, it could end up costing you more, maybe a lot more, in the future.

- **David Golan (iET Solutions):** A good rule of thumb is that you should always understand why you're automating a process before you try to automate it. I've seen examples where companies have automated their existing processes, which were seriously broken in the first place. So they ended up failing, but much faster than they would have failed without the added momentum from the technology.
- **Everton Wallace (Staffware):** It's important to emphasize, though, that understanding these processes is the responsibility of the customer, not the CRM vendor. Customers need to look at their own processes to see if they work well enough to automate. If they don't, the customer must be willing to make changes, sometimes quite substantial changes, before bringing the CRM vendor into the picture. There is no point in automating something that doesn't work.
- **Finn Backer (Software Innovation):** I couldn't agree more. Look, CRM is not a piece of software. CRM is a *strategy*. As part of that strategy, a company needs to revisit its business processes, which means getting management buy-in and sponsorship for the changes that will need to be made prior to system installation. And that management support needs to be ongoing. I've seen situations where the person who brought the CRM system into the company was promoted because the CRM system was so successful, but that created a leadership vacuum that kept the system from growing. CRM is difficult or impossible without a powerful executive sponsor.
- **Jon Van Duyne (Best Software):** It's also important that the decision be made at the right level. In large enterprises, the CRM decision is sometimes made at the boardroom level, which is unfortunate, because the board typically has no idea what the sales force really needs. I saw one case where a multimillion-dollar CRM system was sold to a Fortune 500 company, along with a massive budget for back-end integration, despite the fact that a large percentage of the salespeople didn't even have access to a PC.

The CRM Leadership Challenge

Question: You've hit on an interesting observation, which is that CRM can be a real leadership challenge, because the sales organization will need to work more closely with the rest of the company if the CRM implementation is to have a chance to succeed. But sometimes, sales groups are isolated politically. How do you overcome that?

- **Zach Nelson (NetSuite):** If you're looking at changing or automating the way product orders flow through the company, you have to get the finance people involved, the Web site people involved, the information technology people involved, and so forth. Sometimes this means breaking the barriers in the company, which can be painful. But it's also good for the company, because breaking through the stovepipes tends to focus a corporation outward—on the ability to deliver on customer promises—rather than inward toward the corporate politics.
- **Joshua Lackovic (Clear Technologies):** In a practical sense, getting different groups to work together involves forming a committee or a team of individuals from the company, that helps ensure that different perspectives and different needs and requirements are well understood before proceeding with the implementation. In some cases, it can be almost as important to get input from the receptionists as it is to get input from the CFO. That's especially true if the cooperation of the receptionists is required to make the CRM system into a success.

Convincing the Team to Cooperate

Question: Getting people together is obviously a good idea, but how do you prepare for the internal opposition that is inevitable with any new project? Managing change is always difficult, especially when the change leadership is coming from outside the company. How can a CRM vendor help a customer to change?

- **Jeremy de Silva (StayinFront):** Change is impossible without management involvement. The good thing is that, if you're following management's overall vision of where you need to go, and you've got management commitment and communication, it's difficult for a CRM implementation to go wrong. I've seen plenty of attempts to change a company fail when management commitment is fleeting.
- **William Green (Pivotal):** It's not just management that has to be committed, though. Employee training is extremely important. Your end users need at least a half-day of training on each successive version of the CRM system.
- **Michael Belongie (Axonom):** The executives should be involved in the training sessions as well. When management gets trained along with the salespeople, it gives top management more of a sense of ownership of the final CRM solution. It also communicates in no uncertain terms to the sales staff that the executives are seriously committed to the CRM system.

Convincing Employees to Embrace CRM

Question: There have been many CRM systems that failed simply because the salespeople refused to use the software. What do companies and vendors need to do in order to ensure that CRM actually gets used?

- **Zach Nelson (NetSuite):** The main incentives for any sales rep are fear and greed. (General laughter.) If the CRM system shows the sales reps where and when they're getting commissions and how they are doing compared to their peers, they're a lot more likely to take the CRM implementation seriously.
- **John Durst (Interchange Solutions):** We asked one of our customers in Germany how they planned to make certain that people buy into the system. We were expecting the flowery, "We want to empower our employees" response that we'd normally get in North America. But instead this manager simply said, "We'll fire them if they don't use the system." I'm not sure that's an option in North America, though. (Laughter.) Seriously, the best way to get salespeople to jump on board with CRM is to show them how they can make more commissions.

Question: It seems to me that best way to get people to use a system is to provide an experience where the CRM user and that user's customer both say, "WOW!" Everyone should feel as if they got more than they expected. How do you make that happen in the real world?

- **Bob Tyler (S1):** That's so true. Let me tell you a story. One of our first implementations was in a bank, and I was watching customer interactions—observing, you know—on the first day of operation. A customer came up to a teller to cash a check and the teller suddenly got a big smile on her face. So the customer says, "What's wrong? Did I overdraw my account or something?" But the teller says, "No, no, no. My system says that you have been with us 10 years this month, and our 10-year customers get a special gift to thank them for their business." It seems like a little thing, but that teller was WOWed, and that customer was WOWed. And that system was adopted very, very quickly throughout the entire bank.
- **Finn Backer (Software Innovation):** Every time you try to change how people work, you have to add a corresponding value. All too often, CRM vendors go into a company and try to automate a certain function, but don't give the employees anything in return. It's, "Fill out this electronic form or else." The user doesn't get

any return for his or her effort and doesn't perceive that the system has any value. Under those circumstances, it's very difficult for any CRM solution to succeed.

Return on Investment

Question: Employees are only part of the picture, though. A CRM system must provide value to management as well. In most cases that means showing a solid ROI. What are the best ways to achieve ROI through CRM?

- **Finn Backer (Software Innovation):** That's a difficult question to answer, because the concept of ROI varies from company to company. To find the right ROI equation, it's necessary to interview people at different levels in the organization to determine what they want to get out of the CRM solution. Then you must customize the solution so that it provides an appropriate ROI for all of the stakeholders.
- **David Golan (iET Solutions):** In my view, ROI must be based upon specific measurable objectives. This is key. If a customer can't identify what they want out of their CRM system, then it's impossible to figure out what needs to be implemented. And that, in turn, makes it impossible to measure success, because you don't have anything to measure against. More often than not, companies don't have sound definitions of their problems or a clear idea of the changes they need to make to their internal processes or procedures. So we spend a lot of time early in the sales process in discovering and mapping out the customer's needs, problems, and procedures. The result is a solution that addresses the individual ROI needs of everybody involved.
- **John Durst (Interchange Solutions):** Let's not get all complicated about this. ROI is all about helping companies make more money. That's it. You can accomplish this through improvements in customer service, relationship management, marketing, or whatever. It goes back to what we were saying about implementing for the quick win. When we go into a customer account, we go into the field with the sales reps and ask them questions like "What are you doing?" and "What's bugging you today?" We're looking for the areas where automation can create a quick return.
- **Tony Martinez (SAP):** You have to be careful, though, that you don't run into the pitfall of sacrificing long-term ROI for short-term ROI. The first question that customers need to ask themselves is, "How do I grow my business?" The second question is almost as important: "How can I meet both my short-term and long-term

needs?" The short term, of course, is the functionality that the CRM system can provide today. Long-term needs are likely to be more challenging, such as integrating the CRM system with the internal systems of other organizations inside the company.

- **Jeremy de Silva (StayinFront):** In the end, though, the CRM vendor must own some of the responsibility to ensure that the CRM customer gets a solid ROI. If a CRM vendor can't go back to the VP of sales and marketing and explain what the customer got out of the system, that CRM vendor is out the door. And rightly so. Vendors have to be more involved in the life cycle of CRM systems and take a greater share of the responsibility to ensure that they're successful.

BUILDING YOUR STRATEGY
How CRM Can Help Your Sales

In his book *The Customer Relationship Management Survival Guide*, Dick Lee observes that sales superachievers make selling look so easy. They appear to have a gift. Yet, behind that polished performance lies a foundation built on solid knowledge of what it takes to complete the sale and how to keep customers happy in the long run. One would never guess these sales professionals follow predetermined steps to succeed. And, some don't even require CRM software to get the job done.

But, Lee asks, what about your average performers—the majority of your sales force? "Lacking that rare marriage of personality and process, which part of the equation would you want them to have? If you've ever been a sales manager, you answered 'process' without a moment's hesitation," he writes.

As Lee points out, much of the selling process does not take place in front of the customer—qualifying and researching customers, studying their wants and needs, preparing information, and scheduling meetings. That's part of the process. And here's where CRM offers a great deal for sales success.

- *Qualifying prospects.* CRM database records are much more valuable tools than paper records. The electronic records help qualifiers determine which accounts are worth pursuing, faster and more accurately. Other benefits include branching, or onscreen scripts, built into the CRM software.

- *Sales call selectivity.* Why do salespeople seem to spend more time calling on relatively low-volume accounts rather than key accounts? It could be their resources. A good database can help produce a more productive call list.
- *Call focus.* If you feel as though you're spending too much time on difficult sales calls, concentrating on the wrong products or the wrong needs, CRM can help you plan the right call strategy.
- *Continuity.* Continuity, according to Lee, "is about being buttoned-down, professional, respectful, and competent. It's also about keeping the sales dialogue on track from call to call, not wasting half the time remembering where the last call left off or what was discussed." CRM call histories provide continuity and make the transition from one relationship manager to another easier, without disrupting sales momentum or losing accumulated knowledge of the customer.
- *Increased lifetime value.* CRM is the perfect antidote to "sell-and-run" sales tactics, Lee says. In fact, CRM philosophy emphasizes sales activities after the first sale, stretching the sales cycle over the customer's lifetime.
- *One face to the customer.* Have you ever had customers complain about getting calls from six different reps—all from your company? CRM helps multiline or multidivisional users maintain one face to the customer, Lee says—something like the left hand knowing what the right hand is doing.

THE EIGHT KEYS TO PROFITABLE CRM

1. Take a modular and gradual approach.
2. Get complete support from top management.
3. Keep the implementation simple.
4. Be certain that the sales force participates during the design phase.
5. Consider tying compensation to compliance.
6. Outsource elements of the system to save money.
7. Work with a vendor with whom you feel comfortable.
8. Use the system to measure real-time performance.

Chapter 13

A Manager's Guide to Ethics

THE ETHICAL DILEMMA
How to Do the Right Thing and Get the Sale

Pauline recently started selling office copiers. She is a single mother supporting a chronically sick child and receives little financial support from her ex-husband, so she depends on her sales commissions to help pay the bills. Her most promising prospect is a large company with 10,000 employees and regional offices scattered throughout the Midwest. The company wants to replace its worn-out copiers with brand-new ones, and is accepting bids from Pauline and three of her competitors.

On one sales call to the company's purchasing manager, the manager offers Pauline the order in exchange for 5 percent of her commission on the $200,000 sale. Pauline stands to collect a 10 percent commission, or $20,000.

Pauline knows the kickback to the manager is illegal, but doesn't want to lose the sale. What's worse, her research reveals that his company's founder, a deeply religious man, required all workers to sign a code of ethics as a condition of employment. What should Pauline do?

- Tell the manager she didn't hear his offer and continue her sales call as planned.
- Get flustered and confused, and not know how to respond.
- Consult a fellow salesperson at a different company for advice.
- Meet with her manager for direction.

Ethical conflicts can vary according to the industry and type of selling. While some salespeople rarely face them, others may deal with them regularly. Even salespeople who don't expect to face an ethical dilemma in the near future should have a plan ready to handle one if it occurs. A good ethical plan should (1) help you sort out the ethical issues facing you, (2) help you weigh all your options, and (3) help you make a decision that protects your ethical standards while protecting your sale. It only takes one unethical choice to start a pattern of dishonesty, so be prepared to face any ethical situation with a plan of action.

For help in sorting out the issues involved in ethical conflicts, I consulted Michael Daigneault, president of the Ethics Resource Center in Washington, D.C., and Michael Hoffman, director of Bentley College's Center for Business Ethics in Waltham, Massachusetts.

Hoffman advises Pauline to calmly but clearly tell Joe that she wants to get the sale fairly and honestly. If Joe resists her attempts to sell honestly, Hoffman recommends that Pauline take the matter to her manager and suggest that he call Joe's supervisor to report the incident.

Should Pauline's manager refuse to report Joe or ask Pauline why she didn't just accept his offer, Hoffman maintains that it's Pauline's responsibility to report the incident to a higher authority and see to it that Joe's supervisor is informed of his unethical conduct. Hoffman also emphasizes the importance of having an ethics office and a company code of ethics to protect both the company and the salesperson.

According to Daigneault, Pauline should "raise the issue with her supervisor. At that point, they can decide whether to report the purchasing manager's conduct. Since it is possible that similar offers were made to the other competitors, reporting the purchasing manager's conduct to his company may help to reestablish fairness in the bidding process."

Ethical conflicts like Pauline's leave the salesperson with four primary options: engaging in unethical behavior, ignoring the behavior, confronting the perpetrator, or reporting the behavior. Deciding which option will help you preserve your integrity and your sale requires you to weigh the pros and cons of all your options. To help you resolve the conflict to everyone's satisfaction, handle any ethics conflict with care, and let logic, rather than emotion, be your guide.

- *Option 1: Engaging in unethical behavior.* When dishonest practices guarantee you a big sale and a generous commission, even scrupulously honest salespeople might be tempted to act against their own best interests. Before you do, consider all your options and the consequences of each. Try making a list of what you stand to gain and what you stand to lose if you're caught, or even if you aren't. Consider long-term benefits and drawbacks as well as immediate gains and losses, including possible damage to your reputation or that of your company.
- *Option 2: Ignoring the behavior.* Ignoring selling misconduct may be the easiest option, but it isn't always the best one. Many salespeople want to preserve friendships with fellow salespeople or profitable customers, so they make an emotional decision to overlook the misconduct instead of assessing the situation logically and rationally. Ask yourself questions to help you assess your circumstances: Do your loyalties lie with your colleagues? Your company? Your family? Before you make any snap decisions, make sure your priorities make sense. If anyone exposes the

dishonest actions, some may consider you an accomplice or facilitator because you didn't try to stop it.

- *Option 3: Confronting the perpetrator.* For many ethical dilemmas, a tactful confrontation is the ideal solution. Confrontation often gives you the chance to stop unethical behavior while preserving or even enhancing your relationship with the guilty party. If you decide to confront, assure those you address that you want them to stop what they're doing for their own good, as well as for their company's, colleagues', and customers' well-being. Carefully consider the place and time of your confrontation. To help keep you on good terms with those you confront, address them without self-righteousness and without belittling them.

- *Option 4: Reporting the behavior.* Regardless of one's personal feelings toward a certain person, company, or behavior, some ethical situations leave you little choice but to report them. If your job or reputation are at stake or if your company stands to take a significant loss, for example, you should strongly consider sharing what you know with your company ethics office or supervisor. Reporting the behavior helps keep your name clear of blame in case there's any question as to your involvement.

MARSHALL FIELD'S TEN VIRTUES OF A SUCCESSFUL SALESPERSON

Marshall Field, who founded the world-famous department store Marshall Field's, was one of America's greatest salesmen. A farm boy who left school at the age of 17 to become a clerk at a dry goods store in Pittsfield, Massachusetts, he was destined, by dint of hard work and his unwavering belief that any ordinary job can be made great, to create a vast fortune and a business organization second to none.

After declining an offer of partnership in the dry goods store, he pursued his interest in the fast-developing West and traveled to Chicago in 1856. There he began as a clerk in the city's leading wholesale dry goods store. Only eight years after entering the firm with an initial yearly salary of $400, Marshall Field was the head of a very successful business and boasted an interest in the store of $260,000.

Despite the store's destruction in the Chicago fire of 1871, the ensuing panic of 1873, and another fire in 1877, the success of Marshall Field was not to be denied. The firm's sales totaled $12 million in 1868 and rose to $25 million by 1881. Before Field's death in 1906, sales had reached an impressive $68 million.

What were the key attributes of Marshall Field's success in selling? With his close attention to customer service, he glorified the job of everyday selling and gave it zest and a heroic image. In an era known for its low standard of business ethics, Field stood out as a shining figure of integrity. He insisted all the firm's transactions be handled in the most upright manner. Field established a strict cash system and was the innovator of many principles that are now standard practice in selling. He was the customer's champion by stressing the one-price system and by featuring a personal shopping service and home delivery. In addition, he pioneered the department-store restaurant for shoppers. Field's customer-oriented vision endeared him to patrons who appreciated his introduction of the option of exchanging goods bought on approval.

Field's excellent managerial skill and reputation of fair dealing with employees as well as customers helped to make Marshall Field & Company in Chicago the world's largest retail store. Over his lifespan of 71 years, Field developed a list of 10 fundamentals for salespeople. Listed below, these serve as an excellent guide for salespeople today just as they guided Field himself a century ago.

1. *The value of time.* Time can dry a tear and heal a grievous wound, but it also can make a million of a dime. Time determines whether you are a salesperson or a loafer.
2. *The value of perseverance.* You will always find the greatest sales at the end of the street, at the end of the day, and after ringing many doorbells in vain.
3. *The value of work.* Without work your days are empty and satisfaction flies. There is no pleasure like work. There is no joy its equal.
4. *The value of simplicity.* A sweating racehorse needs no label. A sincere attitude doesn't need words. Simplicity is compelling selling.
5. *The value of kindness.* The service doesn't hide behind a mask of friendliness, for kindness can't be counterfeited.
6. *The value of example.* The salesperson you train with words has nine chances to fail to the one for the salesperson you train by demonstration. The greatest influence you have is built by what you do.
7. *The value of duty.* Like your shadow is always with you in the light, your sense of duty whispers to you through your inner conscience. People who don't listen to conscience act like people without conscience.
8. *The value of talent.* The wise salesperson notes his or her abilities and talents and continually strives to train, expand, and improve them.
9. *The value of character.* The word of some salespeople is greater than the bond of others. Character is so dominant and self-evident that it needs no advertising.

10. *The value of originating.* A salesperson's foremost duty is to point out to prospects new joys and possibilities. He or she originates new visions and sells through them. A salesperson also finds glory in the possibilities that selling offers to the professional.

INTEGRITY IS A SALESPERSON'S BADGE OF HONOR

Long-term professional selling is less about the level of your skill than the content of your character. True professionals know that skill may help you close that first sale, but integrity keeps customers coming back. Integrity may seem like an elusive term, but salespeople who have it share many of the same positive qualities. To check your own integrity level, ask yourself if you . . .

practice sound work ethics. Salespeople with integrity spend work hours working—not chatting by the watercooler or taking long lunches. Because they spend their time wisely, they don't need to falsify call reports. Instead of viewing their territory, prospects, or quota as problems to avoid, they approach them as challenges.

have the courage of your convictions. Do you try to do what's right despite what others might say or think? Having integrity means having the courage to stand up for what you believe in. When you're faced with an ethical decision, decide based on your standards of self-respect—not on how much money is involved.

have character that stands up under scrutiny. Salespeople with integrity are often known for it. Their professional reputation is a primary reason why their customers recommend them to others. Would your colleagues and customers be surprised to hear you'd been accused of professional dishonesty?

offer more value than you have to. Smart salespeople know that holding on to customers often means offering them a little more than the competition. Also, they care about their customers, so they want to make sure they get their money's worth—and then some. Integrity makes you want to do more than you need to for your customers—if only for the satisfaction of a job well done.

make sure the first order isn't the last. To earn your customers' repeat business, you have to take care of them before and after the sale. Your new customers represent a golden opportunity to earn their future sales and referrals—give them the care and attention they deserve to show them just how much you value them.

are confident and assertive. If you have integrity, you have no reason to be underhanded, paranoid, or fearful. When you have the best intentions for your prospects, you have a right—maybe even an obligation—to pursue their business aggressively and ask for the sale.

are disciplined and reliable. Salespeople with integrity set challenging goals, then work hard to reach them. As a manager, you can count on them to put in a full day's work every day and to do whatever it takes to earn their customers' business, satisfaction, and loyalty. Integrity helps keep you focused on your goals and on the right track to success.

make others feel good about themselves. To win your customers' sales and your teams' support, you have to be sensitive to their feelings. Making other people feel good makes them want to be around you, and in sales, the more supporters you have, the better. The kind word you say today may earn you a big sale or valuable referral tomorrow.

For those who want to take shortcuts on the path to sales success, integrity may seem like a burden. After all, it's easier to lie about your product's warranty or convince prospects to buy something they can't use than it is to start over with a new prospect. Sometimes integrity makes it harder to make the sale, but it can make it easier for us to live with ourselves. And in the long run, nice guys do finish first.

ANATOMY OF A CON ARTIST

According to extensive psychological research, sociopathic drives can be found in everyone. There are times and situations where perfectly honest salespeople may sense a temporary thrill when considering keeping the wrong change, by not mentioning the extra quantity discount to a new prospect, or by "forgetting" to remind a customer of an existing credit from erroneous double payment.

When these inner drives are released without the controls of the conscience, the salesperson will take the first step across the boundaries separating right from wrong. When these inner drives become the major mode of operation, the psychopathic con artist emerges.

(*Continued on next page.*)

(*Continued from previous page.*)

Below are 10 typical behavior characteristics of the con artist in selling. If anyone on your team displays these signs, it's time for an intervention and a discussion of the importance of ethical and professional behavior.

1. *Unusual calmness in anxiety-producing situations.* Con artists can act "cool" in situations that would cause a minor heart attack in normal people.
2. *Inability to display deep emotions.* Con artists may go through all motions, even with dramatic flair, but will stay detached as if rehearsing for a performance.
3. *Little respect for other people's feelings.* They view people as fully interchangeable. People are only as good as they are able to serve the pathological need of the con artists.
4. *Highly skilled in establishing exploitative relationships.* An exceptional ability to charm, flatter, and persuade other people allows con artists to win people's trust and confidence in a very short time.
5. *Unusual talent for crafting a nearly flawless image of complete trustworthiness and confidence.* Hard-core con artists carefully dress the part. They are creative in developing a "clean as a whistle" image through legitimate-looking brochures, testimonials from people in impressive positions, and even paid references.
6. *Appearance of perfect psychological health.* Most con artists will appear completely unaffected by the stresses and strains of everyday life. They tell everyone that everything in their lives is absolutely fantastic, terrific, and completely trouble free. They derive pleasure from the effects produced by their masks of sanity.
7. *Unfazed by threats of punishment for their asocial behavior.* They know that risking a jail sentence is part of the game, but their false belief that they are special and outside the rules compels them to press on until they get caught.

8. *Irrational belief that they have been treated unfairly in the past.* (Examples: unhappy childhood, abandoned by parents, mistreated by company, etc.) They have the conviction that their current scams are only designed to "even the balance."
9. *Distorted views of the world.* These include beliefs like: "Everybody has a gimmick," or "Everybody has a price," or "Everyone does it."
10. *Savvy and quick in finding and exploiting minor character flaws in others.* They are always interested in the schemes and techniques used by master manipulators, impostors, and other con artists.

Chapter 14

The Ins and Outs of Compensation

CREATIVE COMPENSATION

The Best Ways to Reward Sales Performance

As more and more sales forces continue to move toward performance-based pay, does that mean a simple shift for salespeople from salary only or a salary/commission mix to straight commissions? In a few cases, yes. But the whole story is more complex.

First, from the company's point of view, what is performance? Is it the same today as it was yesterday? How do managers measure performance?

Does performance mean reaching quota? Going over quota with discounted prices? Increasing number of calls? Punching up the closing ratio? Doing more repeat business? Or does performance come down to some combination of sales closed and a base level of customer satisfaction?

On the salespeople's side, incentives should directly affect things that matter to them and their families. These can differ by age, personality, and career goals. A salesperson just starting out may want the stability of a regular paycheck before establishing a territory and predictable sales. Someone who has been selling for 5 to 10 years already knows the market and what to expect. Such an individual may want the added incentive of commissions to make more sales. A salesperson who has been selling for 20 years may want deferred payments as part of a retirement package to take advantage of tax laws.

For the company to succeed, the compensation plan must satisfy both the company's and the salespeople's objectives. So, in practice, performance pay is not always simple. Fortunately, managers are developing some creative solutions. And they are even tweaking successful compensation plans to improve performance compensation.

Pay for Profits If You Want Them

IBM recently put its 40,000 U.S. salespeople on a new bonus plan tied to customer satisfaction and profits. The old compensation was a "box approach," says IBM's Peter Thonis. It rewarded salespeople for machines and software sold. Now, IBM uses a dual performance compensation measurement tool.

The sales bonus will be 40 percent based on customer satisfaction and 60 percent based on the profitability of each sales transaction. Why not just pay on profits, the "bottom line," and let the salesperson worry about keeping the customer happy? Thonis notes that IBM is no longer happy simply with the maximum profit on each sale but wants satisfied customers for future sales as well.

Well, what business doesn't want profits and continuing relationships? The trick is in making this type of performance incentive measurable and workable. How does IBM plan to cut such a deal? Local IBM managers will survey customers frequently to measure "satisfaction" and will ask customers not just how happy they are with what they have bought but also, "How well does IBM's rep know your agenda?"

In other words, are IBM salespeople keeping up-to-date with what's going on at each customer's site? Are they aware of each customer's changing hardware and software needs? Since the customer's agenda will affect IBM's future, salespeople must keep a vigilant eye not only on the profitability of each sale but also on future trends at each customer's shop. In other words, salespeople must think strategically if IBM is to stay viable in the market.

For this more sophisticated approach to sales force compensation, IBM must measure the profit per transaction. Estimating how much profit a corporation makes on total sales is easy, if it is done once per quarter. It's called *accounting*. But for IBM's system to work, the salesperson should know profits when negotiating the deal. That provides motivation—and builds confidence. So IBM developed a special software tool that takes into account such indirect costs as development. It gives each salesperson a complete corporate picture at the point of sale.

Many customers are also interested in IBM's profits, and for very intelligent reasons. As Thonis explains, nobody in the computer business wants to buy from a company that's losing money—"They may not be around for service, or they'll get you in other ways."

IBM expects its new plan to provide about half of the average salesperson's compensation, and possibly up to 80 percent for the top of the force. However, the key is not fractions, but focus: "We want salespeople to think from the customer's perspective," emphasizes Thonis. And that's just what IBM has found it must do as a corporation.

Dell Computer Corporation is one of the "clone" manufacturers that shaved PC prices by selling direct to users. Dell's Roger Rydell credits the tried-and-true sales-based commissions with tripling Dell's sales over the past two years. But, he notes, "When you're going that fast, you can weather-strip the vehicle."

Currently Dell is more concerned with profits and liquidity. The company has shifted its sales compensation to reflect financial priorities, not sales growth. A simple commission scale, based 100 percent on profits, has been in place for about six months. Dell's 700 salespeople (80 percent sell over the phone) get an estimate of the profit margin on each machine sale, just like IBM's bigger force. And they get a daily estimate of total commissions earned.

Results? "We've seen an immediate shift in selling focus, with salespeople walking away from deals that weren't profitable," comments Rydell.

Pay Salespeople What They Want Most

Another new compensation approach starts with the sales force. In many businesses, the best salespeople are older, experienced hands. They know the product, territory, and have many familiar customers. But some are thinking more and more of Florida, right? The business needs not just veteran bodies. It needs their best efforts until it's their time to flock south. Why not offer them a bigger piece of Florida?

That is what deferred compensation attempts to do. Paid—and taxed—only after retirement, salespeople earn deferred compensation now. That means the company can tie it to performance now, when it counts and it's measurable. And performance may not be just sales. A business may need the most help from experienced salespeople in training new people, in transferring knowledge of the territory, and other "human capital investments." If that's what the business needs, that is, at least partly, what performance compensation should reward.

Deferred compensation is also called "Super Comp" for another reason. Paying taxes on a retirement income is a lot cheaper than being taxed on your best commission years. And the deferred account may also earn interest, just like any retirement provision.

But deferred compensation may not be suitable for all firms. It is usually designed for unincorporated businesses, or Chapter C and Chapter S corporations.

Commissions Can Help Cautious Companies Expand Fast

Some companies start with a distinctive product. Then they develop a distinctive compensation plan to sell the product. National Safety Associates of Memphis, Tennessee, made a small home water filtration unit. No "high tech" or fancy appearance, the moderately priced unit looks like a chubby thermos jug. But NSA knew it was ideal for turning tap water into the softer, tastier liquid—just like spring water—people were grabbing off shelves in fancy bottles during the 1980s. NSA saw a big and booming potential market. What were the risks? The company had been privately held and debt free for most of its history.

NSA went to a multilevel sales force, most of which was on 100 percent commission. Salespeople demonstrated the filters directly to consumers and booked the sale. The company then shipped the product out of its Memphis warehouse directly to the customer. Some salespeople worked only part-time for modest incomes. Others, active and successful at full-time selling, moved up to become regional or national marketing directors. They got a commission on their own sales plus a cut on their recruits' sales. Unlike other such companies, this was a sales organization with products going directly from the company to the customer—no warehousing of stockpiles in down-the-line garages.

Sales of the chubby jugs—and other NSA air and water filtration systems—grew by 3,000 percent, according to company spokespeople. NSA went public and began broadening into Europe and Canada with a diversified line of environmental, safety, and educational products. Commission-only sales helped take the company into the mainstream market and actually fed its growth.

Look At the Jobs That Really Need Doing

Since salespeople are not lone eagles, what about compensating the sales support staff—all those fine folks who keep the home office fires burning? Some companies look at all the tasks needed to get and keep their products in the market and then motivate everybody involved in doing just that. ESP Software Services, Inc., of Minneapolis sells jobs to people and vice versa. It places programmers, lawyers, accountants, and others with firms that need them. The $5 million annual business involves matching some very sophisticated position requirements with specialized individuals.

But, like most selling, job placement also requires lots of market contacts and frequent re-contact. "Everybody on ESP's 10-person office staff shares in performance or results compensation," explains president, Ray Davey. Administrative staff supporting marketing salespeople get a "dollar hit every time somebody is placed.

The Human Resources person has to do orientation and W-4's so they get a cash kicker, too." Compensation of technical staff at ESP has been activity-based for two years.

The company measures and rewards daily calls to potential job candidates, visits to client companies, and developing new leads.

Because of its business, ESP can even "motivate the product." Davey has 75 consultants, the specialists ESP places with firms. ESP offers them an opportunity to work for a straight annual salary—or a salary plus higher hourly rate, depending on how much they are used.

Look At All the Salespeople

Ameritech, a spin-off from AT&T, has all 60,000 employees in its performance incentive plan. The company heavily compensates its "pure sellers" by commissions, according to director of Human Resources, Harry Malone. These are the consultative salespeople who work with big and ongoing accounts. But customer service salespeople also do a lot of selling.

They need to deal with the increasing variety of telephone services, and salespeople should be alert to a customer's personal or business requirements and think creatively about how Ameritech can profitably serve them. So incentives reward these salespeople for results and profits.

To determine if the company as a whole is meeting or exceeding service expectations, Ameritech also surveys customers regularly in 12 key areas. That helps determine management pay in units close to the customer. Ameritech even has a performance element in its union contracts with service and technical staff.

All this is necessary, Harry Malone notes, because so many telephone employees come into contact with existing customers. These are mostly the people Ameritech will be trying to sell new services to in the future. It is an industry where almost all future prospects have been buying something from you for years. So everybody is a salesperson, to some degree.

Innovative compensation plans, like other changes, can start anywhere. But to make them work, managers must consider all the steps. In essence, a comprehensive compensation plan should tie the steps together in a way that works for the company and the sales force. That means: (1) matching sales rewards to company objectives and

(2) clearly focusing on the most important requirements for meeting those objectives. If you can check off both, you have instituted a dynamic, forward-thinking, and practical compensation program.

STEPS IN CREATING A BETTER SALES COMPENSATION PLAN

1. Decide on Major Company Objectives
   - *Example.* Think about future sales compensation based on customer satisfaction and contact activities.

Grow the business	Use revenue-based compensation
Profitability	Use profit-based compensation
Control risks	Make a shift toward commissions

2. Evaluate Requirements to Meet Objectives
   - *Example.* Think about forecasting customer needs; compensate for contacts and assess and reward results.

For early market penetration	Reward leads, prospects, contacts, and revenue
To broaden the market	Reward prospects and contacts
For customer satisfaction	Measure feedback and reward

3. Translate to Satisfy Salespeople's Objectives
   - *Example.* Think about high income; select, train, and compensate top salespeople on performance.

Future (retirement) income	Use deferred compensation
Capital appreciation	Use stock and stock options, perks, cars, expense terms, and so on
Steady income salary base	Use activity-based compensation

HOW TO PAY

Avoid These Seven Compensation Plan Pitfalls

Compensation is the biggest selling cost and by far the most important controllable factor in motivating your salespeople. According to Andris Zoltners, professor of marketing at Northwestern University's Kellogg School and managing director of ZS Associates, Evanston, Illinois, retaining your best performers should be the first goal of a good sales compensation plan. "It must keep the good salespeople, not just any salespeople," says Zoltners.

Just as critically, the good salespeople must be motivated to seek exactly the same goals as the company seeks. "The compensation plan signals the intent of the company, if it's done right," Zoltners explains. "Hopefully, it's a win–win situation."

That can be tricky. "Compensation is always throwing curves at you," Zoltners says. "There isn't a comp plan anywhere that you can't game." Gaming means salespeople figure out how to win at the plan, but the company does not gain much.

Zoltners lists seven common traps in compensation:

1. *Tying individual reps' compensation to customer satisfaction surveys.* Usually, survey results are unreliable at the one-rep level, and reps may give up value for a good customer rating.
2. *Windfall gains, or "compensation monsters."* Reps should not receive big rewards due to external factors. Here is an example from Zoltners: "I sell advertising, and I get a call from Sony. Right away, I pick up $2 million for selling 15 full-page ads." The hefty commission on those sales does not reward effort, it costs the company plenty and it may embitter other ad reps. Examine the volatility of your historical results before you tie commissions to sales, Zoltners advises. Where results are highly volatile—indicating external factors at work—the payout curve should be adjusted to remove the potential unfairness.
3. *Committing to a plan without a good forecast.* Zoltners remembers the start-up phase of the pacemaker market. "The companies hired people whom they thought were really aggressive and gave them nice compensation plans with high upside potential." That made sense initially. The companies had to establish themselves quickly in a promising new market. Sales worked out even better than the companies' forecasts said they would. "The reps just blew away the numbers, they were earning three- and four-figure incomes," Zoltners recalls. Of course, "there were

stock prices windfalls" for investors, so the companies were not unhappy, at first. Then the pacemaker market matured toward a commodity market with slimmer profits and pricing power. Those high sales incomes had become an expectation. "You can't take it away from them, it's an entitlement," Zoltners says. The lesson: forecast your future as well as your current market position so that you can plan for affordable compensation, and let your reps know what is coming up.

4. *Not understanding what your turnover rates mean.* Turnover rates for salespeople average about 18 percent a year in the United States, somewhat higher in a good economy, a bit lower in a recession. In either case, being right on the average is not a good sign for a company that wants to build experience and develop customer relationships. If a company pays a lot of attention to hiring well, Zoltners thinks a turnover rate of 5 to 10 percent could signal happy, effective salespeople in a typical industry. If it is much below that, you may just have stale salespeople.

5. *Extremes on the payout curve.* Plot the payouts to individual reps just for the incentive portions of their compensation. "If I get people making $80,000 above salary and other people making $5,000, I've got a problem," Zoltners says. "This difference cannot be attributed to the people." The obvious place to look is at the sales potential of the assigned territories. Studies consistently show actual sales correlate the best with potential sales, not any other factor. Your reps know this. According to Zoltners, "Salespeople kill for territory." In theory, you could set different goals for different territories and then compensate on goal achievement. Zoltners says this theory is not workable. "Goal setting is a pain in itself. They will battle you on goals." His solution is blunt: "I think you have to give everybody an equal opportunity to succeed. When you pay commissions, get the territory alignment right first."

6. *Paying unnecessarily for "teamwork."* Paying salespeople based on team results is a current trend. Zoltners thinks it can be overdone. "The caveat is that often sales is not a team sport. If you tie me to a team result, I've got to look out for the free riders," he warns. "If team sales are just the sum of individual sales, why compensate for team results?" How about mutual assistance among salespeople? "My view is that should always be part of the culture—you help one another," Zoltners responds.

7. *Providing incentives to managers ineffectively.* The best reps or district managers are often promoted to senior sales management positions. Often, they are compensated with higher salaries but the same commission plans. Thus, according to Zoltners, the true upside potential for the new manager may be reduced. "What happens is, managers have good reps and poor reps. Say, good reps go 20 percent over

quota, but poor reps just hit 90 percent of the quota. The manager may have, on average, just about a 3 percent swing in his [or her] compensation, much less than he [or she] is used to." Take a very close look at managers' compensation plans in light of their importance and the necessity of maximizing incentives so the whole team performs well.

SALES COMPENSATION FORMULAS FOR SALESPEOPLE

Variable Commission

Base salary: $30,000
Commission: monthly
Target pay: $60,000, uncapped

% of Quota	% of Sales Dollar		
	Prod A	Prod B	Prod C
0–100%	3%	5%	9%
101%+	5%	7%	12%

Comments: The mix is 50/50 with a progressive ramp after 100 percent of quota. The strengths of this formula are its simplicity and the fact that it drives the "right" sales volume. The weakness is that, ultimately, sales representatives still can choose what to sell.

Straight Commission

Base salary: none
Commission: monthly
Target pay: $60,000, uncapped

% of Quota	% of Sales Dollar
0–100%	4%
101%+	7%

Comments: The mix is 0/100 with a progressive ramp after 100 percent of quota is met. The strengths of this formula are its simplicity and its ability to drive volume. The weaknesses are that it can result in under- or overpayment, and it may lead to over-selling the customers.

Linked Plan

Base salary: $42,000
Commission: monthly
Target pay: $60,000, uncapped
Commission rate on all
    sales: 6%

Quarterly Profit Incentive	
Gross Profit	Commission Dollar Level
15%	0%
20%	10%
25%	25%

Comments: The mix is 70/30 with no ramping of commission. The strength of this formula is that it links two measures: the payout of quarterly bonuses with commission earnings. The weakness is that it may be too complicated.

Adjusted-Value Commission Point Plan

Base salary: $42,000
Commission: monthly
Target pay: $60,000, uncapped

Product	Point Value/Unit (each point equals 10 cents)
A	5
B	8
C	6
D	10
E	2

Comments: The mix is 70/30 with no ramping. The strength of this formula is it addresses multiple objectives by varying payout by product. The weakness is that including too many products can dilute the sales focus.

EXPERT ADVICE

End Performance Evaluation Anxiety

As a manager, you probably view the performance-review process in one of two ways: It's either (1) an opportunity to engage your staff, highlight strengths, and work on weaknesses to move members of the organization forward toward mutually agreed-upon goals; or (2) a torturous parade of confrontations, each more harrowing and vitriolic than the last. The truth be told, your experience probably lies somewhere in between.

To shape up your performance reviews to bring them more in line with "1" above, make objectivity a key goal of the process. The following are five tips for evaluating with an even hand.

(*Continued on next page.*)

(*Continued from previous page.*)

1. *Keep it simple.* Rather than getting into expansive, detailed analyses of an employee's performance dating back to the Nixon administration, focus on pertinent, recent information. Also, avoid considering dozens of different criteria that may only serve to confuse the issue.

2. *Outsource.* Get input on the employee's performance from others in the organization who are in a position to make an assessment—peers, subordinates, clients, etc.—as well as the employee you're evaluating. These appraisals will help expose your biases and confirm your valid opinions.

3. *Keep the evaluation meter running.* Throughout the year, use a quick and easy short-term evaluation system you can constantly update and add to. Then come appraisal time you will have a database of information to draw from.

4. *Have a metric system.* What are the traits and behaviors your organization values most highly? Find ways to work these characteristics into the performance assessments and you will generate more impartial evaluations.

5. *Put in the time.* One common problem with performance assessments is a lack of data caused by managers who spend too little time with employees to produce quality evaluations. Consider whether you need to make a greater effort to be with your salespeople to gain a more nuanced understanding of their strengths and weaknesses.

—From David DeVries and the coauthors of
Performance Appraisal on the Line.

Chapter 15

Best Practices in Sales Management

WINNING STRATEGIES FOR KEEPING PRODUCTIVITY AND SALES AT THEIR PEAK

Many companies implement standard operating procedures to ensure that salespeople stick to one proven, effective selling system. As time passes, though, methods that once yielded big sales may grow outdated and ineffective. To keep pace with fast changes in your business or industry, you need to review and revise selling practices. Take a close look at your selling methods in all five phases of the selling process, then make changes to help keep your salespeople a cut above the competition.

1. Assessment

To make changes that stimulate sales and productivity, companies must analyze the pros and cons of current practices. Start with questionnaires to gather feedback and manager, salesperson, and customer opinion on company products and practices. Be sure to choose and word questions carefully—their quality determines how well you'll be able to analyze responses and make changes that ensure future success.

The salesperson's questionnaire might ask: What do you sell? Who are your customers? or How do you qualify prospects? Assessments that measure sales process both qualitatively and quantitatively offer a clearer picture of performance.

Customer questionnaires should ask thought-provoking questions to find out why your customers buy from your company, what they like about your service, and what you need to improve. Customers often buy for unusual reasons, so their answers may shed new light on how to improve practices.

To ensure feedback and original ideas from different perspectives, distribute questionnaires to old, big-budget customers and new, more conservative buyers, and all levels of salespeople and management. It doesn't take a veteran manager, a top-performing salesperson, or a million-dollar customer to contribute the ideas that make a difference. Gather all the responses, then compare and evaluate to reach a consensus on the changes to be made.

2. Analysis

Good assessment identifies strengths and weaknesses; good analysis gives you the reasons behind them. Customer feedback often tells you exactly what's wrong (product not delivered on time, customer felt pressured into buying) so managers know immediately how they can make changes to prevent future problems.

Skills and performance analysis poses a greater challenge, because so many factors—motivation, amount and type of training, selling experience, personality, stress, health—can affect a salesperson's performance. To analyze assessment results accurately, ask yourself why your team excels in certain areas and struggles in others.

Your analysis should describe the nature and extent of problems and possible solutions. Look for patterns in the responses to different assessment questions, and ask yourself what might cause them. A pattern of low closing performance may indicate rusty closing skills. Do your salespeople ask for the order? Do they know a variety of closes and how to use them?

If prospecting is a problem, make sure they know how to network, ask for referrals, and cold call effectively or overcome an attack of call reluctance. To help maintain great performance, find out why your salespeople excel in certain areas and create the conditions that foster success.

3. Modeling

After you've carefully analyzed your assessment results, you should have some clear ideas on how to design a sales model—an outline of the selling practices that provide optimum results. Analysis should reveal what works for your sales team and what doesn't—information you can use to recommend effective strategies and techniques for each phase of the selling process. Keep it simple.

The best sales models are prescriptive, easy to understand, and easy to remember. Pay attention to all phases of the selling cycle: prospecting, qualifying, presentation, closing, follow-up, etc., and include techniques of the outstanding performers in each area to design your model. Offer a variety of proven strategies to suit different salespeople and different customers.

To give your model greater impact, customize it with your company's product names. Provide specific instructions on how to implement the selling techniques you choose and examples that illustrate their correct use. Distribute a document outlining the model to your team and make sure they read and follow it.

4. Implementation

You can conduct painstaking assessment and analysis of your salespeople to build the perfect selling model, but to make your efforts pay off, your team must use it.

Talk to your salespeople about how you expect the model to help them and how they should implement it. They're the ones who have to use it, so give them a chance to air their concerns and opinions. Encourage them to adopt the model by showing them that it's based on carefully collected feedback and conclusions drawn from that feedback.

Make the change positive and exciting—a contest or other incentive adds an instant element of fun and motivation and may help change your team's perception of the model for the better.

Set new goals with your salespeople and tell them how much greater their sales potential is now that they're using a model based on the most profitable selling practices. Reassure them that they'll have your support and guidance throughout the process of learning to sell with the new model, and that you'll be monitoring their performance.

5. Measurement

After all the time and energy you've invested in updating and improving your team's selling practices, make sure you know how well your efforts pay off. Before you implement the selling model, let your salespeople know how you'll measure their progress.

To find out exactly how well your team adapts to the model and how sales are improving, track and measure performance carefully. Introduce the new model, then compare sales from the two subsequent quarters to sales from the same quarters last year. You could also compare number of appointments, closing ratios, sales profitability, and sales cycle length.

Frequent measurements allow you to keep close tabs on improvements and help show you where your team needs more practice or coaching. Accuracy counts. Keep thorough, careful performance records on all of your salespeople.

Many selling principles or techniques—customer concern, honesty, persistence—are timeless, but others need frequent evaluation to make sure they still get results. The more quickly your customers, market, and industry change, the more often you should examine selling practices to help you keep up.

Instead of abandoning ineffective methods, try modifying them to fit your present selling situation. Bring your selling strategies up-to-date to make sure that the techniques that worked well in your past don't hold you back today.

TEAMING WITH TROUBLE

Harvey Mackay's Five Sure-Fire Methods for Undermining Your Own Sales Organization

As one of the nation's most sought-after business speakers and authors, Harvey Mackay has become a legendary source of some of the most cogent professional advice around. In his bestseller, *Pushing the Envelope: All the Way to the Top*, Mackay paradoxically offers five guaranteed tips for *ruining* a perfectly good sales force.

1. *Hire more reps.* Many business owners figure that adding salespeople will naturally increase sales. But it doesn't work that way. Adding new salespeople without adding new territories will diminish the original reps' total sales, thereby alienating the very people who helped make you successful.
2. *Have an earnings ceiling.* Salespeople should never have a cap on their earnings. Yet many companies won't let salespeople earn more than the CEO. The message: You're second-class citizens, and it's more important not to step on the CEO's toes than to let you reach your full potential. Good CEOs are happy when the rain-makers earn what they deserve, no matter whose nose gets out of joint.
3. *Hold death-march meetings.* Show me a sales rep who likes sales meetings and I'll show you a rep who can't sell. Meetings should be exciting, targeted, and unpredictable. Make them valuable for every member of your team, but don't put people through a tedious ringer in a vain effort to show them who's in charge.
4. *Promote dead weight.* The sales manager's position is no place to hide your incompetent brother-in-law. Effective salespeople who are ashamed to introduce customers to the boss will take their talents elsewhere—quite possibly to the competition.
5. *Shower them with paperwork.* Salespeople aren't accountants or bookkeepers—they don't like paperwork. Are your reps so laden with detailed record keeping that they barely have time to sell? Why not set them free to do what they're here for? As a test, ask yourself how many orders resulted from your most recent paper-heavy scheme or idea.

Chapter 16

Managing with Psychology

HARNESS THE POWER OF THE MIND TO CLOSE MORE SALES

Sales experts often talk about the importance of understanding the needs of their customers and prospects. By this they usually mean business needs or product needs. While these needs are important, there's another area of needs that goes virtually unnoticed on many sales calls—the mental needs of your customers.

If you could understand the way your customers and prospects think, how their brains work, and what their minds need to make decisions, you could be one step ahead on the closing cycle.

Think of it this way: If you could crawl inside the mind of your customers and look around at how their brains work, perhaps you would be able to pinpoint your presentation, address unstated concerns, unlock real objections, and cement real relationships that lead to committed partnerships. All that, if you could just get inside the mind of your customer. Well, now you can.

According to Dr. Jeffrey Schwartz, research professor of psychiatry at the UCLA School of Medicine and author of *The Mind and the Brain*, a better understanding of how the brain works can teach you a lot about the critical role of attention in the sales process. It can also show you how to create habits that will make you a better salesperson. Once you have this new understanding of how the brain works, you'll understand why walking into a prospect's office and just talking about your product won't hack it.

To become more effective at selling, Schwartz says, salespeople should understand two areas of the brain his research highlights. These are (1) the *prefrontal cortex*, which processes information, and (2) the *caudate nucleus*, which can be used to train yourself to do activities you don't want to do but know you should. He isn't advocating a deep, clinical understanding of these areas; rather, he points out that when you have a basic comprehension of what's happening in the brain during the sales process, you'll be more likely to ask the right types of questions and deliver the right information at the right time to close the sale. Here's how it works.

May I Have Your Attention Please?

Schwartz's work primarily has focused on obsessive compulsive disorder (OCD) patients, but it turns out OCD offers a model that helps answer many of the questions about the mind and the brain. For instance, one of Schwartz's most compelling observations is about the role of attention. He writes, "It is now clear that the attentional state of the brain produces physical change in its structure and future functioning. The seemingly simple act of 'paying attention' produces real and powerful physical changes in the brain." Such an observation can help an OCD patient to recognize that directed mental force could cause changes in the brain that ultimately may help overcome the disorder. But apply the observation to sales and you'll realize something remarkable—namely, that when a prospect is truly paying attention to your presentation, his brain is physically changing. Talk about making an impact on a client!

It all comes down to an area of the brain called the *prefrontal cortex*. This area, located at the front of the brain behind your forehead, is what Schwartz calls the "executive center of the brain." It's the primary information-processing area, and it's used when you think about something. Whether you're adding a column of figures, weighing the merits of going camping or shopping this weekend, or evaluating two different CRM applications, it's your prefrontal cortex that's doing the heavy lifting. With that in mind, your mission as a salesperson is to get clients to use their prefrontal cortices. After all, you need your prospects to think about your product and your proposal if they are ultimately going to buy it.

So how do you activate the prefrontal cortex? Attention. Specifically, you need to gain the prospect's motivated attention to have any hope of closing the sale, but it's not as easy as it sounds. Motivated attention is about more than having a person's eyes and ears. It's about illuminating his or her mind. And the longer you can do that—the longer you can hold people's attention—the more literal, physical impact you're going to have on their brain circuitry, says Schwartz. "Just being in front of people is not enough to make their brains respond. You need to engage their value systems," he says.

Dr. Kevin Hogan, president of www.kevinhogan.com, author of *The Psychology of Persuasion*, and an expert in the neuropsychology of selling, says three things have to happen for attention—or brain arousal, as he calls it—to take place. First, there has to be some kind of emotional stimulus. "If you want arousal, you have to have an emotional impact," says Hogan. "The brain won't pay attention to anything that doesn't have emotional impact."

Second, you have to get the reticular activating system in the brain engaged. That, says Hogan, is the part that picks up the things worth paying attention to—the car that looks exactly like yours, the guy on Wall Street with the purple hair. Generally, these things are novel, seem familiar, or affect your survival. Third, you have to get the buyer cognitively involved in the process. "You have to have thought, cognition," he says. "The thinking part is where people talk themselves into justifying the purchase of what you're selling."

As if it weren't challenging enough to incorporate all those elements into your sales pitch, keep in mind that you're competing for the prospect's attention with everything else in—and often outside—the room. At any given second, says Hogan, there are roughly a million bits of information going into the brain. Those million bits are more than just the biggies like the ringing phone and the secretary popping in to let your prospect know an important meeting is about to start. You're also competing with the sound of the car going by outside the window, the ticking of the second hand on the wall clock, the distraction of your necktie being slightly askew. And you need to compete because, of those million bits, Hogan says, we can only focus on 126 of them, give or take 40 percent. "You'll have impressions or feelings about the other 999,874. But you won't really remember any details except about those things for which you had arousal."

Schwartz makes the same point in *The Mind and the Brain*. "We go through our lives 'seeing' countless objects that we do not pay attention to," he says. "Without attention, the image does not register in the mind and may not be stored even briefly in memory." Our minds, he adds, "have a limited ability to process information about multiple objects at any given time."

The Power of Questions

The salesperson's challenge, then, is to become one of the few objects on which the prospect focuses his or her attention. Remember—if you're going to activate the prefrontal cortex and start making those crucial brain wiring changes that are the precursor to a buying decision, you need motivated attention. And the single best way to achieve it, the experts say, is by asking questions that light up the brain and get the prospect really thinking, thereby getting him or her involved in the sales process.

Jeffrey Gitomer, a leading sales trainer and founder of Charlotte, North Carolina–based BuyGitomer, Inc., has long understood this concept. "My ability to gain attention is determined by my ability to ask intelligent, thought-provoking questions," he says. "I call them power questions. They're questions about other people that make them stop and think. I don't want them to regurgitate facts; I want them to think."

Say, for instance, that you sell copy machines. Chances are, your prospects already have a good idea of what copiers do, so walking in and telling them about your machines is unlikely to gain their attention, which means you won't be making them think, won't be activating their prefrontal cortices, and probably won't get to a yes. The same is true if you ask mundane questions about the types of copiers they use now and what kind of service they're getting. Those are just facts. But what if you can get your prospects to consider the humble copy machine from a perspective they've never considered? For example, what if you could get them to think about copiers as a reflection of their business?

Gitomer says he might approach prospects with a question such as, When a customer gets a copy from you, what do you want them to think about your company? Or, When you have received substandard copies from a business, what have you concluded about that enterprise? "I want them to think 'image' not 'copy.' I want them to think about the copy as a reflection of their business," Gitomer explains. The key word there is *think*. Those kinds of questions get prospects thinking. And when you can do that, you've got their attention.

Get in Gear

The other part of the brain salespeople will find useful to understand, Schwartz says, is an area called the *caudate nucleus*, which, if you're looking at a left side profile of the brain, is located just northwest of center. This is the area that can help you create a habit, whether it be going to the gym every morning, flossing your teeth every night, or cold calling prospects on a regular basis.

Think of the caudate nucleus as a big gearbox, says Schwartz. If you can force yourself to do something repeatedly, such as making 10 cold calls every morning beginning at 9:00 a.m., you'll essentially be creating a gear for the task. After a couple of weeks of doing the task consistently, you'll find that two things will happen: first, you'll begin doing the task without even thinking about it and second, if you try to skip it, you'll find you'll miss it. "You'll find it will get to that time of day and you'll feel like you should be making those cold calls," says Schwartz. "It gets to the point where, even if you don't like doing it, you'll miss it." And when you get to that point, you've created a habit. He cautions, though, that if you really don't like doing a task, it doesn't take skipping more than a couple sessions to get out of the habit, so consistency is key.

The phenomenon can be likened to bringing a grandfather clock into your home. If you've ever done that, you know that for the first few weeks, the slow tick-tocking and deep chimes can distract you during the day and wake you up, crazed with frustration, in the middle of the night. After a couple of weeks, however, you won't even notice the sounds anymore. Eventually, it will come to the point that if you stop the clock, you'll miss it. Habits like cold calling every morning work the same way, thanks to the caudate nucleus.

Carrie Beam made that discovery shortly after she started her own business, Carrie Beam Consulting, an enterprise based in the San Francisco Bay area that offers services in data mining, performance measures, and decision support. With no clients and lots of bills, she recognized that she needed to start dialing if she was to have any hope of getting the business off the ground. For the first few weeks, she spent most of her day and all of her energy cold calling prospects. At the end of the day, she frequently was exhausted, frustrated, and still client-less.

Then Beam modified her approach to cold calling. She decided she would do the task for one hour each day—from 7:30 a.m. to 8:30 a.m.—and no more. The night before, she would set out her list of contacts, their phone numbers, background information on their companies, and her script. And she would call 10 people, then call it a day.

Establishing that routine turned things around. For starters, she was able to bypass gatekeepers and catch many of her target prospects in the office. And by completing her cold calling early in the day, she found she didn't spend the rest of the day dreading it and so had more energy to pour into other aspects of her company. "The one hour a day has been the lifeblood of my business," says Beam.

In essence, Beam has created a "gear" for her cold calling. You can do the same thing with going to the gym, writing thank-you notes to your clients—whatever habit you want to establish. So the brain is complex, but understanding how it can help you in the sales process doesn't have to be. Get the prospect truly thinking, and your chances of making the sale skyrocket. Need to establish a cold calling habit? Create a "gear" in your brain for it. It's that simple. And it's worth every bit of your attention.

EXPERT ADVICE

Use Psychology to Increase Your Confidence in Selling

Cognitive dissonance is a psychological term that clearly explains some of the problems salespeople experience, problems like call reluctance, low closing success, and job turnover.

Simply stated, *cognitive dissonance* means that an inner conflict occurs when a person views behavior that is expected of him or her to be inconsistent with his or her ability or values. And often this conflict negates or torpedoes creative performance.

To salespeople, this means that when they view the sales process or their expected sales behavior as being inconsistent with their values or skills, a conflict results that derails their effectiveness. We see this destructive force at work in many sales organizations.

With this in mind, let's think for a few moments about these two subjects:

1. What causes conflicts within salespeople?
2. How is their performance damaged?

Recent studies have found that where the sales process is taught to salespeople as a bag of tricks or gimmicks, a natural dissonance results. Even in the most manipulative selling, salespeople don't feel good about what they're asked to do to people. They feel an inner conflict.

This dissonance causes an extremely high rate of turnover. That's how salespeople ordinarily deal with the conflict. Where salespeople aren't taught to regard customers' wants or needs, but to sell them whatever they can sell them, a dissonance results.

This dissonance increases call reluctance and a failure to ask closing questions. Most of the time when salespeople are taught strategies and techniques, with little regard for ethics, their selling becomes manipulative. And ... manipulative selling causes cognitive dissonance.

(*Continued on next page.*)

(Continued from previous page.)

On the other hand, when salespeople are taught values and ethics—when they see the sales process as creating value for people—they tend to feel good about themselves and what they are doing for others.

Then the result of this value-focused selling is congruence, the quality of agreeing or coinciding. The salespeople feel good about themselves. They feel good about what they're doing. They feel good about feeling good!

A result of this integrity selling is that salespeople experience reduced call reluctance as well as reduced job turnover. They want to share what they have with people because they know that people will respect them and eventually be glad they dealt with them. Their performance is enhanced.

Here are three suggestions that will reduce salesperson conflict and increase confidence:

1. View the sales process as one that creates value for people—a process where you do something for and with someone instead of to someone.
2. Set goals that specifically state the value you'll create for customers.
3. Take regular inventory of the value you've created for real people in the past.

These suggestions can help you develop a positive mind-set. As you internalize these ideas and they become values you possess, your selling habits will be influenced.

You'll feel better about yourself. This will translate into greater self-confidence, which will translate into increased customer respect.

—From Ron Willingham, author of *The Best Seller:*
The New Psychology of Selling.
He works as a sales and
marketing consultant conducting
Psychology of Selling and Goal-Achievement seminars.

DIARY OF A SALES PSYCHOLOGIST: BY DR. DONALD J. MOINE

The loneliness and parental harangues combined with excessive drinking and drug use pulled Bill down into a maelstrom of self-pity and doubt. Here is his true story.

Bill stared into the darkness and saw the clock's reflection in his bedroom mirror. It was past 2 a.m. and still he didn't feel like going to sleep. The thought of his breakfast sales appointment with a wealthy prospect sent a shiver down his spine.

"I've got to be rested for this one," Bill thought, but a nagging voice inside reminded him he was never able to sleep on nights like this. He decided to do a few more lines of cocaine and watch another movie on cable TV.

He fell asleep two hours later and woke up with a start just after six o'clock. After taking a quick shower, pulling on his custom-made suit, and rushing for his downtown breakfast meeting, his own reflection in the restaurant's window caught Bill's eye. He was surprised by how good he looked. "Good genes," he congratulated himself, "No one will ever know."

He thought his presentation was much better than it actually was. Near the end of the hour, he realized his timing was off, he was talking excessively and nervously, and had asked few questions. He felt an urgency to close but sensed he wouldn't succeed. He was right. The prospect was completely cold, and Bill didn't know what to do. "I've lost the touch," Bill mumbled to himself as he slumped out of the restaurant. "I don't know how to light the fire anymore. I've got to get back in shape."

Bill dropped the drugs and began to exercise fanatically. He joined two health spas and played racquetball almost daily. He read self-help books and primers on power closing techniques. However, his sales slump persisted and he still couldn't sleep at night.

His sales manager was becoming alarmed at Bill's decline in productivity. He talked with Bill and offered good advice. He coached Bill on prospecting, on qualifying prospects, on doing powerful sales presentations, and on closing—all the basics. He gave Bill pep talks. Still the slump dragged on. Months passed with no sales. The sales manager began to feel guilty whenever he saw Bill. He knew Bill was using up the last of his savings and would soon be completely broke. Eventually he gave up and avoided seeing or talking with Bill as much as possible.

Bill felt worse than ever. He knew his manager had tried to help and had given up in exasperation. "What's wrong with me?" Bill asked himself over and over.

Finally Bill's company called in an industrial psychologist who specialized in working with troubled sales executives.

Bill approached the first session with great suspicion. He knew he needed help, but he wasn't sure a "shrink" could assist him in solving his problems.

Nine months earlier, Bill's girlfriend, Jean, had walked out on him. He thought of Jean obsessively and begged and pleaded with her to return, even proposing marriage. Jean had found a new boyfriend and laughed cruelly at Bill, stating flatly she had lost all interest in him.

Bill traced the beginning of his depression to his breakup with Jean. However, there were other, earlier signals of danger. Bill's parents had been calling frequently to suggest Bill leave sales and return to the "respectable" profession of accounting for which he was trained. The loneliness and parental harangues, combined with excessive drinking and drug usage, had pulled Bill down into a maelstrom of self-pity and doubt.

During his first visit with the industrial psychologist, Bill was surprised he wasn't asked to reveal his entire life story and all his secrets. Instead, he was put through two hours of testing and psychological assessment.

Bill found the procedure fascinating. He asked himself questions and examined issues that had remained buried for years. Bill was even anxious to see the test results. "I wonder if they'll be able to find out what's going on inside me?" Bill mused to himself.

During the second session, Bill and the industrial psychologist went over the results. "These tests are frighteningly accurate," Bill blurted out at one point during the session. It amazed him that any tests, even ones he himself had filled out, could be so accurate.

Bill's strengths and weaknesses were pinpointed. The tests measured extroversion, leadership, self-acceptance, stress tolerance, energy, well-being, competitiveness, reserve, self-esteem, optimism, honesty, and guardedness. In addition, his motivations were examined, including need to be active, need to be correct, desire to do the exceptional, need to stay impersonal, need to have close personal relationships, desire to meet and make new friends, need to be noticed, need to have status, need to be respected, and desire to maximize team effectiveness.

Bill was surprised that the tests did not ask about his early upbringing, religious beliefs, or attitudes towards sex. "These questions are basically tests of my strengths," Bill noted, "and all this is related to my work performance."

Bill measured well in most dimensions, compared to other salespeople in his field. Since there is a large database of over 40,000 people for the sophisticated H.R. Chally tests that Bill had taken, results can be given percentile comparisons. The tests pinpointed Bill's weaknesses and indicated the improvements needed. Overall, Bill found the tests' results reassuring. The task of recovery and the return to excellence now seemed manageable.

For the second part of the assessment, the industrial psychologist went on actual sales calls with Bill. The psychologist, who had himself worked as a salesman for nine years, noticed a strikingly consistent sales style. Bill didn't read his customers well. He used nearly the same approach on all prospects. He lacked flexibility and self-awareness.

While his presentation covered all the basics, it lacked a persuasive or motivating force. It also lacked mathematical "dollars and sense" justification. Ultimately, the canned presentation only increased Bill's stress level, as it failed to bring in orders no matter how loudly or persistently it was delivered.

From seeing and listening to Bill's actual sales calls, the sales psychologist learned that Bill was weak in handling questions, stalls, and objections. While he occasionally came up with brilliant ways of handling particular stalls or objections, he failed to write down any of his lines. Consequently, he usually forgot his own "best material" on the next call and doomed himself to reinventing the wheel time and again.

The assessment results from the tests and the ride-along calls were used to tailor a therapeutic action plan. Bill took specific training in neurolinguistic programming methods of reading prospects. He was coached by the psychologist in persuasive language techniques, in how to use sales arithmetic to prove financial benefits, and was assisted in writing a sales script book of his own most powerful ways of handling questions, stalls, and objections. In addition, he was taught a quick effective method of self-hypnosis, combined with meditation, which enabled him to relax deeply at night, and he now slept soundly without the aid of chemicals or alcohol.

Did it work? How successful were the interventions? While a few of the personal details of this case have been changed, the financial facts that follow are precise. Bill had gone nine months without a sale. After the program, he began to pick up a few orders, and his income went from nothing to several thousand dollars a month. June of 1982 was a breakthrough month. Bill earned approximately $30,000 in commissions. But even this didn't prepare Bill or his manager for July's performance.

Bill was no longer a problem salesman, but both he and his sales manager decided to voluntarily continue the intervention program with the industrial psychologist. The issue was no longer one of making a living. Bill now wanted to make a killing. He felt in his heart he deserved the money and he was willing to work as hard as necessary to make it. And, importantly, he was in one of the areas of selling in which it is genuinely possible to make a financial killing.

There was one major problem left. Bill was afraid to call on the CEOs and top lawyers and physicians who could place the big orders he needed to make the maximum commissions. In strategic psychological counseling sessions, Bill's fear of rejection, his fear of power figures, and his procrastination were dealt with.

Bill prioritized all his accounts and prospects and set up a "Top 10 Hit List." His growing sales script book, containing his most powerful and persuasive lines, gave him increasing self-confidence in dealing with top executives and professionals. The big orders started coming in.

On July 15, Bill set a sales record that neither he nor his industrial psychologist is ever going to forget. On that day, he earned $48,000 in personal commissions. During the entire year, he earned more than he had earned in the previous 10 years of his working life combined.

How do I know this case so well? I was the industrial psychologist.

(Dr. Donald J. Moine, listed in *Who's Who in Business and Finance*, is a member of the American Psychological Association's Division of Industrial and Organizational Psychologists. A consultant and sales psychologist to Fortune 500 companies, Dr. Moine is the president of the American Association for the Advancement of Communications Training in Redondo Beach, California.)

Chapter 17

Navigating Change Management

BE A CHANGE AGENT

Management Guru Peter Senge Reveals How to Make Change Work for Your Company

Nobody wants to change. Yet change marks the American way of business more than any other single element. Note the Industrial Revolution, the communications revolution, and the technological revolution. Not to mention the Web. With all the changes over the past hundred years, you'd think that managers and workers would have gotten used to continual change in markets and methods.

Yet the facts tell a different story.

The nation's corporate highways are littered with the wrecks of hundreds of failed management-driven corporate transformation programs. Studies show that the disaster rate for total quality management and corporate reengineering initiatives hovers at around 70 percent, with only a small fraction rated as "very successful."

Look Out Below

So how does a company create positive long-term organizational change? According to Peter Senge, MIT professor and author of the fabulously popular *Fifth Discipline* book series, the issue is not merely an unwillingness to change. Among the many factors that contribute to organizational stagnation, he says, is that people neglect to look below the surface.

"We tend to look at problems at a very symptomatic level," Senge explains. "As a result we waste our time fixing those symptoms instead of sustaining significant inquiry and trying to build understanding of the deeper problems. In any complex system, you can always do a lot to improve things in the short term. But usually they have no impact in the long term and maybe even make things worse in the long term. So we end up with a whole new set of symptoms, and then we occupy ourselves, again, dealing with symptoms. It's a huge vicious cycle for keeping everybody busy doing very trivial things."

At the same time, Senge notes, when people do make these sorts of small, incremental changes, they feel that since something is being done, the problem has been solved and everything can return to normal. This, he says, is how complacency sets in.

"People get to feel that they have the answers," he says, "and that they can keep doing what they're doing. We tend to think, 'Well, this is the way we've always done things; this is the way we'll always do things.' Everybody becomes resigned. Even the things that people hate about their organizations—the stress, the game playing, the politics—they won't change in any substantive way. So it isn't just complacency about things we like and are comfortable with, it's also complacency around things we don't like."

Senge views this complacency as more than just a personal problem shared by many; he finds the roots of our cultural malaise in the American educational system.

Learning Philosophy

"It is terribly important that we start recognizing the connection between the way the institutions we create work and the way schools operate," he says. "In school we are introduced to a philosophy of learning that's all about getting the right answers and avoiding wrong answers. Learning becomes about 'knowing things' and if we don't know, pretending that we do. Learning becomes a big game of pretending that we are competent, pretending that we know. The consequence is that we destroy the innate curiosity and risk-taking behavior that all of us displayed as children. All children are curious and risk-takers. Children don't start with the notion that there are right and wrong answers—they start off with the notion that the world is a mysterious place.

"So as adults we live as the by-products of that contamination. We're all still waiting for the answer. And all that kills a willingness to take risks and kills our natural curiosity."

Anti-Learning

Senge adds that in our society's organizations and institutions, the people who fill the most senior and influential positions are the consummate products of what he calls "the system of anti-learning."

Though our risk-averse educational system and the leaders who perpetuate it may stack the odds against a change-driven organization, Senge suggests that there is a saving grace, a way to get back in touch with that childlike sense of wonder and curiosity: Have children of your own.

"Being a parent helps in two ways," he says. "The obvious one is that you get to be around young children and feel the tremendous curiosity and orientation toward experimenting. The second is that parenting is a great learning process because it is the quintessential setting where you really do know that you don't know. There are no right answers. Of course a tremendous amount of very useful research has been done, but when it comes right down to it, there are no simple answers. There is ambiguity, ambivalence, indecision, and messiness, and in that way it's a lot like leading an organization. But there's no boss, either. So we're not trying to prove ourselves to anyone else. And that helps you accept the ambiguity. I have found that this willingness to accept uncertainty is the key to learning."

According to Senge, there is another element that makes parenting an excellent model for organizational change: caring. Members of an organization should care about the company or institution's mission.

"As a parent," he says, "of course you always care. Caring is part of the whole compact. You care deeply about your children; you care deeply about their growth and development. That's a source of energy helping us confront the ambiguity. That caring attitude is equally important in any setting where learning is possible. It's a tremendous detriment when corporations act as if their purpose is maximizing shareholder return, because nobody really cares about that very much. It creates a context where deep caring is compromised.

"But if we are insightful about identifying the mission for which society really has a need, and if we're really competent in pursuing that mission, then the consequence of all of that is we get economic resources that allow us to stay in the game. Making money is terribly important, but it's not the purpose. It's the by-product of having a purpose."

Clear Mission

Inspiring people with a clearly defined mission or purpose is a leader's responsibility, Senge notes, adding that leaders today are often guilty of paying lip service to the idea of a mission statement without recognizing the power of purpose for organization-wide change.

"This is a timeless aspect of leadership," he says, "to help people make meaning of their situations, so they can discover where their genuine passion and commitment is. You can't manufacture commitment. Commitment comes when we are engaged in something that has real meaning for us."

Contrary to the traditional image of the powerful leader who commands troops like a field general, Senge suggests that today's effective leaders recognize their own shortcomings and openly pursue ambiguity.

"Besides having a real mission or purpose, what creates self-reinforcing change in an organization is an environment where people feel there is a degree of authenticity and where truth is not just a slogan we put on a corporate value statement," he says. "Leaders need to be willing to be wrong, to tell the truth about difficult situations. Shell CEO Phil Carroll put it beautifully. He said that his greatest learning lesson in six years as CEO was that his unique power and ability to influence the organization had to do with his willingness to be vulnerable, to be imperfect. He was willing to tell people, 'I don't know what the answer to this problem is.' As you can imagine, that can drive people nuts because they say, 'You're the boss. You're getting paid all this money. How can you not know?'

"But his experience points out that as a leader you have to put yourself in a position of vulnerability if you want to earn the trust of other people. The more you're in a position of hierarchical authority, the more this is true. It sort of turns the hierarchy on its ear. You can use your influence, not so much to provide the answer, but to get people focused on the right questions."

Thinking Unboxed

Beyond the lofty theories of change management, Senge also offers tactical advice for the leader eager to sustain the kind of outside-the-box thinking that characterizes a learning organization.

"The first rule of thumb is to be very open and broad," Senge advises. "If you have a favorite solution—where every job you've been in you went in and did X, Y, or Z—I would always be very suspicious of that. Because that's one thing that makes you closed to the specific situation you now face and where the best starting point might be.

"Second, look for colleagues who share your concerns and values. No individual working alone ever produces change. It's always the product of relationships, the two, three, or four people who share some real joint commitment that becomes a nucleus for a growing, larger purpose. I always worry when I see talented but isolated leaders trying to change an organization.

"Third, treat your own behavior, questions, and confusion as a source of learning. Often you need friends to help you do that, people who say, 'Bill, in that meeting I think I understand what you were trying to say, but what came across was very different from what you intended.' That's good because you can't see that. The eye can't see the eye. It is very hard for us to see our own shortcomings and our own assumptions.

So the reason colleagues are so important is that the actuality of change has a very personal dimension, and you have to be prepared for that. If you are the leader and you are not prepared to change yourself, forget it. You need people who are close to you who can tell you the truth."

Channel the Change

In his bestselling book, *The Dance of Chang*, Senge lists the 10 common challenges companies face when trying to institute long-term, organization-wide change. Here are his tips for meeting these challenges head-on:

- *Challenge 1: Time crunch.* Participants lack control over their own time to plan and follow through on change initiatives.
  Solution: Upper-level management must allow schedule flexibility, giving participants the discretionary time to pursue every aspect of change, from idea generation through implementation.
- *Challenge 2: Lack of support.* Innovative groups are given inadequate coaching, guidance, and support.
  Solution: Develop coaches and a support network well ahead of time, then encourage people to seek these outlets and ask questions.
- *Challenge 3: "What's the point?"* The greater organization fails to understand why the change effort is relevant or necessary.
  Solution: Hardwire relevance into the pilot group, then maintain the focus so that participants keep relevance in mind as a critical objective.
- *Challenge 4: Translating talking into walking.* Leaders are not perceived as reflecting the values of change that they espouse.
  Solution: The leaders must articulate meaningful goals that resonate with what people value, then demonstrate management's commitment to those values to build credibility with honest partners who can expose contradictory behavior when necessary.
- *Challenge 5: Resistance.* Expanding the pilot program to the greater organization draws fire from those fearful of or anxious about change.
  Solution: Address anxiety by building momentum in small doses, avoiding explicit confrontations, establishing clear lines of communication, remaining patient about slow but steady progress, and accepting that fear is a natural reaction to innovation and learning.

- *Challenge 6: Coming up short.* By traditional methods of assessment, the new program is not meeting expected results.
  Solution: Build new assessment policies into the overall initiative, get buy-in to new assessment tools from executives, then recognize and appreciate the progress you do make.
- *Challenge 7: Converts confront the established culture.* Misinterpretations crop up between "True Believers" and the greater organization, increasing the pilot group's isolation.
  Solution: Leaders must anticipate concerns of both the larger community and articulate all changes in terms of the common values shared by the entire organization.
- *Challenge 8: Chain of command.* The pilot group's desire for autonomy confronts the prevailing organizational structure.
  Solution: When boundaries need to be crossed, focus on business results, incorporate other executive leaders into the creative-thinking process, develop cross-functional teams (where possible), avoid creating new hard-and-fast rules, and then use small, effective changes as their own most persuasive advocates.
- *Challenge 9: "Look at this new wheel I just reinvented!"* The same changes must be repeatedly transmitted to new institutional divisions.
  Solution: Understand and respect the informal cultures and practices within divisions, develop better media for distributing information, expose your ideas openly to allow potential collaborators to come to you, and, whenever possible, ignore arbitrary boundaries that discourage the free flow of information.
- *Challenge 10: The long-term purpose.* Rethinking the organization's role, identity, and place in the greater community.
  Solution: Envision future possibilities to investigate blind spots, match decisions to optimum outcomes, continue to engage people to discuss strategy and purpose, and consistently expose assumptions behind strategy to develop better strategic and ethical thinking capabilities.

EXPERT ADVICE

Kathleen Reardon's Five Tips for Positive Organizational Change

1. *Establish a clear picture of where you want the company to go.* This means verbalizing how the company should operate and how its people should feel about working there and about each other. At Accountants Overload I asked Richard E. Lewis what kind of a company he wanted. He described a place where everyone felt comfortable yet able to handle the intense pressure, a place where competition gave way to cooperation, a place where service to the customer and to the internal organization was the paramount job. In addition, he wanted to build a company where its people would want to stay there for life.

2. *Develop a mission statement and action plans.* The mission statement should reflect the philosophy of your company. Be sure that it is accompanied by action statements. A mission without clearly articulated methods for action is of little use. Include employees in the development of both the mission statement and action steps. Organization change is most effective when people are involved in planning it and have a stake in making it work. Prior to my work with Accountants Overload, a consultant had advised that women be given less visible roles and grey-haired men be hired to improve company image. There are few things more damaging to a company than divisiveness. For a mission statement to be successful, people must feel valued and included.

3. *Get to know who works in the company.* Since people are every company's most valuable assets, what they think, how they feel, and what ideas they have for improvement are the building blocks for the company's future. When I arrived at Accountants Overload, I interviewed all of the managers. I interviewed CEO Richard E. Lewis as well. Through educational sessions, I met many of the salespeople and staff. We developed a relationship, and I acquired information important to helping them in their efforts

to be the best company of their type. I shared my impressions and recommendations with management, and they implemented them. We also began a series of training sessions. Deby Lewis arranged regular meetings with Richard E. Lewis, Peggy Baggott, and myself to assure that we were on track and were continuing to implement the change plan.

4. *Begin the job of culture change with intensity.* Change is usually a challenge. People often cling to the status quo even when it is dysfunctional. It helps if people are at a point where they recognize that change must occur if they are to operate effectively. The great thing about Accountants Overload was the sense of dedication and motivation everyone brought to the task. We became a team with me as a member. In the beginning my presence was more frequent than it is now. The goal of change is for the people in a company to be able to sustain it on their own. The consultant's role is to provide guidance, to be available, to provide training, and to assist when challenges arise.

5. *Establish a set of checks and balances.* Companies must have a way of assessing how far they've come, what is working and what is not. Feedback is key. And it must come from every level. Organizational change is an ongoing task. Once committed to it, companies should stay committed. Otherwise, the results are disappointing. Organizational change involves initiation, implementation, and maintenance. The last part is often neglected. When that happens people lose sight of the mission.

One final note for managers wondering if their company needs change. Here are some telltale warning signs:

- Trouble on the bottom line
- High turnover, especially among one group such as women or minorities
- Inordinately high stress
- Backstabbing and infighting for turf
- Complaining that has little focus on real issues
- Low motivation

(*Continued on next page.*)

(Continued from previous page.)

- Unaccounted-for absences from the office or the territory
- Poor communication among workers
- Long work days but low productivity
- High levels of fear

—From Kathleen Reardon, Ph.D., a professor of management at the Marshall School of Business at the University of Southern California. She is also the author of several acclaimed business books and a highly regarded consultant who has worked with Toyota, Xerox, AT&T, and other leading corporations.

BE EFFECTIVE FOR A CHANGE

Tips for an Organization-Wide Great Leap Forward

Executives struggling to overcome employees' instinctive resistance to change have discovered a new ally in author Brian D. Molitor. In his classic book, *The Power of Agreement*, Molitor suggests a five-step program for helping your people move forward into the unknown.

1. *Clarify the future.* People are much more willing to accept change when they understand how the new programs will help them attain their goals. Instead of highlighting ways the new policy will benefit shareholders or the company's bottom line, talk about such issues as decreased paperwork, shortened sales cycles, and improved customer service.
2. *Costs of inaction.* Just as there are benefits to change, inaction carries costs. Talk about these costs in terms of lost opportunities, diminished market share, and the uncertainty involved in failing to respond to changing market conditions.
3. *Before you launch it, plan it.* There are plenty of great concepts and proposals floating around the ether. The shortage is in effective, thought-out strategies for turning these ideas into plans of action. Even those who agree with the need for change may remain skeptical without seeing your plans for how to get there.

4. *De-accentuate the negative.* No matter how much explaining and convincing you do, some negative Nellies will inevitably emerge to challenge the decision. Molitor suggests three steps for dealing with the nabobs:

   - Make sure people understand the effort and how they will be affected. Then ask, "Why are you resisting this effort? What will you gain if the program fails? What about if it succeeds?"
   - Next, ask if they have a better idea for tackling the challenges ahead. If so, why isn't their program already in place?
   - The first two steps will typically take care of most of the remaining doubters. But if any do remain, consider asking them to leave the organization. Allowing an ardent voice of negativity to stick around can undermine your project before it even begins.

5. *Information, involvement, encouragement.* Although it may seem unnecessarily time-consuming, keep your people informed on the effort's progress. Leaders must remain personally involved in transmitting the vision, mission, core values, and critical issues facing an organization. Make constant encouragement a regular habit.

Chapter 18

Above All, Be a Leader

QUALITIES OF TOP SALES MANAGERS

If you think becoming a sales manager is easy, here's the lowdown from seasoned sales managers who look back at what they learned—the hard way.

Dave Anderson has something to say to the first group of sales reps that he managed 13 years ago. "I am so, so sorry," he says.

"I didn't know what I was doing."

Like many new managers, Anderson was promoted to his position based on his sales ability—but he didn't have a clue about dealing with people. So he held reps accountable but didn't communicate what was expected of them. He managed by intimidation, instead of motivation. Rather than coach his team, he stayed aloof, locking himself in his office and immersing himself in administrative tasks.

"I could close deals and do budgets, but I was just horrible when it came to leading people," he admits. "I didn't teach anyone anything—I managed by command control and whips and chains. I don't know how anyone could stand to work with me."

Nowadays, Anderson is a lot savvier about sales management. In fact, you could say he wrote the book on the topic: he's the author of *Selling Above the Crowd* and *No-Nonsense Leadership*, and he's president of LearntoLead, a sales and leadership training company in Los Altos, California.

As Anderson's experience proves, being a top rep doesn't mean you can manage people. But what does it take to succeed? We asked managers who've built great teams, reps who report to them, and executives who direct the whole sales organization. Here's what they said.

1. Become a Master of Change

The biggest and most challenging task of a sales manager is to prepare the sales team for the constantly changing marketplace. "Every organization," management legend Peter Drucker once said, "has to prepare for the abandonment of everything it does." Great sales managers are the arch role model for change. Business is never a straight series of predictable evolutions that will produce a happy, boldface chart pointing north. Today's business is the result of uncontrollable, unpredictable eruptions of simultaneous financial, technological, and economic revolutions. The ideal sales manager will calmly face chaos, enthusiastically embrace change, and always adjust to whatever tough challenges lie ahead.

That's why great managers set the bar high with their own work ethic, and they lead in change management. Leilani Lutali, a rep with Comforce Technical Services, a Woodbury, New York–based consulting and staffing company, says her first manager did just that. "Diana expected as much of herself as she did of her sales force. And she wasn't afraid of her reps' surpassing her—in fact, she encouraged it. Through her mentoring, she helped us rise to our highest levels of excellence."

Troy Berns, a rep with All Copy Products, a Denver, Colorado–based dealer for copiers, printers, facsimile machines, postage meters, and scanners, says he appreciates that his current manager works just as hard as—or harder than—the reps he oversees. "My manager gets in the office before I do, and when I stay late he's right here strategizing with me. He won't ask me to do anything that he wouldn't do himself."

"When we're faced with change," says Tom Miller, a sales-training consultant, "salespeople will automatically focus on what they must give up. To them, virtually all change will be perceived as loss. That's why good sales managers add value when it comes to selling the pain of gain. They help the salespeople vividly imagine the raisins in a huge cake, and then they will tell them that they will lead them personally through a potentially unnerving gauntlet that ultimately gets them unscathed into a big cake factory."

2. Earn Their Trust

Salespeople do not pay so much attention to what their sales manager says; they judge their managers by what they do. Trust is the foundation of any relationship. Trust means that your word is as good as gold, that salespeople don't have to second-guess anything you tell them, and that they can count on you. Trust is not what you preach to your team; it is what you do when nobody is watching.

"Managers who have a reputation for changing their views based on who was in their office last have no credibility," says Lawrence B. Chonko, a professor of marketing at Baylor University in Waco, Texas, and founder of the school's Center for Professional Selling and Sales Management.

That means if you set rules and deadlines, you'd better enforce them. If you schedule meetings, you must hold them. "Otherwise you become a joke," says Doug Stevens, a sales-and-marketing consultant with Carrera Agency, a talent management firm in Aliso Viejo, California.

Most importantly, reps must believe their manager is working for the good of the team and will go to bat for them when needed. If you become complacent, have a bad attitude, make rude or abusive comments, or are caught lying or cheating, you betray their trust and end up with a demoralized, unmotivated sales force.

"You may think that you are watching your reps," Anderson says. "But actually, they are watching you. Reps won't buy into what you say unless they buy into your character, your competence, and your consistency."

When you make a mistake as a manager, don't hide it, don't gloss over it, but admit it quickly by saying, "I blew it. I made a mistake and I take full responsibility for it." Your honest response will silence the critics and everyone who has ever made a mistake will understand and respect your honesty. If you are too proud to admit your mistakes, you will lose people's trust. When you lose trust, your team will no longer be able to function smoothly, and your ability to manage will suffer.

3. Give Feedback

Good salespeople stop working hard when the sales manager fails to provide objective feedback. Without the pat on the back or the celebration of a stretch goal achieved, salespeople will ask themselves, "Why am I working so hard?" If there are no consequences for goals missed and no rewards for goals exceeded, sales productivity will decline.

Good managers set clear expectations and realistic goals. Give plenty of feedback and let reps know where they stand—and not just during annual or quarterly reviews. "Delayed consequences lose their punch, so you should give feedback on the fly," Anderson says. "Reps will try to hit a standard if they know what it is. If you don't create clarity, how can you create accountability? How can reps know if they are cutting it if they don't know what 'it' is?"

In one company, the VP of sales was so preoccupied with moving up the ladder— and fishing for compliments from the CEO—that he overlooked the need for complimenting and thanking his regional managers for their extra efforts. Every time they achieved their goals, he asked them to set their expectations higher and told them that their salespeople could do a lot more. Within a year, 5 of his 12 regional managers moved out of his division; sales suffered; and when a new CEO took over, he was let go. Remember to balance criticism with elegant, positive reinforcement. "Managers who give only criticism without building us back up don't help," Berns says. "They just make us feel less motivated."

Diego Lombardo, an account manager for MobilSense Technologies Inc., an Agoura Hills, California, company that provides cost-management solutions for the wireless industry, remembers his first sales manager fondly. "He was completely honest and put everything on the table with no facades," Lombardo says. "He would tell us if we weren't doing the job. When we asked him for help, he never pushed us off to someone else."

4. Build Enthusiasm

"I want to keep the salespeople happy and engaged," says Brad Knepper, CEO of All Copy Products, who brought his company's revenues from $1.2 million to $11 million during the three years he's been in charge. He says creative competitions keep enthusiasm high. For example, during a recent week-long *Survivor* contest—complete with palm trees, grass skirts, and tiki torches—reps earned points for making calls, setting appointments, and demonstrating products, and those with the fewest points got booted off their tribal teams.

"I really wanted people to get into the theme—and they did," Knepper says. "Productivity jumped, people stayed extra late at the office, and they shared tips and ideas across the cubes. The contest made it less about cold calling and pitching and more about competitive spirit."

The contest also showed the reps just how much they were capable of producing, Berns says. "For that week, we worked hard, but we enjoyed it. People stepped up to the plate and were doing quite a bit more than in the past. Then they realized that they could do that every week."

In companies that went through the pain of layoffs during the recent economic recession, it was much harder to maintain a high level of enthusiasm. "We went though a really tough period," said a sales manager at an online media company. "In one week, our entire marketing team and half of our sales force was let go. After the initial shock wore off, I decided to have an honest conversation with every member of my team. I told them that there was no guarantee that our company would make it. There are no guarantees in life. I told them that if they wanted to quit, I would understand and accept their decision. But, if we worked as a team and gave it our best effort, and adjusted our approach, we'd have a good chance at winning. Within the next nine months, we recovered, our company broke even, and we lost only one salesperson."

5. Get Involved

Many salespeople are overly preoccupied with their efforts rather than with results. They worry about what their sales managers would or should do for them. They'd rather complain about the poor quality of sales leads instead of taking the initiative through cold calling. Instead of taking total ownership of their jobs, they feel that their managers owe them. As a result, they become ineffectual.

Management guru, Peter Drucker, once said, "The manager who focuses on contribution and who takes responsibility for results, no matter how junior, is in the most literal sense of the phrase 'top management,' for he holds himself accountable for the performance of the whole."

The key to great sales management is to get involved and be highly visible to your customers and highly accessible to your sales team. Don't get so immersed in paperwork that you forget about how people work. Armchair managers don't cut it. "Poor managers hide in their offices. Good managers are visible and accessible. They are down in the trenches showing their people how to get the job done," Anderson says.

That kind of involvement breeds loyalty. "My previous sales manager didn't play an active role in my job," Berns says. "He didn't work with me one-on-one; he didn't go on appointments with me; he kept his distance. He had no interest in anything except what I was going to close and when I was going to do it."

In contrast, Berns's current manager frequently accompanies him out in the field, teaches by example, provides honest feedback, and coaches him on how he could have done better. "I feel loyal toward him because he is involved," Berns says.

Vital involvement of the sales manager at the customer level keeps sales organizations more rooted in the marketplace, and, as a result, customers feel more connected to the company. For example, it is not uncommon for the room manager or the catering manager at a Ritz Carlton hotel to greet customers at the door and thank them for visiting. Why? Research shows that customers feel honored by the presence of management.

6. Grow and Develop Your Team

We live in a knowledge-based society where information moves at lightning speed. The speed and volume of information create new challenges. Salespeople have deeper access to a company's knowledge universe than their customers, but customers have a deeper knowledge of their own situations. While information suffers from inflation, quality human contact has become a rare commodity. The best sales-training strategy is to encourage salespeople to spend more time learning about their customers' situations and then invest more time digging deeper to create better-fitting solutions for their customers.

Great managers provide ongoing coaching, training, and development. "You can't expect people to be up and running after their two-week orientation. Sales training is a continual investment," Anderson says. "Don't leave the development of your people to chance. Create a focused plan. Objectives for skill proficiency should be set and progress measured."

But that doesn't just mean signing up for sales seminars. Great managers "stretch us outside of our comfort zones," Lutali says. Encourage reps to join associations, create community-based relationships, or continue their education. "My first sales manager encouraged me to finish my degree. That alone helped my production," says Lutali.

Good managers also separate career development from skills development. While a sales negotiation course may give a salesperson a short-term boost, it will not improve the salesperson's long-term career. A career development process should aim at stretching a salesperson's business acumen, judgment of people, and business behavior.

In the end, successful sales managers have mastered the delicate balancing act of getting the job done for the company while advocating individual growth for each rep—and that's as much an art as a science. "You have to hold people accountable to quotas and hard measurements," Stevens says. "That's the science part." But, he adds, "you also have to build people up, give them hope, and help them make money."

And that's where the art—and the heart—comes in.

7. Lead People to Never-Ending Improvement

Excellence in selling means engaging every salesperson in a never-ending and ongoing improvement process. While it is easy for a new sales manager to implement a few quick and effective changes, it is difficult to keep the momentum going. Why? Sales managers often worry more about reaching their quarterly sales goals, which requires innovative, last-minute changes in sales strategies that often strangle the idea of ongoing improvement.

There are subtle, yet profound, differences between innovation and ongoing improvement. Innovation demands big steps leading to breakthroughs and fast results. Ongoing improvement depends on small steps, relies on conventional common sense, pays great attention to process, and teases out results in small doses over time.

When business prospects are positive, the innovation-focused sales manager will roll out a new CRM solution, train the entire sales staff, or create a lavish incentive plan. In other words, cash in the pocket fuels the motivation for innovation. Unfortunately, these managers mistake innovation for improvement. In today's challenging economic environment, ongoing improvement may be a more desirable alternative.

Here are five areas sales managers can focus on to perpetuate improvement efforts.

1. Improve your measurement methods. Start with better sales forecasting, measure the closing ratio per salesperson, research how many leads you need to close one sale. Better measurement of activity leads to a better understanding of what causes better results.
2. Improve your sales process. Look at every component and get your team to identify a better way to perform each task.
3. Look at your management process. How much time do you spend with top performers, helping them do better, work more efficiently, capture more opportunities? How much time do you invest in coaching poor performers who are unable to grow?
4. Examine how you motivate your people. Ask your salespeople, "How am I doing?" or "What can I do to help you win?" or "How can I help you grow?" They will tell you where improvement is needed most—you only have to ask.
5. Commit yourself to never-ending improvement.

YOU GOT A PROBLEM WITH THAT?

How to Dissolve the Three Key Pressure Points Between Reps and Managers

If one thing is true in sales, besides that it's a tough profession, it's that reps and managers often complain about each other. It's part of the job. Something reps and managers have to learn to live with. Or is it? Let's take a look.

For instance, here's a true story from an ad sales rep for a national consumer magazine.

"I was on a call with my manager. The setup was low chairs around a coffee table. I was wearing a dress and had my legs crossed above the knee. I was gesturing and wanted to point to something in the magazine, so I leaned over, still with my legs crossed, and found what I was looking for.

"It ended up being a positive meeting, and we did get some business. But as we left, my manager felt compelled to find something wrong: 'You shouldn't have crossed your legs like that. If you were going to lean over, you should have uncrossed your legs and put your right foot behind your left.' I mean, come on! It's not enough for a manager to see that what her salespeople are doing is working. For her to feel in charge, she needed to impose her preferences." (Hypercritical manager—sound familiar?)

Conversely, here's a true story from a sales manager for a software company.

"I had a rep who was extremely successful. He built relationships and was very good at what he did. But he was also very negative. He would complain to my team that he was getting screwed on commissions and that the company wasn't doing enough for him. I had numerous discussions with him, appealing to his ego and trying to make him a leader. 'Look,' I told him, 'you know what you're doing out there. I don't need to babysit you. But your younger teammates are looking up to you, and you are influencing them in a negative way.' Unfortunately, he didn't react well. He had his laundry list of issues. I had to make a decision: Make one guy successful and contribute to the other 10 failing, or make 10 guys successful. I ended up having to fire him." (Loud-mouth complainer—do you know one?)

See what we mean? Both sides have issues. But there are solutions, and they're worth a look. Because smoothing out the problems between reps and managers can make a team stronger, more efficient, and much more effective. And that translates to—you guessed it—overall success of the sales effort.

There's not a boss–subordinate relationship in the world that's friction-free. Stick two people in a room, give one authority over the other, and human dynamics will kick up enough squabbles to keep a behavioral psychologist busy for years. The battles range from internal meetings ("Why doesn't Joe ever contribute?") to sales calls ("How can I get my boss to stop hogging the spotlight?"). Salespeople want their managers to stop breathing down their necks. And managers wonder why Susie doesn't keep them informed on her progress. It's a dance between forced partners, and the two aren't always in step.

Part of the problem is that salespeople and their managers face challenges not found in other disciplines—like the fact that most salespeople toil far from the direct eyes of their supervisors. "Managers believe their salespeople are loose cannons. Since they're out of sight, they think they're getting into all kinds of trouble," notes ArLyne Diamond, Ph.D., a management consultant in Santa Clara, California. Managers, meanwhile, struggle to get reps to submit to training or any kind of oversight. "I hate to be harsh about it, but sales is not a democracy," says Robert Tas, vice president of sales and marketing for Tacoda Systems, a New York firm that makes software to help marketers and publishers manage their audiences. "It's my butt on the line too, so we'd better figure out how to make each other better."

But isn't that what everybody wants? In the following three sections, salespeople and their supervisors talk about the issues that derail a smooth-running relationship—and how to get back in one another's good graces.

Problem: Accountability

You already know that most salespeople hate accountability, but what you probably didn't know is that they hate it in all its forms: ride-alongs, call planning, and most of all, paperwork. "I hear it all the time: 'It's boring. It's hard to do. It's redundant. I don't have the time,'" says Tas.

From their side of the desk, though, reps feel justified in balking at busywork. For one thing, it takes them away from their core competency—getting in front of people and being persuasive. And sometimes, the policies they're asked to uphold seem arbitrary, or worse. Consider this incident, recounted by a star salesperson for a food brokerage: "I use my cell phone frequently while on the road. My phone bill was higher than that of my colleagues. But my expenses for dinners out and entertainment are low, because I'm a single mother and choose to spend as much time as possible with my child. My manager repeatedly complained about the cell phone bill, and at one point even took the phone away from me." That gesture affected not only her morale, the rep says, but also slowed her down, since she is now forced to look for pay phones while on her route. (Sticky policy—have you gotten stuck?)

Call it a classic case of enforcing the letter but not the spirit of the law—a common problem in all fields but especially in sales, says Diamond. If demands for accountability and paperwork disintegrate into nasty confrontations, Diamond suggests that managers consider the following:

- Ask reps why they find the policy onerous. If the manager in the above example had probed further, he could have responded with an alternate policy—say, capping total expenses at a percentage of the rep's volume rather than focusing on the phone bill. And the relationship would have remained intact.
- Provide clerical support if possible, especially if paperwork is devouring too much of a rep's schedule.
- Explain to your reps why you need the data or procedure—and don't make capricious or arbitrary demands.

Sometimes, simply explaining why you need the information is enough. Robert Tas is a case in point: He's developed a call-reporting and planning system that, he says, fills in all the holes that can sink a sale. His reps get such pieces of information as who the major players and influencers are and the prospect company's marketplace position, among others. "If I have 30 salespeople operating this way, I can take this data to management and say, 'Here's what we're going to do and why.' It's a lot more predictable than 'My rep took the client to a basketball game and says we're going to get the deal.'"

Tas sells the system to his reps by proving that it will make them more successful—which it has, judging from the firms' list of blue-chip clients including *USA TODAY* and the *Chicago Tribune*. "I think a lot of managers make the mistake of saying, 'Did you get the deal or not?'" he says. "The call-reporting system helps me to help them. I can look at the details and strategize with them."

Take-away tip for managers: Explaining the "why" behind a policy can ease reps' grumbling. When rules aren't being followed, figure out the reason—and see if there's another solution.

Take-away tip for reps: If you find a rule onerous, ask your manager why it's in place. See if you can suggest a better, more efficient way to meet the objective. Even if the rule can't be changed, asking "Why?" will help you better understand how administrative tasks feed into the company's operations.

Problem: Stress

Global unrest. An anemic economy. Pressure on your team to make its numbers. Customers aren't buying. Need a little more stress?

Patricia Schneider doesn't. She's sales manager for Community Investment Services, Inc., a Lockport, New York, firm that provides brokerage services to banks. With so many consumers gun-shy about the current market, it's getting harder just to maintain the status quo, she says. "Where before you had to make 20 calls to find a customer, now it takes 40," she explains. For many of the products her firm sells, commissions have been sliced in half.

Schneider can't control the economy, but she can prevent stress from driving a wedge between her and her 13 reps who are scattered across the state. Her solution? Calling reps once a week and letting them vent. "Salespeople always have to be 'on,'" she says, "and I don't want them taking the pressure home or internalizing it." During her calls, Schneider listens, empathizes, and then steers the rep toward a solution. For example, she'll say, "Three weeks ago you had a dynamite day and closed three sales. Tell me about that day. Was there a referral from a CPA or a lawyer who you can go back to?" Replaying previous wins will usually put the salesperson back on track.

And when she senses that a rep is reaching the boiling point, she'll offer to come work with him or her for a few days. "There's a relief at handing the ball off," says Schneider. "You're temporarily removing the burden, and they realize they've got someone on their side."

Support takes different forms for different people, and it's up to managers and reps to speak up about how they can help—and be helped. Donna Firman, director of business development for Inktel, a direct-marketing firm in Miami Lakes, Florida, looks to her manager to clear client complaints from her path so that she can spend time pursuing new business. If, for example, she hears that a delivery date is in jeopardy, she leans on the manager to apply his resources and clout to speed things up. And when responding to RFPs, she asks him to recruit the firm's client services, accounting, and IT departments to contribute. "He needs to coordinate all this so I can do what I need to do, which is develop my relationship with my client," Firman says.

Sometimes, though, stress comes from sources outside the office. When it starts to affect job performance, managers may need to step in—delicately. Scott Testa, CIO of software maker Mindbridge, Inc., in Norristown, Pennsylvania, manages a sales force of 30 and recently noticed that one of his top performers was enduring a five-month slump. Testa asked the rep's manager about the slide, and the manager said he'd already talked to the rep—but that the "talk" consisted of a warning to get the numbers up. Testa instructed the manager to go back and ask the magic question: "Why?" It turned out that the rep was grappling with a family issue and needed time off. The rep is now back on track. "Sometimes you have to find out the need behind the need," says Testa. "A lot of times it's personal stuff that can be dealt with."

Take-away tip for managers: Check in with your reps more frequently during tough times. Offer a sympathetic ear. Ask what you can do to help take the pressure off, and be sensitive to the fact that the stress might be personal.

Take-away tip for reps: Don't suffer in silence. When the tension builds, it's more important than ever to use your manager as a sounding board. Be specific about how you'd like your manager to help you.

Problem: Culture Change

For a glittering example of sweeping culture change, look no farther than the banking industry. Over the past several years, giants like Wachovia and Citicorp have swallowed up smaller banks around the world, giving themselves economies of scale and a range of products that leaves their smaller brethren fighting for air. Meanwhile, all banks large and small are battling other financial services companies, such as insurance firms and securities brokerages, for a share of consumers' dwindling assets.

As a result, what was once a service culture—fielding Mrs. Jones's complaint about her bounced check—is now a sales culture. Bankers who were hired to assess risk and serve clients at their local branches are now being told to make cold calls and chase business. Many aren't happy about it. Says James A. Ellis, senior vice president and regional manager of Citizens Business Bank in Orange, California, "Any time you're going to change a culture, you're going to have pain."

Pain indeed. Citizens Bank has set some aggressive goals for itself, including bottom-line growth of 15 percent a year. As Ellis ominously intones, "We do not miss our objectives." But how do you ramp up an essentially nonsales staff to sell?

There are literally hundreds of books on engineering change (*Managing Transitions* by William Bridges is one of the best), but much of the expert advice centers around one concept: setting short-range goals for people to aim at. Ellis, for example, has fixed monthly goals for branch managers of 30 sales calls a month—"and someone coming up to your desk in the bank doesn't count," he says. But he's not leaving them to fend for themselves. At weekly sales meetings and periodic training, he provides leads, walks them through the steps of a telephone sales call, and discusses getting meaningful referrals from customers, attorneys, and CPAs. He also allows them to progress in baby steps, suggesting that they start devoting half an hour a day to selling and then move up to 45 minutes three times a day.

That deconstruction of the sales process is what sales consultant Jack Hubbard, a principal with St. Myers & Hubbard in Chicago, teaches to all his clients. Hubbard believes in stressing process over results—an odd stance for a sales consultant, perhaps, but one that he says is critical to weathering cultural change.

Most sales organizations hand down a quota from on high, and say, "Go get'em tiger," he maintains. But a manager's job is to give reps the skills and tools they need to be successful. And that means focusing on behaviors and activities rather than outcomes.

The distinction between behaviors and activities is an important one, says Hubbard, and is often misunderstood. An activity is, "Make five telephone calls to your top customers each week." The behaviors, however, are the individual components that make up the act: What question will I ask? How am I going to take notes? How will I redirect questions that too quickly focus on price?

"Most organizations measure outcomes, but they don't measure activity and behaviors," he says. "But I believe that's the key to success. It's not staring at the scoreboard until you're scared stiff—you just glance at it every once in a while to see how you're doing."

Take-away tip for managers: Don't just hand down quotas from on high. When your company or industry is in flux, help your team focus on the things it can control, namely, activities and behaviors.

Take-away tip for reps: The same thing goes for you. Train your radar toward factors you can control, and ask for your manager's help with activities with which you feel uncomfortable.

HAVING THE TOUGH CONVERSATION WITH YOUR DIRECT REPORTS

Teenagers who've suffered through the throes of dating know that "We've got to talk" usually isn't followed by good news. The same holds true in the workplace, where confrontations about job performance and personality conflicts are about as enjoyable as, well, dancing with the class geek at the prom.

Laurie Schloff isn't immune to the agony of the tough conversation. As an executive communication coach at The Speech Improvement Company in Boston, she's made a career of helping people through all sorts of communication crises, from telling a pesky coworker to buzz off to informing a loyal staff about layoffs. She offers these tips to help salespeople and sales managers settle their beefs.

- *Lay the groundwork with ongoing meetings.* Any discussion about your relationship is going to be a lot less squirm-inducing if you've been having ongoing status meetings. If the last time you met with your rep or manager was, oh, last Christmas, start now. Get together every few weeks for 20 minutes to talk about what's going well and what needs to change.
- *Start with a "check-in" conversation.* If you sense trouble brewing, set up an appointment to talk—and watch the language you use. Notice the difference between this: "Hey Jim, I really need to talk to you. Why is Susan getting all the good leads?" And this: "Hey Jim, when you have a moment I'd love to check in with you about something. I've noticed that when an opportunity to work on a major account comes up, I'm not the one chosen. I'd like to hear your input on how you're viewing my work."

  The first example is "babyish" and puts the other person on the defensive, Schloff notes. But the second example uses more objective language. "You're stating what you observed," she says. "You're not being accusatory or making a judgment."
- *Use the "sandwich" technique.* Once you're face-to-face, describe the problem and its impact on you. To use the sandwich technique: Open with a positive statement, introduce the complaint, and then close with a positive statement. One example: "Steve, what you said about dealing with the nurses at Mass General really turned things around for me. One thing I want to share with you is that when I bring up an idea, there are times when I'm not able to get out my whole opinion. You're jumping in with a strong suggestion. I'm not sure what that means: Should I still bring up my idea? Or does it mean your idea is the way to go? I want to make sure I understand your intent, because your suggestions have been so helpful."

  What this really means, of course, is "stop interrupting me." But the tone is much more professional—and more apt to get results.

FOUR COMMON MANAGEMENT MISTAKES AND TACTICS FOR FIXING THEM

1. Assembly-Line Management

If you treat everyone on your team exactly the same, you'll end up reaching no one. "You can clone sheep, but you cannot clone people," says Bob Senatore, senior vice president of Comforce Corporation, a Woodbury, New York–based consulting and staffing firm. "Each rep has his or her own style and rate of growth."

Customize your management approach to play to individual strengths, weaknesses, and personalities. "Every salesperson responds to different incentives and has different hot spots," says Diego Lombardo, an account manager for MobilSense Technologies, Inc., an Agoura Hills, California, company that provides cost-management solutions for the wireless industry. "Great sales managers are flexible enough to adapt to each person they support. They know when to tighten the reins and when not to."

For example, Lombardo says he is on "self-drive"and doesn't need—or want— someone looking over his shoulder. Others may need a little push or more hand-holding. But be careful not to play favorites. Each member of the team must ultimately be held to the same set of standards.

2. Micromanagement

Want to squash sales? Then, micromanage your team.

"A lot of new managers really try to micromanage their people, and it's just a turnoff," Lombardo says. "It builds in extra steps and takes the focus away from the goal of selling product."

That doesn't mean that managers shouldn't keep up-to-date with what's going on. But you are not managing if you find yourself constantly bombarding reps with questions like "Have you done. . .?" "Have you called on. . .?" or "When will you. . .?" You are nit-picking.

3. Doing the Reps' Work for Them

As a sales manager, you should be the reps' coach. But that doesn't mean you should get in and play the game.

Doug Stevens, a sales-and-marketing consultant who serves as vice president of sales for MobilSense Technologies, admits that he occasionally falls into the trap of doing the reps' work for them. "I remember one rep who was always saying, 'I can't get this done.' He wanted me to call customers to solve problems," says Stevens.

But after a while, Stevens realized that he was working for his rep—not the other way around. "Salespeople can expect help, but they shouldn't be managing the manager," he says. "A sales manager who takes over and runs the sales call doesn't build trust and doesn't coach."

Troy Berns, a rep with All Copy Products in Denver, Colorado, appreciates that his manager frequently accompanies him on sales calls. "But it wouldn't be helpful if he went out on every close," he says. "I have to go out on my own, or else I wouldn't grow."

4. Doing All the Talking

Good salespeople learn that they should do 20 percent of the talking and 80 percent of the listening when interacting with customers. Follow that maxim with your sales team. "Listen to us before you go off on a tangent," Lombardo urges.

Rather than ramming your opinions down their throats, understand where the reps are coming from. Not only is it your place to give feedback, but to get it, too.

THE ABCs OF SALES MANAGEMENT

Alertness—Vigilance, promptness, and attention to detail
Boldness—Willingness to act with audacity
Courage—Moral strength to venture, persevere, and withstand danger or difficulty
Decisiveness—The ability to make prompt decisions
Dependability—Doing what you promised and planned to do
Endurance—The capacity to continue and complete a task
Enthusiasm—Positive emotion injected into the task at hand
Failure—A bad outcome that is not to be repeated, but is a lesson to learn from
Generosity—The art of letting your heart speak at the right moment
Humility—Freedom from arrogance and boastful pride
Humor—The capacity to look beyond the seriousness of life
Initiative—Acting decisively in the absence of a definite plan
Integrity—Absolute fidelity to the truth
Judgment—The ability to weigh ambiguous information and make a wise decision
Justice—Equitable and impartial bestowing of favors and issuing of reprimands
Knowledge—The capacity to organize information into a basis for sensible action
Loyalty—Being faithful to the promises you make
Motivation—Inducing action within yourself and others

Negotiation—Reaching for a satisfactory agreement that lasts

Opportunity—Recognizing a favorable situation and taking action

Persuasiveness—The capacity to communicate your fervent beliefs

Renewal—Regeneration, rejuvenation, and reenergizing of yourself, your ideas, and your action plans

Sympathy—The capacity to share your feelings with those who encounter difficulty

Tact—The ability to deal with people in a respectful and appropriate manner

Unselfishness—Avoidance of providing for your own comfort at the expense of others

Virtue—The embodiment of good qualities that allows you to influence people on the basis of your character

Wisdom—Soundness of thoughts, action, and decisions

Zeal—Eagerness in pursuing your plans, your goals, and your vision

RETURN TO GENDER

Tips for Women in Sales Who Are "Movin' On Up" into Management

Twenty years ago, women sales professionals were a rare breed and limited to just a few corners of the marketplace. Today, women have made such strides that they now dominate sales management positions in industries that were previously closed off to them. Despite the progress, however, women managers still face gender-related challenges in the workplace. So says Margie Caballero, sales manager for the past three years with the Embassy Suites hotel in Austin, Texas.

"The main issue as a woman manager in dealing with men is a lack of respect," she says. "It's not that men don't feel that a woman should be in charge of a man—that may have been the issue in the past. Today, it's that people experience so much female management turnover because of family issues that when a new woman manager comes in, there's an attitude of, 'Here we go again.' When we try to implement new programs, there's a sense of, 'Are you even going to stick around long enough to implement that?'"

To combat this attitude, Caballero recommends a few tactics to her fellow women managers. "Regardless of gender, when you come into a new position you have to communicate that you know what you're talking about and that you understand what it means to implement policies," she explains. "Learn everything possible about every area of your job and about other areas you may want to move into, and find out precisely what your policies will mean for the people below who will have to actually put them into practice."

Caballero's other tip for new women managers? Be firm. "You can't be wishy-washy," she warns. "That's a stereotype about women that you need to be aware of. Particularly with men, don't back down on deadlines or your expectation levels. Men respond to firmness with respect. With women, your approach should be more nuanced."

Finally, Caballero suggests that women managers seek out colleagues and others in related industries. "There are workshops, magazines, support groups, and all kinds of networking opportunities out there," she advises. "Pursue those networks in your area and your industry. You can learn a great deal from others' experiences, so I feel women should take the initiative and seek out these opportunities."

Chapter 19

Success Tips

This chapter provides final success tips on key aspects of sales management. Refer to these lists when you have a specific problem or just when you need a little motivation of your own. Above all, let each idea guide you toward your ultimate goal: Being the best sales manager you can be!

UP WITH PEOPLE

Tips for Maximizing Performance from Your Organization's Most Important Resource

Sales managers are not accountants squirreled away in a cloistered office meticulously counting out nuts collected by the front-line sales force. No, sales managers are judged by the quality of the performance their people produce. The key word there is *people*, observes noted author and sales trainer Chick Waddell. To help managers remember the critical tactics at their disposal for maximizing salespeople's performance, Waddell offers the following acronym excerpted from his booklet *Coaching 2 Win*:

P *Philosophy-focused.* What are your core beliefs and values? Have you ever written them down? What do you believe about the importance of winning? Integrity? The nurturing of talent? Hard work? Know your beliefs and then let them guide your management practices.

E *Establish standards.* What are the standards you expect from yourself and your people? Do they know what they are, or do you expect them to read your mind? Share your standards of dress, conduct, and performance with your team and then let them meet or exceed those standards.

O *Objective-driven.* By their nature, people want to be a part of something bigger than themselves. A corporate mission can fulfill this need. Communicate the company mission to your people and then explain how each person's individual objectives contribute to the successful achievement of that mission.

P *Paradigm shifting.* The vogue phrase in business today is thinking "outside the box." Whatever you call it, it means considering a new approach to an old problem. Set an example as an idea generator and then encourage solutions from your team. Even if an idea is impractical, praise people for trying to come up with new ways of thinking.

L *Let them know you care.* Nothing builds morale and encourages productivity like a manager who genuinely cares about his or her team members and shows it. When your people feel like valued members of the organization, that sensibility will show in the way they communicate with your customers.

E *Encourage and build belief.* Do you believe in your people? Do you recognize their strengths and share that recognition with them? Specific personal words of encouragement and faith in a person's abilities can provide the difference in determining whether someone becomes a success or a failure.

HANDLE WITH FLAIR

Tips for Managing Your Best and Brightest Sales Staff

When Mark McCormack talks about managing superstars, everyone listens. Frequently recognized as one of the most powerful figures in the world of professional sports, the best-selling author and chairman of the world's largest sports marketing organization has represented some of the top athletes—and biggest egos—the world has ever seen. In *On Management,* McCormack offers the following tips for handling superstars:

- *Measure by their yardsticks.* Many top performers are motivated by money, but don't assume that's the only important factor. Determine what else may stoke your hot shots—status, recognition, autonomy—and find effective ways to feed that need.
- *Let them breathe the air up there.* Invite top performers to participate in a senior management meeting. This not only sends a message to the reps, but also to the executives attending the meeting, that they are special.
- *Feed them opportunities.* Many organizations stifle top performers by asking them to put out fires and right sinking ships. Instead, give your eagles the chance to spread their wings and fly with burgeoning new opportunities. Superstars should be building your company's future instead of getting mired in its past.
- *Promote early and often.* Top performers who don't go up the chain go out the door—to competitors. Promote good people early and you reward them with increased responsibility, a new title, and the desire to prove your decision right.
- *The stars are always greener.* Hiring superstars away from the competition is risky—and lazy too. Just because someone performs well in one arena doesn't mean lightning will

strike under your roof too. Plus you risk alienating your existing staff. Better to groom tomorrow's superstars from your current crop or hire an unproven but promising "Young Turk" than to raid someone else's pantry.

SEVEN SUBTLE CLUES TO MAKE YOU A BETTER MANAGER

1. *Set the tone.* Are you a model for professional behavior? Do you scream and yell? Do you take long lunches and duck out of work early? Bear in mind that your attitude and behavior, good or bad, will infect the entire organization.

2. *Turn your customers into do-it-yourself types.* From self-service gas stations to fast-food restaurants, all kinds of organizations have learned to cut costs by asking customers to take on minimal tasks. Don't be afraid to ask for this kind of assistance from your customers, too.

3. *Turn your trainees into trainers.* When you spend thousands of dollars to send sales reps to be trained, let them know you expect them to come back ready to teach the rest of the sales staff what they've learned. That ought to get them to pay attention.

4. *Don't lie down with dogs.* When you do, you get up with fleas. No matter how airtight the contract, don't go into business with disreputable individuals or operations.

5. *Give decisions the time they deserve.* You are paid to be right, not to be quick. Important decisions should never be made hastily. Give yourself the time to mull it over. Sleep on it. Then, once you decide to act, be decisive.

6. *Let the liars lie.* When customers give you excuses, they may well be lying. Rather than browbeat the truth out of them, accept the short-term no instead, so you can position yourself as the number two supplier for whenever something goes awry with number one.

7. *Do the postmortem.* Everyone knows preparation is important, but what's the best way to prepare? One surefire method for improvement comes from going over every presentation afterward and analyzing what went well and what went not-so-well. Knowing precisely what happened last time will help you determine what happens next time.

EXPERT ADVICE
I Came, I Saw—Idea!

EXPERT ✓ ADVICE

As a famous business guru once said, "Get the change out of your pockets and into your organization." OK, no one famous ever said that, but the sentiment remains true regardless. In *Thunderbolt Thinkers: Electrifying Ideas for Building an Innovative Workplace*, author Grace McGartland suggests the following nine tips for keeping your mind flexible and open to the type of groundbreaking ideas that can transform an organization.

1. *Attitude is everything.* Try altering your physical frame of reference. For an entire day do your work while standing.
2. *Right brain, left brain.* Let both facts and feelings hold equal sway over your thought processes. Acknowledge both sides without losing your ability to think clearly.
3. *Look up.* Risk being positive about your own thoughts. Instead of immediately thinking why something won't work, start asking yourself questions that will lead to a genuine solution.
4. *Prioritize!* Think about what your primary goals are for your organization. Then focus on this issue as you consider alternatives for the future.
5. *Make it your business.* Whenever you identify a problem or challenge, take the responsibility for finding a solution. Solidify your resolve by saying it out loud and writing it down.
6. *Reach out and talk to someone.* Call trusted friends and let them know that you're facing a challenge. Say that you're not looking for a solution, but rather a sympathetic ear to listen as you talk things out.
7. *Choose the unusual.* Recognize that some of the greatest ideas are also the most radical or off the wall. Give yourself permission to be different.
8. *Project X, Y, and Z.* Embark on a number of unrelated projects and enterprises at once. Release yourself from any anxieties and let the ideas come to you. Then run with them.

(*Continued on next page.*)

(Continued from previous page.)

9. *Swap perspectives.* For a day, whether at home or at work, trade responsibilities with someone. Just this simple change in perspective can open a world of ideas and broaden your worldview.

—From Grace McGartland, the principal and founder of GM Consultants, an organization that has helped hundreds of Fortune 500 organizations break through mental barriers to see new opportunities.

A COLLEAGUE OF THEIR OWN

Hints for Managing Your Former Teammates

There's an ocean of difference between being a deckhand and running the ship. That's doubly true when the new captain is charged with overseeing a team of former shipmates. So what's the best way to smooth the transition from being just one of the gang to assuming the wheel? For advice straight from the captain's chair, Darren Dunay, a regional sales manager with *Metal Bulletin*—an international publication covering the world's metals markets, shares his top five tips for just such a scenario.

1. *Lay the groundwork.* "When you're still a sales rep, rather than being just 'one of the guys,' goofing off and taking two-hour lunches, try to establish yourself as a leader and a go-to guy for your peers. This will also put you first in line when that management position comes open."

2. *No favors.* "When you become a manager, some of your former peers may expect you to be more lenient or grant them special favors. Don't do it or you'll diminish the others' respect for you. It may be a little uncomfortable at first, but be straight and tell them, 'You know I can't do that and you shouldn't even be asking.'"

3. *Give people space.* "It may be difficult for some coworkers to deal with seeing you promoted. People you thought were your friends may become unpleasant and begrudge you the promotion. Don't show that person special favors—you're there to do a job. If they're mature enough, they should eventually come around and accept the new situation, and at that point you can likely resume being friends and work well together."

4. *Play to your strengths.* "Managing your former peers is actually a plus because you already know the team so well. You know their strengths and their weaknesses, plus you know what motivates them. So if someone is a big baseball fan, you know you can motivate that person with Yankee tickets—that's the kind of insight another supervisor doesn't come to the position knowing."

5. *No blind eyes.* "Management is all about making tough decisions. Inevitably you're going to be confronted with an unpleasant task or a confrontation you won't relish. Frontline reps don't have these issues. You're torn between coming across as a jerk or letting something go on that you shouldn't. Whatever you do, resist the temptation to say, 'Go ahead, but I don't know about this,' because that will come back to bite you later."

HOW A *SMART ONE* MANAGES
Success Tips for Effective Critical Assessment

When a Japanese soldier emerged from the jungles of the Philippines some 30 years after the end of World War II, most people attributed his perseverance to tenacity and grit. It turned out, however, that he was merely going to extreme levels to put off his workplace performance review. Salespeople and sales managers dread performance reviews too, and as a result the review process is often put off indefinitely. But as Frank McNair points out in *It's OK to Ask 'Em to Work*, useful feedback from management is one of the most effective keys to improving sales performance. Instead of putting off the review, McNair suggests following the SMART ONE path.

S *is for Specific.* "Good job" or "Bad job" doesn't tell an employee much. Spend the time analyzing the reps' performance to ferret out precisely what they are doing well and where there is room for improvement.

M *is for Measurable.* Let your salespeople know ahead of time what metrics will be used to determine performance (total sales, margins, new accounts, etc.) and then how that performance will be measured (percentage increase, dollar increase, number of new accounts, etc.).

A *is for Actionable.* Give your reports suggestions that they can follow through on immediately. A rep can, for example, dress more appropriately the next time, but cannot grow taller—without expensive, painful, and time-consuming surgery, that is.

R *is for Relevant.* As you offer criticism, explain precisely how the adverse behavior blocked the sale or the positive actions helped close the sale.

T *is for Timely.* Whenever possible, offer up your criticisms, both positive and negative, immediately following the actions you're commenting on. This will help cement them in the sales rep's mind and make positive change easier.

O *is for Objective.* Objective criticisms deal with behavior, which can be changed, and not with conclusions you reach about a person. Calling reps stupid is a conclusion (and a nonobjective one to boot). Instead, note that they have achieved only half the proficiency of their peers with the same training.

N *is for Nonthreatening.* Feedback should be unequivocal and honest, but shouldn't sound like a threat. Be clear but nonthreatening about both the carrots and sticks the future may hold.

E *is for Encouraging.* Effective managers are always encouraging—challenging top performers to keep up the good work and sitting down with underachievers to find solutions to what's run them aground.

Chapter 20

Test Your Skills

To be effective, sales managers must assume many roles. To see how well you have mastered these roles, answer the questions below using the following rating system:

5 for agree always

4 for agree often

3 for agree sometimes

2 for agree rarely

1 for disagree

1. I know what motivates my salespeople.
2. I am familiar with the challenges they face in their jobs and in their personal lives.
3. I understand their professional skills.
4. I set realistic goals, based on stretch goals, for my team.
5. I am good at planning my work and organizing my team.
6. I am a great salesperson, but I resist the temptation to play the super-salesperson for my team members.
7. I keep up-to-date with the latest technology to help my sales team stay productive.
8. I hire salespeople who complement each other in strength and attributes to create a diverse team.
9. I am a firm but fair leader.
10. I always deliver on my promises, and my actions inspire trust in my sales team.
11. I am a good coach, and I use every opportunity to inspire and develop people.
12. I motivate with generous praise in public and offer constructive criticism in private.
13. When problems arise, I challenge my team for solutions and offer direction as needed.
14. I create a positive and exciting environment to continually reward my team for excellence.
15. My communication style with the sales force is honest, open, and focused.
16. In one-on-one meetings I listen more than I speak.
17. I share my overall strategy with my team so that they know where they're heading.

18. I am aware of the major challenges within the company, and I contribute effectively to meet those challenges.
19. I am able to gain the full support of other departments to help my team perform at peak levels.
20. When it becomes necessary, I act quickly to handle terminations with tact and dignity.

ADD UP YOUR SCORE

- If your score is below 39, you should take immediate action and sign up for a management or leadership course.
- If your score is between 40 and 64, note your weakest areas and develop a personal improvement plan. You may discuss certain issues with your manager or with an HR professional within your company.
- If your score is between 65 and 90, you are a good manager, but you could still improve and obtain even better results.
- If your score is between 91 and 100, you are doing exceptionally well. Be careful not to become overconfident, and remain vigilant.

Credits

The following excerpts of chapters were originally published in *Selling Power* and written by …

… Lisa Gschwandtner
  "What Makes an Ideal Sales Manager"
  "Double the Benefits"
  "Test Your Skills"

… William F. Kendy
  "The Whole Picture"
  "Tips for Successful Hiring"
  "Quick Tips to Become a More Effective Sales Coach"

… Howard Stevens
  "Smart Hiring"

… Malcolm Fleschner
  "Make Your Next Hire Your Best Hire"
  "Always on the Lookout"
  "Annual Focus"
  "Even Top Dogs Need Leaders"

"Meet Up and Heat Up"
"Peaks, Not Plateaus"
"End Performance Evaluation Anxiety"
"Teaming with Trouble"
"Be a Change Agent"
"Be Effective for a Change"
"Return to Gender"
"I Came, I Saw—Idea!"
"A Colleague of Their Own"
"Up with People"
"Handle with Flair"
"How A SMART ONE Manages"

... Henry Canaday
"Testing the Waters"
"Which Is the Best Test for You?"
"What It Costs to Test Sales Recruits"
"Process Is a Snap"
"Creative Compensation"
"How to Pay"

... Alan S. Horowitz
"How the Right Training at the Right Price Provides the Right Results"

... Christine Neuberger
"Invaluable Training"
"Keep Workers Happy"
"Incentive to Perform"
"Ignite Your Sales Team—from the Bottom Performer to the Superstar"
"Rewarding Tips"

... Heather Baldwin
"Knowledge Is Power"
"Winning Alternatives to Meetings"
"How to Harness the Power of the Mind to Close More Sales"

... Kim Wright Wiley
"Don't Hesitate, Motivate"

... Joan Leotta
"SKILL SET: Tips for Recharging the Sales Engine"

... Steve Atlas
"Top Performers Motivate Others to Excel"

... Ken Liebeskind
"Profitable Meetings"

... Wes Van Slyke
"Ten Rules for Successful Meetings"

... Catherine Sheppard
"Celebrate Success"

... Bob Nelson
"An Added Incentive"

... Gerhard Gschwandtner and Dr. Donald J. Moine
"How to Manage the Seven Most Difficult (but Promising) Sales Personalities"

... Renee Houston Zemanski and Sandra Gurvis
"Oh, Grow Up!"

... Renee Houston Zemanski
"Six Tips for Effective Employee Relations"

... Sandra Gurvis
"Simple Steps to Sales Success"
"The Marine Corps Way to Manage"

... Arnold L. Schwartz
"For Success in Coaching: Know When to Hold Back"

... Brian Azan
"Defining Your Role as a Coach"

... Karen E. Starr
"Perfect the Process of Selling"

... Geoffrey James
"Enthusiastic Acceptance"
"Roundtable of Top CRM Industry Leaders"
"The Eight Keys to Profitable CRM"

... Dana Ray
"The Ethical Dilemma"

... Ronald S. Tartarella
"Integrity Makes for Great Sales"

... Thomas Fee
"Winning Strategies for Keeping Productivity and Sales at Their Peak"

... Ron Willingham
"Use Psychology to Increase Your Confidence in Selling"

... Gerhard Gschwandtner and Maryann Hammers
"Qualities of Top Sales Managers"

... Betsy Wiesendanger
"You Got a Problem with That?"
"The Tough Conversation"

Index

About the Author

A dual citizen of both Austria and the United States, Gerhard Gschwandtner is the founder and publisher of *Selling Power*, the leading magazine for sales professionals worldwide, with a circulation of 165,000 subscribers in 67 countries.

He began his career in his native Austria in the sales training and marketing departments of a large construction equipment company. In 1972, he moved to the United States to become the company's North American Sales Training Director, later moving into the position of Marketing Manager.

In 1977, he became an independent sales training consultant, and in 1979 he created an audiovisual sales training course called "The Languages of Selling." Marketed to sales managers at Fortune 500 companies, the course taught nonverbal communication in sales together with professional selling skills.

In 1981, Gerhard launched *Personal Selling Power*, a tabloid-format newsletter directed to sales managers. Over the years the tabloid grew in subscriptions, size, and frequency. The name changed to *Selling Power*, and in magazine format it became the leader in the professional sales field. Every year *Selling Power* publishes the "Selling Power 500," a listing of the 500 largest sales forces in America. The company publishes books, sales training posters, and audio and video products for the professional sales market.

Gerhard has become America's leading expert on selling and sales management. He conducts webinars for such companies as SAP, and *Selling Power* has recently launched a new conference division that sponsors and conducts by-invitation-only leadership conferences directed toward companies with high sales volume and large sales forces.

For more information on *Selling Power* and its products and services, please visit www.sellingpower.com.

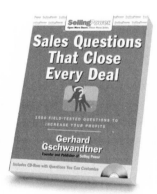

Subscribe to *Selling Power* today and close more sales tomorrow!

GET 10 ISSUES – INCLUDING THE SALES MANAGER'S SOURCE BOOK.

In every issue of *Selling Power* magazine you'll find:

■ **A Sales Manager's Training Guide** with a one-hour sales training workshop complete with exercises and step-by-step instructions. Get a new guide in every issue! Created by proven industry experts who get $10,000 or more for a keynote speech or a training session.

■ **Best-practices reports** that show you how to win in today's tough market. Valuable tips and techniques for opening more doors and closing more sales.

■ **How-to stories** that help you speed up your sales cycle with innovative technology solutions, so you'll stay on the leading edge and avoid the "bleeding edge."

■ **Tested motivation ideas** so you and your team can remain focused, stay enthusiastic and prevail in the face of adversity.

Plus, you can sign up for five online SellingPower.com newsletters absolutely FREE.